6/06

Restoring the
American Dream

Restoring the American Dream

A Working Families' Agenda for America

Thomas A. Kochan

The MIT Press
Cambridge, Massachusetts
London, England

MIT Press books may be purchased at special quantity discounts for business or sales promotional use. For information, please email special_sales@mitpress.mit.edu or write to Special Sales Department, The MIT Press, 5 Cambridge Center, Cambridge, MA 02142.

This book was set in Palatino by SNP Best-set Typesetter Ltd., Hong Kong. Printed and bound in the United States of America.

Library of Congress Cataloging-in-Publication Data

Kochan, Thomas A.
Restoring the American Dream : a working families' agenda for America / Thomas A. Kochan.
  p. cm.
  Contents: Work, family, and American values—Integrating work and family life—Contributing and prospering in a knowledge economy—Good jobs—Building knowledge-based organizations—Portable benefits—Restoring voice at work and in society—A working families' agenda for government—A call to action.
  Includes bibliographical references and index.
  ISBN 0-262-11292-2 (alk. paper)
  1. Work and family—United States. 2. Quality of life—United States. 3. Family policy—United States. 4. Social planning—United States—Citizen participation. 5. United States—Economic policy—21st century. I. Title: Working families' agenda for America. II. Title.

HD4904.25.K634 2005
306.3'6—dc22
                                                                    2005045103

10 9 8 7 6 5 4 3 2 1

To my family—generations past, present, and future.

Contents

Preface   ix
Acknowledgments   xvii

1 Work, Family, and American Values   1

2 Integrating Work and Family Life   17

3 Contributing and Prospering in a Knowledge Economy   49

4 Good Jobs   69

5 Building Knowledge-Based Organizations   101

6 Portable Benefits   127

7 Restoring Voice at Work and in Society   141

8 A Working Families' Agenda for Government   175

9 A Call to Action   203

Notes   223
Index   231

Preface

I grew up on a small family farm in Wisconsin where work and family were inseparable. I have on a wall at home a picture of my four siblings and me with our grandfather standing together in a field on our farm at harvest time. This picture is a reminder of how farm life taught us the values of cooperation, community, responsibility, initiative, leadership, and, of course, hard work. With these values came an equally deep conviction that hard work should generate its just rewards—a psychological feeling of accomplishment and pride, recognition from others of a job well done, and fair compensation. I was lucky to have parents who recognized that the world was changing in ways that required their children to move off the farm to go where job opportunities might take them. My parents encouraged us to get as much education as we could so that these opportunities would be open to us and to our children.

Because of its progressive traditions, Wisconsin gave us this chance. We received a solid foundation of basic education from our local parish school, an excellent public high school, and a world-class public university system that has now served two generations of our family very well.

The education I received enabled me to devote the last thirty years to studying, teaching, and advocating innovations in work and employment relations in search of ways to improve both our nation's economic performance and the quality of work and family live. Over these years I've been fortunate to work on these issues with many talented academic, business, labor, government, and community leaders. What I value most from these experiences is the mutual respect and satisfaction that develops when diverse parties work together to solve a difficult problem or resolve a conflict.

But in recent years, I have grown more and more concerned that these work and family values were eroding in a world in which people had turned inward and selfish in the booming 1990s and then were shattered by the layoffs, restructurings, wage and benefit cuts, and corporate scandals of recent years. The social contract at work that allowed so many of us in the postwar, baby boom generation to realize the American dream had broken down. I've made this point before in academic papers and at professional conferences but I've come to the conclusion that real progress in reversing these trends requires engaging the American public. This book is an effort to do just that.

Government leaders have done little or nothing to address these problems in recent years, in part because they are paralyzed by the ideological impasse between business and labor, the two interest groups that have traditionally dominated policy making on these issues, and in part because American politics in general has become more polarized and divisive. Somehow, American business, labor, and government have lost sight of their responsibilities to workers and their families.

It is as if America has lost both its moral and economic footing, unsure of how to take on the major problems of our day. This, indeed, is very un-American. Since the French philosopher Alexis de Tocqueville visited the United States in the 1830s, we have been told that Americans are a highly pragmatic people, capable of rolling up their sleeves and working together without much concern for divisions of class, ideology, religion, or even race and gender to find workable solutions to whatever problems we face. It is this pragmatic determination, respect for each other, and willingness to work together for the common good that must be restored.

So what can be done? The central message here is that the solutions must start with ourselves—with working families taking the steps needed to raise our voices so we can restore faith in the American dream, if not for ourselves, then for our children. Why? Because these problems are too important to leave, as we have in recent decades, to the "market." That solution, standing alone, will deepen the divide between a privileged few and the rest of society that has widened over the past two decades. Our democracy and social fabric are already wearing thin by the income and wealth inequalities found in America today. Making them worse will indeed risk the type of "class warfare" politicians fear. We also cannot expect a return to the days in which government takes care of our problems. The deficits government leaders face will limit their ability to spend their way out of the mess policymakers have created. Indeed, in the short run, government leaders could make things worse, especially if they stand idly by and watch families experience the stress, frustration, and hardships of being caught in a world where the old jobs that supported them in the industrial economy are disappearing without providing them the tools and opportunities to prosper in the economy of the future.

To be sure, we need a change in the direction of government policies. But as I will argue throughout this book, we also need new ideas and a new approach. I will argue for one that encourages community groups, labor organizations, businesses, and state government officials to work together to address these problems. We need to return to a strategy that has served America well in the past— empowering those closest to the problems to invent solutions that work for them. Then, when we discover new workable solutions, we can translate them into national policies and institutions.

Nor can we trust top business leaders and executives acting on their own to lead us to the promised land of the knowledge economy. This is not just because a few of them have engaged in scandalous behavior that has broken the workforce's trust in them. A deeper problem is that they are making decisions in an environment where their main and most powerful pressures are coming from Wall Street's demand for short-term returns to shareholders while there is no voice from Main Street holding executives accountable to workers and their communities.

Some business leaders and their firms are trying to restore trust and build the knowledge-based corporations that see employees more as assets than as costs to be controlled. Many of these same firms are leading the way in introducing flexible policies the modern workforce needs to meet their dual work and family responsibilities. But these leaders need the pressure of working families to sustain support for these policies within their organizations and in the broader business community. Indeed there is a debate raging in corporate America today over which model of management will dominate in the future. Will we stay fixated on Wall Street's view that stock prices are all that matter and employees are costs to be controlled and traded like any other commodity? Or will we see knowledge as an asset, organize work so employees can fully make use of their skills, and recognize that when employees invest and put at risk their human capital they should have the same rights to information and voice in governance as those who invest their financial capital? Working families have an enormous stake in the outcome of this debate and need to add their voices to it.

In the past, these realities would lead many to turn to the labor movement. After all, throughout much of the industrial era, unions and collective bargaining helped millions of working families move from destitute wages and working conditions into the middle class. But union membership today has declined to a point that unions no longer serve as a powerful or effective voice for the full range of working families in the country. Nor would resurgence of a labor movement in the mirror image of the one now in decline serve the needs of people or an economy entering an era in which putting one's knowledge to work is a more important source of power than withholding one's labor by going on strike. American workers, for their own benefit and for the welfare of families, the economy, and our democracy, need a renewed labor movement to help restore their voice at work and in society. But the next generation of unions and professional associations needs to be better matched to the diverse aspirations and needs of today's workforce and help speed the transition to a knowledge economy that benefits all working families.

This leaves it to working families to be the catalysts for action, to raise their voices to reassert the values on which the American dream is based. But they cannot and do not have to do this alone. I believe many progressive leaders in business, labor, government, and civil society share their concerns. By taking actions outlined in the chapters that follow I believe working families can build alliances with these progressive leaders to get access to the tools they need to contribute to and prosper in the knowledge economy. As the examples sprinkled throughout this book will illustrate, a good deal of this is already happening in different communities and workplaces. More than anything, this book is a call to move these local innovations to a scale large enough to benefit the overall economy and society.

Any campaign to regain control of our future must rest on a strong and broadly shared moral foundation, one that our parents taught us, is consistent with our various religious traditions, shows a concern for the common good, and is inclusive of the diversity we find and value in the American community. So in what follows, I will draw liberally on the values I, and I believe many others of my generation, had passed on to us. Our job is to embed them in our actions, institutions, and policies and by doing so pass them on to generations to come.

Why bring *families* so directly into this discussion about workplace issues and policies? Why not follow the more conventional approach of treating work and family as separate areas of inquiry, teaching, and policy making? After all aren't family matters really just our personal, private concerns and responsibilities? And shouldn't business stay out of our personal lives and focus on the business of business? And don't we have separate government policies governing the world of work and the social welfare of families?

The basic reason for using "working families" is that today, as in my days on the farm, work and family life are once again nearly inseparable. Because most mothers and fathers are now working more hours than in the past, we cannot understand the full consequences of the changing nature of work without considering how families are affected and without considering how family structures and needs influence decisions about when, where, and how much to work. Moreover, modern technology has blurred the lines between work and personal/family life. I first typed these words on a holiday using a laptop in my living room!

But you might ask a final question: If Wall Street and its favorite CEOs are where the power now lies, why not take the standard business school approach and call on these business leaders simply to be more responsible? As a professor at MIT's Sloan School of Management, I've always been uneasy with the top-down perspective of business books and teaching. Even my own field—what used to be called industrial relations, then became human resource management, and now is work and employment relations—gradually shifted from being taught from a neutral perspective in recognition of the need to balance the interests of employees and employers to more and more of a management perspective. Then, in the 1990s, we witnessed an explosion of business books extolling the wisdom and leadership of what my friend and colleague Rakesh Khurana called the "charismatic CEO." The media looked to these highly visible and powerful people to lead the transformation to the fast-paced, knowledge-based economy of the future. For a long time I've wondered what it would look like if we analyzed this transformation from the perspectives of workers and their families. Their voice seemed to be sorely absent in these discussions, and the view from the top of organizations downward being presented seemed far removed from the realities of the American workplace. This book is an effort to help working families find their voice and to bring a more balanced and fair perspective back into discussions about how to shape the future of work and the future of our economy.

Acknowledgments

Many friends contributed to this project. Lotte Bailyn, Tom Barocci, Phillip Beaumont, Fran Benson, Ann Bookman, Susan Cass, Lee Dyer, Mona Harrington, Malcolm Lovell, Richard Locke, Robert McKersie, Paul Osterman, Phillip Primack, Dennis Rocheleau, Saul Rubinstein, and Arnold Zack read and, in some cases, reread and commented on several drafts of this book. Individually and collectively they helped shape the message, tone the rhetoric, and fine-tune examples (some of which they have reason to know quite well), and offered plain good advice. I hope they will see their imprints in the final product.

My colleagues at the MIT Workplace Center deserve special thanks. Recognition of the increased interdependence of work and family led the Alfred P. Sloan Foundation to ask Lotte Bailyn, the dean of the work-family field of study, and me to combine forces and create the MIT Workplace Center. Our center's mission is to find better ways to integrate work, family, and community needs by bringing together all the groups and institutions that share responsibilities for these issues—workers, employers, labor organizations, community and family advocacy groups, and government. This mission is carried out by a dedicated and talented team whose work I draw on throughout this book. Along with Lotte, they include Ann Bookman, Mona Harrington, Susan Cass, Cicely Dockett, Joanne Batziotegos, and Kellie Donovan. A considerable amount of the raw material for this book comes from the work of our graduates and PhD students: Forrest Briscoe, Kate Kellogg, Matthew Bidwell, Isabel Fernandez-Mateo, Kyoung-Hee Yu, and Adam Seth Litwin. As she has done for so many of our projects, Susan Cass did an excellent job of editing and shaping this manuscript at various stages of its development. I hope everyone at the center sees some evidence of limited progress in their project— teaching me about the family dimensions of the work-family issues discussed here.

Kathleen Christensen and her colleagues at the Sloan Foundation have my unqualified thanks and respect for first inspiring us to create this center and then for staying the course. I have benefited enormously from the support of the Sloan Foundation over the years. I continue to be grateful for its confidence in us and its tolerance of our approach to research. As always, the views expressed here are my own and should not be attributed to either the Sloan Foundation or the Workplace Center.

Jackie Curreri runs our office, manages the faculty and student community in our Institute for Work and Employment Research, and makes my hours at work both enjoyable and productive. Her good humor and organizational skills get us both through some seemingly impossible days, all the while listening for my calls (or other phrases) for help with some computer glitch or puzzle that only members of a younger generation seem to be able to fix.

All of the above, I'm sure, will be pleased to have this project done. I thank them for helping to get it there.

This book is about families and their working lives so it is appropriate to dedicate it to my family. Family to me is something that spans generations and is carried on in person and by traditions, memories, and stories. Over the course of writing this book we experienced this first hand in the loss of my father-in-law John Otis and my mother Loretta Kochan.

John Otis was a model of the small-town business leader America is at risk of losing. He was a sales executive in a local electronics company and an active community leader, serving over the years on the Chamber of Commerce, the City Council, the Library Board, and his Church Council. For most of his career he and his family benefited greatly from the post–World War II social contract in which his hard work and loyalty were rewarded with respect, security, and opportunity. Then late in his working career, he experienced first-hand the effects of the breakdown in this implied contract. When a large conglomerate took over this local company, he watched it slowly but surely replace his peers, relocate production to lower cost areas, and lose interest in the community. He retired early but the community never forgot his many years of service. Nor did his dedication and leadership get lost on his children and grandchildren.

Loretta Kochan died as this manuscript was going through its final revisions. Her children, grandchildren, and great-grandchildren were able to celebrate her passing in a way that demonstrated the strength that comes from strong family bonds and a close-knit, supportive community. One of her favorite comments in her later years was a question: "What would I ever do without my family?" She never had to answer that question, and by the example she and her family set, my guess is neither will generations to come.

The direct burden of this project, others that came before it, and ones that will likely come in the future continue to be carried by my wife Kathy and our children Andrew, Sarah, Sam, Jacob, and Ben. They have been partners in this project in some obvious and less obvious ways. They provided the kind of comments and suggestions on segments they read that only those you love would dare make, such as "put stories of real people in here not just your normal academic abstractions," or "nice words but be sure to tell people how to make this happen." After being disillusioned by the

2004 elections one suggested using a takeoff on Dante's *Inferno* in the title: "Abandon all hope ye who enter here!" And finally, "How about just getting it done this weekend!" This is what families are for—to offer support but to keep things in perspective. I thank them for their tolerance of my work habits and for all they contribute to my work and family life.

I'll end this note with a word about a close friend, former graduate student, and gifted teacher, scholar, and activist who also died about the time I was trying to decide whether or not to turn what was then a short memo into this book. Susan Eaton was an inspiration to everyone she touched in her all-too-brief life. She embodied the spirit, ideas, and values expressed in this book. Remembering what she stood for and how she encouraged us all to say and do what we think is right helped make the decision to go ahead with this project.

1   Work, Family, and American Values

Our faith calls us to measure this economy, not only by what it produces but also by how it touches human life and whether it protects or undermines the dignity of the human person. Economic decisions have human consequences and moral content; they help or hurt people, strengthen or weaken family life, advance or diminish the quality of justice in our land.

—*Economic Justice for All*, U.S. Catholic Bishops' Pastoral Letter, 1986

Debate over values is alive and well in America today. Much of it serves more to divide than to unite the country. In doing so the debate misses the deep values about matters of justice, fairness, families, and work that bind us together and that are deeply embedded in our moral traditions. Statements like the one above can be found in Jewish, Protestant, Islamic, Hindu, and Catholic social teachings. What divides America today are not our values, but the conditions so many people face in trying to earn a good living, have a satisfying career, have the time needed to care for their families, and participate in community life. The reality is that too many families are working longer and harder only to fall further and further behind. As a result deep pressures are building up in our workplaces and communities that, if not addressed soon, will explode. The day of reckoning is likely to come, if not sooner, when many of our young people realize they will never achieve, much less surpass, the standards of living they experienced growing up.

American workers are telling us this story in the numbers in table 1.1, figure 1.1, and figure 1.2. Table 1.1 appeared in *Business Week* at the peak of the booming economy in 1999. Remarkably, even in that period of prosperity, three-fourths of Americans felt the benefits of the "new economy" were being distributed unevenly. More surprising, less than one-third of Americans felt that they were experiencing improvements in their wages and job security and only half saw their lives as being better. These perceptions were backed up by fact: Income inequality was growing throughout most of the decade.

Figures 1.1 and 1.2 show what happened after the dot-com bust, stock market declines, and corporate scandals. By 2002, two out of

Table 1.1
Business Week/Harris Poll "Survey of Discontent"

Question	Percent agreeing
Thinking about the impact that this economic productivity boom has had on you personally, do you think that it has or not:	
Raised the level of your earned income	34%
Raised the value of your investments	50%
Increased your job security	30%
Generally speaking, would you say that the recent economic boom had made your life . . . better, . . . had no impact, . . . or worse?	
Better	53%
Had no impact	37%
Worse	8%
Do you feel that the benefits of the New Economy are evenly distributed or unevenly distributed?	
Evenly	20%
Unevenly	70%
How would you rate the job business is doing of raising living standards of all Americans?	
Excellent or Good	29%
Fair or Poor	69%

Source: "Hey, What About Us?" *Business Week*, December 27, 1999, p. 54.

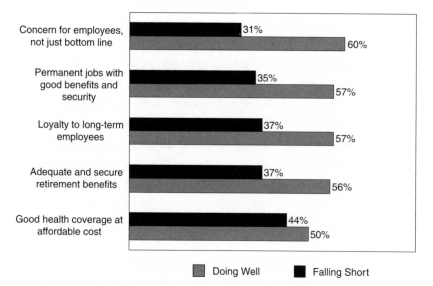

Figure 1.1
View from the Workplace: Employee Views of Their Employers. Source: Peter Hart Associates, 2002.

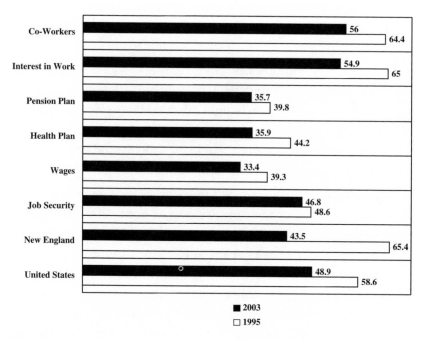

Figure 1.2
Job Satisfaction. Source: The Conference Board, September 2003.

three Americans viewed their companies as doing a poor job of rewarding employee loyalty, attending to anything beyond the bottom line, or providing good wages and benefits. A national survey conducted in 2003 by the Conference Board, a leading research organization supported by business, showed American workers' satisfaction with their pay, health insurance, and retirement savings had plummeted since the mid-1990s.

Who Are America's Working Families?

Just who are America's working families and why are they so upset?

• They are the average two parent families that have increased the hours devoted to paid work by approximately 15 percent between 1985 and 2000. Together, the parents in these families now work over 3,800 hours a year, nearly the equivalent of two forty-hour-per-week jobs and more than any other country in the world.

• They are the middle-class wage earners whose hourly pay declined between 1985 and 1995, then finally started rising again for the five years of extremely tight labor markets prior to the stock market bust in 2000, and since then have once again stopped growing. So the median wage earner in America today is in about the same position as he or she was a generation ago.

• They are the middle-aged, white-collar professionals and managers who watched as their firms changed from defined benefit to cash balance and defined contribution or 401(k) programs. Because these plans shift the risks from employers to employees, those covered by these plans experienced significant declines in the value of their retirement plans. One estimate puts the decline at about 14 percent since 1990. A more graphic figure is that the value of pensions declined by $7 billion, or about $28,000 for every man, women, and child in America.[1]

• They are among the 45 million Americans without health insurance coverage today.[2] Many of these uninsured are young employees working in small firms or temporary jobs that either do not provide health insurance or that have premiums that are beyond reach. Or they are employees and employers who are struggling to figure out how to share the costs of health insurance that have been rising at double-digit rates in recent years. Or even worse, they are the retirees that face increases in the costs or loss of coverage of the plans promised to them while working.[3]

• They are the 34 million "working poor" whose hourly pay is not enough to get the average family out of poverty. These families need to work two or three jobs just to meet their basic needs.

• They are among the more than three million people who lost their jobs and have either given up finding another or are working part time or for less pay and fewer benefits in jobs well below their skill levels long after the end of the last recession. Or they are professionals in highly skilled information technology jobs who thought their careers were secure only to watch jobs like theirs being "offshored" to a lower wage country. They read in the business media that another three million high-tech jobs could be outsourced to India or other countries in the next decade. These reports lead them to worry: "Is my job the next to go?"[4]

• They are union members who watch the labor movement decline to its lowest level of membership and influence since prior to the Great Depression (below 9 percent in the private sector). Despite significant efforts, unions have not been able to reverse their declining numbers and influence. As a result, collective bargaining can no longer move workers and families into the middle class, as it did for so many over the past half century. Workers and their families have lost their voice at work.

• Or they are among the 40 million nonunion workers who would join a union if given the chance, but are not able to do so in the face of determined management opposition and a labor law that fails to protect them if they tried. Or they are among the over 70 million workers who want a more direct and cooperative voice at work and access to the information they need to decide whether to continue investing their human capital in their firm, but who have no channels for gaining this information or voice.[5]

• They are citizens of our communities that are now absorbing the effects of the federal government's tax cuts and deficits, forcing cutbacks in schools, family and child-care services, and even public safety. They fear the effects will be increased crime and rising tensions and conflicts among groups opposing cuts in their particular services, programs, and jobs.

• Finally, they are parents worrying that they are passing on to the next generation many economic and community problems and the costs of dealing with them. This is something that no parent wants to do. At the very least, our children should be able to attain the standard of living that our generation inherited from our parents.

Yes, we are *all* members of America's working families. Families across the full socioeconomic spectrum share a stake in reversing the course of our country.

What Is at Stake for the Economy?

The stakes are equally high for our nation's economy and democracy as they are for workers and their families. America is in the midst of a transition from an industrial to a "knowledge economy," one in which human capital is becoming the most valuable resource and strategic asset for any nation or company that wants to compete in a global marketplace at high standards of living. This means that we must fully develop and use the skills, abilities, motivation, and creativity of the workforce to invent and deliver new products and services efficiently, quickly, and safely. We cannot build a sustainable, stable knowledge economy with a highly stressed, frustrated, insecure workforce and with workplaces that are fraught with conflict, tension, and distrust.

Creative knowledge workers need and want to work together cooperatively in teams, organizations, and professional networks where they are empowered to use their skills and abilities and are encouraged to take risks. They have been taught that this is the workplace of the future and are prepared and motivated to work in this way. But they also want to make sure that they will not experience the same fate of their parents and older peers whose lives were shattered by the corporate restructurings and market meltdowns of recent years.

Mike Amati, a student in one of MIT's midcareer management and engineering programs, captured this sentiment well in a letter commenting on an op-ed I wrote on the pressures building in America's workplaces:

What you are describing in the article—increasing work hours, less security, shrinking benefits, lack of portability of benefits, etc.—really hits home to me as I prepare to begin my job search for life after [graduation]. It is very important to me to find a job where I have some control over the amount of time I spend at work, the amount of travel I do, and the opportunities I have to control my career. Certainly I expect to work hard and realize I will never have complete control over my situation, but I compare what I saw my father and grandfather experience to what I've seen around me in my own work experience, and stories from my peers, and I can't help but conclude that every generation is "living to work" a little more and "working to live" a little less. It scares me for my personal future and the future of our country.

Mike captures the energy, creative potential, and willingness to work hard, along with the uncertainties and skepticism that young people bring to their jobs today. They want to do their part to turn this country around and are searching for a way to regain control of their destinies, for their own sake and for the sake of their country.

The Growing Call: Restore Trust!

Workers and families cannot reverse the course of this country acting alone, nor do they need to. A growing number of leaders in business, labor, and government recognize that America needs to rebuild the trust at work and in society that was lost in the 1990s. Alex d'Arbeloff, retired CEO of Teradyne, one of New England's leading high-technology firms, opened his speech to a convocation of MIT Sloan School Alumni in 2002 by saying:

Trust in free market capitalism is based on trust in the collective integrity of the companies that make up the market. A company's integrity depends on trust—the trust it shows its employees, its customers, its suppliers, its stockholders, and all the other constituencies that surround it. This trust is not just a matter of virtue for virtue's sake; it is an indispensable element for any business that wants to survive over the long haul.[6]

At the same meeting, United Nations secretary general Kofi Annan called on leaders of business, labor, and civil society in America to join him in a Global Compact committed to learning how to promote economic development and improved living standards.[7]

So there seems to be a broad-based yearning to build a new social contract at work that is attuned to the realities of today's economy and provides all who work their just rewards. This time around, however, no one is going to make the same mistake of putting his or her destiny in the hands of others. To borrow a phrase from Jack Welch, who until his recent fall from grace was one of the business press's favorite CEOs, it's time for working families to "Control Their Own Destinies, or Someone Else Will!"[8]

What Can We Do?

Here is a thumbnail sketch of what we need to do. Each of these points is developed in more detail in the following chapters.

We have to start by taking seriously the need to reduce the stresses on working families. This requires seeing work and family for what they are today, namely tightly coupled issues. Empowering working families to regain control of their destinies requires us to reframe the ways we think about, study, and shape policies and practices governing work and family life.

Since the emergence of the industrial era, work and family have been treated as separate spheres of activity. Family was viewed as an exclusively personal domain, not to be taken into consideration in business decisions. Work and business activities, on the other hand, were treated as private enterprises and enshrined with property rights that kept government and "outside" interest or pressure groups—such as unions, environmentalists, or more recently women and family advocates—at bay. Employees worked fixed schedules at workplaces outside the home. Gradually, a division of labor took shape in which the male breadwinner went off to paid work and an image of the "ideal worker" evolved as a male, full-time employee who could commit long hours and his full energies and loyalties to work because he presumably had a wife at home attending to family and community responsibilities.

None of these assumptions fits contemporary work and family life. Today, as back in the days of the farming economy, work and family are once again tightly coupled spheres of activity. Work is always with many of us, thanks to the wonders of modern information technology and our 24/7 economy. Today, most people work at work and at home and while traveling, even sometimes while on "vacation." And less than one quarter of American households today consist of two parents in which one is the "breadwinner" and the other is the "homemaker."

So there is a dire need to adapt workplace policies and practices, and the way we think about their relationships to family decisions and life, to accommodate this new reality. The good news is many of our leading companies are trying to do this. The buzzwords are that we need to make our workplaces "flexible" and "family friendly." But we need to go beyond the buzzwords to realize truly flexible work and employment practices that are capable of meeting what my colleague Lotte Bailyn has coined the "dual agenda," meaning the need to design work systems, organizational practices, and community institutions to support productive work and healthy family life.

Labor unions are also quite active on this front. Some are trying to negotiate limits on working hours and particularly nonmandatory overtime. In some cases, unions and employers are working together in joint programs funded through collective bargaining to deliver a range of services to help working families better integrate and meet their dual responsibilities. These, unfortunately, are too few and far between. But they point us in the right direction by bringing these two potentially powerful stakeholders together to work on these issues.

A number of family and community groups are promoting expansions in child-care and related family services and paid family leave policies. Congress and state legislatures are considering or, as in the case of California, enacting limited forms of paid leave and minimum staffing levels for essential services such as nursing.

Unfortunately, most of these efforts are working completely independently. We need to bring these different groups together and insist they work toward coordinated solutions. How to reframe our thinking to reflect the tight coupling of work and family life and how we might work toward more coordinated solutions are issues taken up in chapter 2.

With this reframing in mind, we can begin preparing working families with what they need to be successful in today's labor market and to add value to a knowledge-based economy. We need to go beyond the rhetoric about the "knowledge economy" or the oft-stated phrase that "human resources are our most important asset" by holding workers, families, and our institutions accountable for investing in education and life-long learning.

This starts at home with the type of good parenting that creates a learning environment for children. It requires adequate and equitable funding of early childhood development, elementary, and secondary schools and education programs—fulfilling the promise of the "No Child Left Behind" legislation. Business leaders have a special stake in improving educational opportunities in low income, minority, and immigrant communities since they will inherit the shortages of knowledge workers that demographic and college graduate trends suggest are coming as the baby boomers retire. Women, African Americans, and Hispanics are underrepresented in the talent pool of scientists, engineers, and other technical specialties, and few young people from these demographic groups are going into these fields of study. Only by starting early in life to get children dreaming about what they might do in these fields and providing the opportunity for them to realize their dreams will America have the supply of knowledge workers needed to fuel a robust economy in the future.

We also need to rethink *what* knowledge and skills are needed to translate advances in science and technology into products and services that serve society and help industry prosper. An innovative economy requires a scientifically and technically literate workforce that is skilled and motivated to work effectively in teams and to communicate and resolve problems and conflicts effectively, and that is empowered to put their knowledge and skills to work. The education system most of us graduated from was built to serve the industrial economy's needs for discipline, specialization, and deference to authority that corresponded to the prevailing organization of work and growing bureaucracies of the industrial era. An overhaul of how we teach and how we integrate knowledge from different technical and behavioral science disciplines will be essential to prepare the workforce to add value to today's knowledge economy.

Educational reforms are most quickly and effectively implemented when those who hire graduates work in partnership with schools, colleges, and universities. Many American universities are moving in this direction, overcoming their qualms about losing their "academic freedom" to outsiders. The key to making this work is to ensure that those getting involved are a representative cross section of the "customers" of education—industry leaders and entrepreneurs, but also leaders of professional associations, unions, and working families themselves. All these parties have a stake in educational reforms and should be part of the process.

What about the current labor force? Are those already working destined to experience the same fate as their parents who were victims of the restructurings and downsizings of the last two decades when many firms were laying off older employees while hiring younger workers because the skills needed were changing? Firms judged that the cost of retraining and retaining older workers far exceeded the cost of hiring younger workers who had or could more quickly learn the new technical skills in demand. History will repeat itself unless we get serious about "life-long learning."

Life-long learning will not be translated from rhetoric to reality for most workers if we continue to depend on individual companies as the source of training and education. Nor can we expect our government with its monumental budget deficits to fund the investments that workers will need to keep their skills current. In chapter 3, we explore ways for workers to fund and engage in life-long learning.

Calls for young people to invest in education and training will fall on deaf ears unless there are jobs out there to reward those who make the investments. America is going through as big a jobs scare as at any time since the Great Depression of the 1930s. While the official unemployment rate as of this writing is 5.5 percent—neither extremely high nor low when judged in the long stream of history— three things are scaring people today. First, it has taken nearly three years of an economic recovery to get back the jobs lost to the last recession. This is an unprecedented slow rate of job growth. The great American job machine of the 1990s seemed to have ground to a halt; only recently has it begun to show signs of reappearing. Second, the more than two million Americans who have lost good paying middle-income jobs in manufacturing have taken big and most likely permanent pay and benefit cuts. Third, job losses are now spread more broadly across the blue- and white-collar labor force, leading to the concern of many people who thought their education and training protected them from insecurity to ask the "is my job next?" question.

Working families have achieved a milestone in American politics. They have put the issue of job creation and retention on the front pages of newspapers and at the top of the nation's political agenda. There is no guarantee it will stay there unless the public insists on it. And, unfortunately, there is no single silver-bullet strategy for creating and sustaining an adequate number of good jobs in America. Instead, it will take the combined efforts of policy makers at the national and state level, business leaders, entrepreneurs, and university researchers to generate the ideas for the next-generation products, services, and jobs. The question we need to ask is: Are these groups prepared to work together in pursuit of this common goal? We should insist that they do.

Suppose parents, families, and our educational systems do their part and supply industry with the knowledgeable and skilled workforce needed to fuel a knowledge-based economy. Does this ensure that today and tomorrow's organizations will use this knowledge effectively in the "organizations of the twenty-first century"? Not necessarily. Despite the rhetoric about "human resources being our most important resource," in American corporations today, as in the past, finance and cost control trump investments in human resources and empowerment of the workforce to use its skills. We carry over the legacy of the corporate design and governance doctrines that rose to prominence during the early stages of the industrial economy when pools of financial capital were the key resource needed to build the large modern publicly traded corporation. For human resource considerations to now rise to the top of corporate priorities and decision-making, employees will need to find new avenues to exert their voice and to participate as equals with those representing financial concerns in management. Moreover, American corporate governance will have to come to terms with a new principle: Just as it is the right of investors to gain a voice in corporate governance by putting their financial capital at risk in a firm, so too should employees who invest and put at risk their human capital. More on this in chapter 5.

These changes in organizational practices and governance structures are necessary but far from sufficient for workers and families to regain control of their futures. The reality today is that no individual organization can guarantee lifetime jobs or careers. So changes in labor market policies and institutions are needed to ensure that workers can move more easily across jobs if and when they either choose or are forced to do so. This means we need to slowly but surely wean ourselves from depending on firms as the institutions through which we fund and deliver standard benefits such as health insurance, pensions, leave benefits, educational and training opportunities, unemployment insurance, worker representation, and other services that employees need regardless of where they work. How to do this is taken up in chapter 6.

None of these changes will be accomplished unless America restores the independent voice workers have been losing as union membership falls to its pre–Great Depression levels. This does not, however, mean that we should simply try to bring back unions in their industrial-era mirror image. To be sure, for the sake of our democracy and our economy, America needs a strong, independent, and forward-looking labor movement. There is much in the legacy of unions and labor management relations to build on since efforts to transform labor relations and reinvent unions have been underway for some time. But more innovation and new thinking are needed. Indeed, a growing number of labor leaders, activists, and academics are calling for and experimenting with ways to invent the "next-generation" unions and employee associations and other institutions for giving workers the voice they need to prosper and add value in a knowledge-based economy. In chapter 7 we take up this challenge, discussing both what unions need to do to reinvent themselves and by exploring complementary forums and institutions for giving workers a voice that are emerging in selected settings.

Chapter 8 turns to the hardest part of the challenge—the reforms needed in government to support working families. A working families' agenda for a twenty-first century workplace policy is laid out. American workers, families, the economy, and indeed our democratic society have suffered from a twenty-five-year stalemate over how to update and modernize workplace policies because of an impasse between two ideological behemoths: business and labor. The gridlock will be broken only if the American workforce itself demands change and is guided by a clear vision for what changes are necessary. Only then will elected leaders, Democrats and Republicans, take notice and respond accordingly.

To borrow and adapt slightly a phrase from the late Tip O'Neill: "Not all policies are national." As in the early years of the past century, local and state governments are beginning to experiment with new approaches to developing their economies and meeting the needs of modern workers and families. Historically, most innovations in American social policy have come from experiments at the state level. Progressive states like Wisconsin, New York, Massachusetts, and California brought us the models for unemployment insurance, industrial safety regulations and workers compensation, welfare reform, and women and child labor protections that are now part of federal law. We may be in a similar phase of policy development and experimentation from which we can learn and eventually extend nationwide.

The final chapter is a call to action for all of us—workers, spouses, community and family activists, business, labor, and government officials and leaders, and even university professors. It is a call for all of us to reexamine the core values we hold for work and its relationships to family and community life and to our democracy. Americans have always believed in the value of hard work—for religious and moral reasons and for the economic value generated by efficiency and innovation. Judging from the number of hours devoted to paid work, this has not changed and will continue to serve our economy and society well in the future.

But as the quote at the beginning of this chapter indicates, we expect more than efficiency and productivity from work. We must restore the dignity that all who work deserve. This begins with making sure that all who work are rewarded with a living wage. We must ensure that the opportunity to learn and gain access to good jobs is open to men and women of all races, family backgrounds, and cultures. And, perhaps, most of all we need to renew our sense of solidarity by working together for the common good so that the gains and hardships of economic booms and busts to come are shared in an equitable fashion. The agenda laid out here is a starting point for reversing the disastrous course of our nation in hope for a better tomorrow for our families, and especially for our children.

Integrating Work and Family Life

Julie describes herself as "the engine" of her family. . . . She works hard at her paid job, carrying significant responsibilities in her company's research and development efforts. She works hard at home, doing most of the childcare and housework. And she struggles to be involved in her community, though she minimizes what she had done and worries about what she is not doing. Next year, [her two daughters] will be in elementary school, making involvement in their school even more compelling, although Julie does not know how she will get the time off work to volunteer.

—Ann Bookman, *Starting in Our Own Backyards* (New York: Routledge, 2004), p. 7

Julie is one of the 70 percent of mothers in two-parent families with children now working in the paid labor force.[1] As Ralph Gomory and Kathleen Christensen from the Alfred P. Sloan Foundation put it: "In today's two-career family, there are three jobs, two paid and one unpaid, but still only two people to do them."[2]

Today these two-parent working families are on average contributing over 3,800 hours to the paid labor force, nearly the equivalent of two full-time jobs. This amounts to about a 15 percent increase in family working hours since 1980. The stresses and strains on family life and community activities are apparent.

Wives and mothers were America's safety valve for the past twenty years. Without the hours they added to the labor force, family incomes would have fallen precipitously. In fact, three-fourths of the increases in family incomes in the past two decades came from the additional work hours contributed by wives and mothers. Looking ahead, the problem is obvious. These families are exhausted, literally and figuratively. They have no more hours to add to generate future increases in family income.

For single parents who have been working hard all along, the problem is worse. They had few available hours to add to work and so they fell even further behind.

Linda's typical day started at 6:00 A.M. when she got her daughter ready for school. Her job at Kessel [a grocery store] started at 7:00 A.M. and ended at 3:00 P.M. . . . . She came home, changed, and went to her job at H&R Block at 5:00 P.M. and got off at 10:00 P.M. Linda lives in what she describes as a "rough neighborhood. There's gambling, drinking and drugs in the neighborhood." . . . She wants to move but she can't afford it. Even working full-time it's hard to pay the bills. . . . After six years as a breadwinner, Linda admits she's discouraged. "I work hard. . . . I have a child to raise. I want my daughter to have a future, go to college, have the opportunities I didn't have. But it is hard when you can't save for her future."[3]

Welfare reform in the 1990s did bring approximately 3 million more single mothers into the labor force and cut welfare rolls roughly in half. For some, moving from welfare to work produced some of the benefits we expect from work, such as greater pride and dignity and learning and human capital development. A living wage proved more elusive. Follow up studies found that 58 percent of parents that moved from welfare to work earned wages that failed to move their families above the poverty line. Half were in jobs paying less than $7 per hour. The new workers whose families did best were ones in states like Minnesota, Illinois, and Wisconsin that provided child-care supports, education and training opportunities, and continued health-care coverage through Medicaid or a similar state program.[4] So the challenge lies in combining the job requirements of the welfare to work policies with adequate income and family supports parents need to meet their work and family responsibilities so that the children of these families can break out of the cycle of poverty they inherited.

These are just some of the stark facts that demonstrate why work and family issues now need to be seen as an integrated phenomenon.

How can we do this?

Recasting the "Ideal Worker"

The workforce and employment policies that still govern work today were put in place as part of the New Deal in the 1930s and were designed to fit the industrial economy of that era. They were built around a caricature of the ideal worker as a long-term employee of a large firm who could devote his total commitment to work because he conveniently had a wife at home attending to family and community responsibilities.[5] This view drew a clear separation of work from family life; family life issues were personal choices and private matters, not issues of concern for corporations, communities, or governments.

That was not the view of work and family issues in the earlier agrarian economy. Women and children's labor were essential to the farming economy and so work and family issues were considered part of the same social policy fabric. The school year, for example, was designed so children would be available to work in the summer (and no one thought it inappropriate for us to take a day off from school to help with time-sensitive fall harvesting or spring planting needs). Where I grew up, even our parish priest would, without hesitation, absolve farm families from observing the commandment to rest on the Sabbath when there were crops to harvest!

We now find ourselves in a situation similar to the farming economy. But to rethink public policies and organizational practices, not to mention religious rules and doctrines, to fit the realities of current work and family life we first need to shed the industrial-age notion that family issues are purely personal and private matters of no concern to business, community, or government. If it now takes two incomes for many families to make ends meet, and if society demands that even single parents work rather than stay at home, then society and business need to provide the flexibility and services people need to balance and integrate their work and family responsibilities.

The failure to reframe our thinking about the ideal worker perpetuates the default solution: Women simply absorb more of the burden of long hours of care at home.[6] Unless they adopt the ideal male worker model and postpone or forgo having children, their earning power and opportunities for advancement in their organizations and professions are limited. This is where society and labor markets are today. Despite some shifts in the family division of labor, surveys report that women still spend about twice as many hours doing care work and related duties at home as do men. Moreover, despite some gradual improvements in women's wages, a male-female gap persists. In 1998 women's average annual wages were approximately 72 percent of men's; average hourly wages were 78 percent of men's. Most studies now find that the difference that remains in male and female earnings has less to do with overt gender discrimination than to who gets access to higher level positions within organizations and occupations. These high-level positions continue to be influenced by the image of an ideal worker. Movement in and out of the labor force or between part-time and full-time career attachment lowers one's chances of getting to the top of most organizations and occupations.[7]

The point here is not that all residual differences in division of labor and male-female wage differences will be or should be eliminated. Some of these are still matters of personal and family choices and reflect deep cultural norms that neither business nor society should attempt to eliminate. Instead, the point is that we need to make these choices explicit and see them for what they are, namely closely coupled, so we don't simply continue to shape workplace policies and practices assuming there is a "care workforce" that no longer exists. A broader and more realistic vision is needed that recognizes the heterogeneity and shared nature of work and family arrangements and obligations.

Engaging All the Stakeholders

Rethinking and reframing the links between work and family will not be successful if each of the stakeholders involved goes it alone. We need to encourage all the groups that share responsibilities for integrating work and family life to work together to change this view and to bring their collective energies to bear on work and family issues. As my example in box 2.1 illustrates, doing so requires overcoming some ideological blinders that, if not shed, risk growing into insurmountable barriers.

Ships in the Night: Hospitals and Health Care

Failure to bring different stakeholders together results in the ships passing in the night phenomenon, each going their own way, most of the time to no avail and little consequence, but every once in a while blundering into a costly and avoidable clash. Consider how one such issue is playing out in the health-care sector: the challenge of the widespread shortage of nurses. Everybody recognizes the need to do something but, to date, each interested stakeholder is acting independently of the others.

Employers are engaged in recruiting and raiding wars. An ad in *The Boston Globe* in midwinter from Las Vegas hospitals touted jobs in the sunshine, with hiring bonuses to boot! Unions in two hospitals in Massachusetts went on strike to try to eliminate mandatory overtime.

Hospitals are turning increasingly to companies that supply "travel" nurses who move around the country, working in particular hospitals for limited blocks of time. Other hospitals turn to

Box 2.1
The Power of Bringing Together Diverse Stakeholders

Several years ago, I was invited to lead a workshop at a meeting of corporate human resource and work-family executives. I decided to try an experiment to see if this group could think collaboratively and outside their corporate boundaries. I asked them to assume that sometime in the foreseeable future America would pass some form of paid family leave. I asked them to role play about how to best do this, assuming that at their table were people such as themselves representing corporate America and others representing small business, labor, women's groups, and family advocates. Their task was to recommend to their governor and state legislature how (not whether or not) to design a paid-leave policy that dovetailed with current organizational fringe benefit and leave policies and operational concerns that was acceptable to all the stakeholders involved.

What happened? First, the participants balked at the way the problem was framed. They wanted to debate whether such a public policy should be adopted. I told them this was not theirs to decide. Then some said, "but I can't imagine dealing with labor leaders on this or any other issue in a collaborative forum. What could they possibly contribute? [Others echoed these sentiments for women's groups as well.] And, besides, if our bosses heard we were engaged in such discussions we'd be fired!"

"Ah," I said. This is the first lesson of this exercise. Is the knee-jerk reaction of American managers to oppose any form of collective action on behalf of workers—an infectious ideology that is a root cause of the adversarial history of union-management relations in this country—now about to be carried over to how business responds to women and family groups as they find and raise their voices on these issues? Or can we find a better way?

Since I can be persistent, the group eventually decided to go along with the exercise. Once they started brainstorming, the floodgates opened and all sorts of innovative, flexible arrangements that could fit with different organizational and business settings began to be proposed. And many of the ideas came from those playing (effectively I might add) their roles as labor and women's advocates. They held their corporate counterparts' feet to the fire.

This simple exercise demonstrated to the group, if only for a moment, the power of bringing together diverse stakeholders with different perspectives on work-family issues. But as the session ended, several participants said that this was fine and interesting, but they could never go back and advocate that their companies engage in a similar process in their communities.

immigrant nurses trained in other countries to meet their staffing needs.

Bills were introduced both in Congress and in a number of state legislatures to set minimum staffing ratios and/or limit mandatory overtime, or apply some other uniform "solution." California passed a staffing ratio bill; Washington and New Jersey enacted mandatory overtime limitations for nurses.

Meanwhile, nearly 20 percent of all registered nurses in the country have left the nursing profession.[8] This is a tremendous loss of human talent and skills. While some of these nurses are retired, most left nursing because of the stresses associated with the hours, working conditions, shortage of staffing, and lack of respect they experienced on the job.

Imagine how the nursing shortage might be addressed if all these groups—hospital and health-care employers, nursing unions and professional associations, and state governments—got together to work on coordinated solutions to the shortage. I suspect creative ideas and solutions would emerge, similar to those that came out of the multistakeholder discussions simulated at the workshop described in box 2.1. Even some of those nurses now in retirement, if given a voice in these discussions, might be enticed back to help out on a part-time basis if jobs were designed and scheduled to better fit with their personal and family roles and life stage.

Getting these stakeholders together does not mean individual organizations or groups should wait for others to take the lead. Employers, unions and professional associations, colleges and universities, and government all need to do their part, individually as well as collectively. Some of these groups are already doing so. Box 2.2 describes an innovative career ladder educational program for nursing assistants designed to move them to higher-level nursing occupations.

finding child-care services. So the same income and status differences as one finds in access to other fringe benefits is being replicated in access to firm initiated policies designed to help workers
address family needs.

Moreover, the evidence is that these policies are grossly under-
used by those covered by them because the culture of most firms
has not changed to support the formal policies. Employees
fear their careers will be hurt if they use these flexible options
because they won't be seen as conforming to that old "ideal worker"
image.

Consider the experience of a young Boston lawyer, his wife, and
family:

My husband's first law firm, one of the most prestigious in the city, offered
a three-month paid parental leave to anyone who had just adopted or had
a baby. When Jacob was born my husband took his full leave because it
coincided with the term I was finishing my PhD dissertation and lecturing
for the first time in the Sociology Department. There is no way I could have
accomplished these things without him at home. It allowed me the
maximum amount of time to devote to my writing and teaching. But it was
so unusual for men actually to take advantage of the leave policy that it
hurt him professionally and he eventually realized that he was going to
have to leave the firm if he was going to advance.

He was at a new firm (equally well known and prestigious) when June
was born. This time he did not dare to take advantage of their equally gen-
erous leave policy.

I faced a different type of problem when I was still planning an academic career. After Jacob was born, it became clear to me that I was only
going to be able to devote a typical work day (9 to 5) to my profession if I
wanted to live up to my own standards of parenthood. But those who are
most successful in academia are the ones who have the freedom to read,
think, and work from the moment they get up until they go to bed. This is
not going to change, even if it becomes more acceptable to split one's time
between work and family. My guess is the same could be said of careers
in business and medicine. It is certainly true in the world of law, where
one bills by the hour. I find it hard to envision a world where entire fields
reduce their standards of excellence when even a fraction of its practition-
ers are willing to make that extra effort.[9]

When this comment was made in 2001, nearly 90 percent of law firms in the country had already implemented formal part-time policies for associates and partners. Formal policies regarding time and criteria for promotion, part-time compensation arrangements, and related human resource policies were in place to support individuals choosing to take advantage of a reduced hours or part-time option. So most firms thought they had solved the problem of providing flexibility for their young associates to integrate their work and family responsibilities.

But the reality was something else. A study by the Women's Bar Association of Massachusetts[10] found, for example, that:

1. Consistent with the national pattern, over 90 percent of major Boston firms offered a part-time or reduced hours option;

2. Less than 5 percent of associates took advantage of it; less than two percent of all partners used it;

3. One-third of those who used it (and an equal number who did not) believed that it hurt the careers of those using this option because they were perceived as being less committed to either the firm or their profession than those who continued to work full-time, long hours;

4. The biggest barrier to use reported in both surveys and focus groups of lawyers was the stigma attached to breaking the norms of the profession, and;

5. Women constitute 28 percent of the attorneys in Boston law firms but account for 40 percent of attorneys leaving these firms. Approximately 40 percent of those who left their firm reported that the attitudes toward the reduced hours arrangements affected their decision to leave.

Thus, the above quote, written in response to a work-family report,[11] reflected the experiences of others who took the option. The problem was far from solved. The formal policies failed to overcome the informal norms or culture that penalized these professionals for deviating from the image of the "ideal worker" that was engrained in the minds of senior partners and perhaps in the minds of others in the profession.

Yet there continues to be evidence that a substantial proportion of lawyers would individually prefer to work shorter hours. But as one study demonstrated, no individual is likely to take this action as long as others do not follow suit.[12] Thus there is a collective action problem at work here.

This is the state of affairs today, among lawyers and perhaps among other professionals as well. Many organizations offer reduced hours options for family reasons; few people take it. Those who take it—and those who would like to but don't—worry about the negative career stigma it connotes. Meanwhile, the inability to manage these policies effectively appears to induce high rates of turnover and all its associated costs of recruitment, training, and lost productivity.

Clearly, this is a problem with multiple stakeholders—employees who, given their family needs, would prefer shorter hours; managing partners who are concerned about attracting and retaining talented professionals; clients who want high-quality services when they need them; and family members who bear the costs of unusable policies or policies that add more stress to those who use them.

What can be done? My codirector at MIT's Workplace Center, Lotte Bailyn, and her coauthors have invented a solution to this problem.[13] They call for redesigning work to meet the "dual agenda" requirements of workplace performance and personal and family roles and responsibilities. They see the design of work as the root cause of the problem and redesign of work as the place to start searching for solutions. This requires a very special kind of negotiations—a collaborative exploration involving front-line employees, supervisors, and perhaps even spouses in search of options that meet dual agenda objectives. Box 2.3 provides examples of how

Box 2.3
Dual Agenda Action Research Projects

The emphasis of these projects has been on identifying work practices and assumptions underlying them that create difficulties both for people's personal lives and for organizational effectiveness, and then to try, on an experimental basis, to change these practices.

To achieve this double goal researchers collaborated with local work units to understand the assumptions that underlie current practice and to experiment with new ways of working geared to helping employees' lives and helping the organization become more effective.

In one case, for example, the structure of daily time was altered in order to allow software engineers to better plan their work; in another case, a 360° performance review was introduced in order to allow the nonmeasurable "invisible" coordinating work of some employees to be recognized and valued; in still another case, a form was developed so that systems people could have a clearer view of what was requested of them and thus eliminate many of the "redos" they had previously encountered. In each case, the work of the unit was enhanced while at the same time giving employees more control over their work and thus easing pressure on all.

In one case, creating a cross-functional team of service and sales employees produced double gains: increased sales, because service workers had customer information that helped sales, and greater control over time, since both groups benefited from sharing information on installations and service.

These dual-agenda action-research projects have shown that it is possible to design work that integrates work needs and family needs in a positive, synergistic manner. But they have also shown how very difficult this can be because it goes against the deeply held beliefs about the separation of work and family spheres, some of which are embedded in law and personnel regulations.

Source: Lotte Bailyn, Robert Drago, and Thomas Kochan, *Integrating Work and Family Life: A Holistic Approach*, MIT Sloan School of Management, 2001, pp. 24–25.

Bailyn and her colleagues have applied this dual agenda strategy in different workplaces.

The key to starting these negotiations lies in legitimating the dual agenda. That means American business executives and their organizations need to see work and family as legitimate business issues. Paul Osterman, another MIT colleague, estimated, based on national survey findings, that about half of American businesses see work and family as values that are legitimate business issues.[14] How do we bring the other 50 percent along?

One way to do so is for market forces to send a clear message to firms that do not engage the dual agenda as a business issue. This will happen if valued employees, like the lawyer-spouse described earlier, are attracted to firms that take the dual agenda approach seriously. One innovative law firm in Boston, Sullivan, Weinstein & McQuay (SWM), is testing out this approach. Bob Sullivan, the firm's founder, designed his firm to appeal to lawyers who wanted flexible schedules and were willing to trade off some amount of income. Box 2.4 describes how this firm competes in its niche in the market for legal services. The fact that SWM recruits young associates after they have been trained and worked for several years in one of the big Boston firms has not gone unnoticed. Senior partners in several of the biggest firms are now asking what changes they need to make to retain this talent. The open question, however, is whether the same type of flexibility and variation in work hours could work in the large firms.

Another strategy would be for law firms to address this issue collectively. Indeed, in 2000, at the peak of the tight labor markets for lawyers, a group of senior partners from Boston's leading law firms began to meet to discuss what might be done. They were prodded to do so by the well-organized and persistent efforts of the Boston Bar Association's Work-Family Task Force. Each partner listed the various things his or her (mostly his) firm was doing or planned to do to reduce the work and family tradeoffs associates face. They

Box 2.4
The Part-time Law Firm

Sullivan, Weinstein & McQuay (SWM) is a firm of 17 lawyers founded in 1995. Its goal was to create a new type of law firm focused on providing better value to clients and more responsibility and flexibility for their attorneys. Eight years later, there is widespread belief at SWM that this is exactly what they have achieved.

Bob Sullivan describes the firm's strategy and culture: "We don't have many rules here. Our only rule is that you must be responsible in meeting your obligations to your clients and your coworkers." Attorneys can control their work schedule, work from home, negotiate a part-time position, and take leaves of absence. SWM also provides a home for lawyers in a variety of places in their professional careers with a variety of goals.

Eleven of the firm's lawyers are women, and six of them are on part-time schedules. All but one anticipates staying at the firm into the foreseeable future; however some were considering increasing or decreasing their workload.

SWM relies heavily on information technologies to increase productivity and keep costs low. The firm relies exclusively on the Westlaw online legal library; through a secure virtual private network the lawyers can work from their home offices. A traditional firm might have as many as 23 support staff for 17 attorneys. SWM has only 3.5 nonlawyers on their payroll, helping to reduce labor and associated space and management costs to approximately 50 percent of the costs in a traditional firm.

In one SWM lawyer's words:

What I saw at SWM when I was applying was a group of professionals all of whom were respected and treated like professionals by each other, with people responsible for their own work and their own time. It's a supportive group of people: we help each other out when someone's in a pinch and there's support for getting and handling cases on your own. [Lawyers at SWM get 10 percent of gross revenues received from clients they bring in.] No one has ever said anything about what hours I was in the office or not in the four years I have worked here. What I was told up front was: "you need to be responsive to your clients and as long as you are doing that, you know best what you need to do." And that's the way it's been.

Source: Brendan Miller, Thomas Kochan, and Mona Harrington, *Beyond the Part-Time Partner: A Part-Time Law Firm?* MIT Workplace Center Teaching Case, WPC# 100, 2003.

met several times, but by mid-2001 interest dissipated as the labor market shortages turned into surpluses when the big firms considered layoffs and slowed down their hiring in the face of the recession and the evaporation of the dot-com market that had been attracting young talented lawyers. So much for the collective efforts of these employers—their attention span is only as long as the labor market is tight!

Fortunately, the Women's Bar Association is picking up where the senior partners dropped the ball. The association is following up on its earlier study to see what, if anything, has changed. And a number of leading law firms are again beginning to discuss ways to reduce the high rate of turnover of women lawyers. This shows the power of collective action by a group of determined and potentially powerful professionals.

If collective action is required to alter the professional norms of lawyers, change will need to start where these norms first get formed—in law schools. And the change will come if women lawyers continue to organize and fight for change in professional norms, firm-specific practices, and cultures, and if they continue to vote with their feet and leave the big practice firms for more organizations like SWM.

Watch the lawyers—they have started something by raising these issues. While their efforts reflect a start-and-stop pattern, they may be ahead of others. Since almost 50 percent of current law school graduates are women, they might yet show the way for themselves and for other professionals who are facing the same pressures and obstacles to change.

The same challenge faces the health-care professions and industry. Like their counterparts in legal services, some health-care providers are indeed responding. Forrest Briscoe, an MIT Workplace Center PhD graduate, examined how physician careers have changed over the years in one particular large-scale health-care organization. For physicians, the problem of finding time for family life is doubly hard because patients never stop getting sick and never go away. Yet Briscoe reports that a sizable and growing number of female and male physicians found it possible in this organization to pursue part-time medical practice. This organization has been able to offer multiple career opportunities for physicians at different points in their life and family stages.[15] Yes, there are income and career trade-offs, but over time as more women and men take up these options the image of an "ideal career" will change.

As a doctor said in a *New York Times* article that focused on the long hours physicians have taken for granted as part of their profession: "I want to have a family. And when you work 80 or 90 hours a week, you can't even take care of yourself."[16]

And again, for widespread change to occur, the medical profession itself will have to change its norms. Kate Kellogg, a PhD student in our center, studied resident surgeons who are now being required by the board that certifies hospitals to reduce their hours from 120 to 80 per week. She reports one of the biggest obstacles to overcome in implementing the hours reduction is the "Iron Man" image that surgeons have cultivated for themselves. To accept the reduction somehow attacks their self-image and in the view of some, would downgrade the status, power, and dominant role surgeons hold in the medical circles and organizations.[17]

Kellogg's study also identifies critical but mostly silent stakeholders in debates about long work hours—the spouses of the residents. They are the ones who often feel the brunt of the fatigue and stresses that follow these long workdays.

In an interesting gender role reversal, one of our midcareer students who is married to a resident surgeon made this comment in response to a class discussion of work and family pressures:

In spite of the fact that she [his wife] was putting in all this effort, the head of the program, coming from a time when surgeons were men, with wives at home taking care of everything, could not understand how this lifestyle was not maintainable for her. There were no support programs or other alternatives available. Surgeons were supposed to do their job, not complain, and stick it out.[18]

Even in universities, faculty who want to be at the top of their field and make their careers in renowned universities often resist accepting that colleagues might have family aspirations or obligations requiring time and attention. One senior male MIT professor made the following comment at a promotion and tenure meeting several years ago: "Well, there are lots of other [read less prestigious] places that people can teach and do research than MIT." The notion was that it takes a commitment of long hours of work to make it at a place like MIT. I am happy to report that five years after making this comment the same professor has, as our kids would say, "gotten it." He recently became a vocal advocate for young women and men taking junior sabbaticals to have the time they need to extend the tenure clock and better balance their family and career responsibilities.

Universities like MIT still have a long way to go, but more and more now have policies in place to make it possible. Making it commonly accepted and standard practice without negative connotations and repercussions will require continued informal negotiations to change the culture of organizations, including the most elite ones. The good news is that labor market competition for the best and brightest talent is on the right side of this issue.

The Business Case for Flexibility

These market pressures help to strengthen what some call the "business case" for integrating work and family responsibilities. Indeed, there can be clear business benefits from reducing turnover and recruitment costs and for the increased motivation, commitment, and loyalty that is returned to employers by employees who have successfully worked out flexible arrangements.[19] Box 2.5 describes

Box 2.5
Luring Moms Back to Work

As more working mothers seek lengthy leaves to care for their families—or quit jobs entirely—some companies are devising new ways to lure them back to work.

After years of steady increases, the rate of working mothers with young children is declining. The percentage of new mothers who work fell to 55 percent in 2000 from 59 percent in 1998—and it hasn't risen since, according to the U.S. Census Bureau.

This development is likely to persist. According to a survey of about 3,500 workers, more than one quarter of women who are planning to have children think they will stop working for more than a few months.

Traditionally, many employers wrote off women who quit work to become stay-at-home moms. Now companies are experimenting with ways to retain moms or even would-be moms. Some are allowing employees to take leaves that can last as long as five years. Others are trying to recapture workers who have already left. (Many of these programs are open to men as well, but women tend to be the target audience.) The retention efforts go way beyond the offers of flexible hours and telecommuting that companies have used for some time to keep workers happy.

Deloitte & Touche LLP, the accounting firm, is preparing to launch a "Personal Pursuits" program sometime in 2004, which will allow employees to take an unpaid leave of absence of as long as five years for various personal reasons. The firm will run training sessions for employees on leave, assign them mentors, and periodically check to see if they are still planning to return to work. A major goal: further cutting turnover costs. Deloitte says flexibility programs already in place allowed it to save $41.5 million in such costs in fiscal 2003.

International Business Machines Corp. is a rarity; it has long allowed selected workers to take leaves of as long as three years. While open to both sexes, 80 percent of those using the program have been women, and the most common reason cited for taking a leave is "parenting," the company says. The leave is unpaid, though workers retain a major perk: They keep their health benefits. And while they're not guaranteed their old jobs when they return, IBM makes an effort to get them something comparable.

Source: Ann Marie Chaker, "Luring Moms Back to Work," *Wall Street Journal*, September 30, 2003.

the savings Deloitte and Touche and other companies estimate that flow from allowing employees to take extended "sabbaticals" to attend to family responsibilities. We have seen it in our own office at MIT as the example in box 2.6 illustrates. In some ways, the loyalty for flexibility trade may be a key component of the new social contract at work that will evolve.

In the 1990s, arrangements like this had to stay informal, below the radar screen of MIT's personnel policies. Since then, MIT has begun to encourage this type of arrangement by issuing formal "flexibility guidelines." This is a major step forward. But, alas, we still hear stories from secretaries and other staff members around

Box 2.6
Flexibility Close to Home

In 1991, I was lucky to hire an extremely competent and in many ways overqualified new assistant, Susan Cass. I knew that in the next few years I would face the challenge of organizing an international congress for our professional association. To do this I would need the support of a person of considerable creativity and energy, especially since our budget would require us to run this on a shoestring. Susan took charge of coordinating this event. My colleagues from around the world are still marveling at the standard she set for putting on a world-class congress.

Over the course of these years, Susan went through a series of personal and family transitions, including having a baby. Since I continued to need and value Susan's help, we worked out (despite MIT's rigid personnel policies at that time) a flexible arrangement. We both knew what work needed to be done. We used whatever technologies were available—first just a fax machine, then a home computer, and later email—to support and enable this flexible arrangement. Most of all we had the trust that didn't require either of us to count specific work hours or days. If Susan needed to stay home if her daughter woke up ill, she could do so. In return for this flexibility we not only retained Susan for this time period, I am convinced we got the productivity of much more than one full-time professional.

MIT that they encounter supervisors who resist requests to use the flexibility promised in the guidelines. Supervisors worry that "if we did it for them, everybody might want their own deal and I just don't have the time to manage all this."

Like MIT, most organizations have lots of creative and talented people who need and could benefit from flexibility and would provide handsome productivity and performance benefits in return. There are mutual gains to be found for those who pursue them. The challenge lies in making these opportunities available to all employees, not just those in the high income and occupational ranks or who happen to have supportive supervisors.

The key to *finding* these mutual gains opportunities lies in opening up discussions of how people work together to get their jobs done. The key to *sustaining* flexibility lies in ensuring that everyone shares in the benefits of flexibility in a fair way—including the supervisors, shareholders, and employees with diverse family needs and responsibilities. These ongoing, collaborative negotiations are essential to changing workplace cultures and empowering people to take advantage of the flexibility that a growing number of leading firms now offer.

Unions and Professional Associations

But, once again, individual firms cannot do this alone. Nor do they need to. Some unions have taken the lead in introducing family-care benefits and programs into collective bargaining at both firm and local industry levels.[20]

Local 1199 of the Service Employees International Union (SEIU) represents approximately 250,000 maintenance, clerical, and professional employees who work for hospitals in the New York City region. Based on a 1989 membership survey showing 80 percent of their members wanted the union to pursue a child-care benefit program, the union and 16 health-care institutions created a joint child-care fund financed by a 0.3 percent payroll contribution. By 2003, the joint program expanded to include 380 employers providing benefits to approximately 8,000 children per year. A joint labor-management board of trustees and local committees of parents and rank and file members manage the program.

The program runs several child-care centers, provides tuition vouchers and subsidies based on salary and number of children in a family, and more recently added a summer camp and career counseling and educational assistance for teenagers.

Similar joint programs have been negotiated in a number of other settings, such as the hotel association in San Francisco and the Hotel, Entertainment and Restaurant Employees; and the United Auto Workers and Ford, General Motors, and Daimler Chrysler. The UAW-Ford Family Services and Learning Center was created in 1999 and takes what it calls an "intergenerational" approach by providing programs from early childhood development to family educational services, and community service and outreach that draw heavily on the voluntary services of UAW retirees.

The Harvard Union of Clerical and Technical Workers (HUCTW) takes a different approach. It has made work and family a central theme in its organizing, bargaining, and membership service activities. Its contract with Harvard University provides for 13 weeks paid maternity leave with flexibility to use additional time accrued in vacation or sick pay, prorated benefits for part-time workers, and child-care subsidies. The union estimates that it resolves approximately 1,000 workplace problems informally or through mediation each year, about half of which involve scheduling flexibility. And it believes strongly in the need to take a dual agenda perspective to work design. HUCTW's Kris Rondeau puts it this way:

Work design is a core family issue and without redesigning work we are not going to be able to take care of our families. Work is structured badly—it is not flexible enough, interesting enough, nor meaningful enough. Power relationships are unhealthy, and the work design consultants who say we should redesign work in America to improve quality and productivity are off base. While I care about quality and productivity and am interested in those issues, work-family is just as important. The family is in trouble and people are suffering and it is because work is broken.[21]

These are examples of what is possible when two key stakeholders—workers and employers—work together to integrate work and family responsibilities.

Community and Family Groups

A growing number of groups are working to highlight the need for community, cross firm, and public policy initiatives on working family issues. In January 2004, for example, a coalition of 14 sponsoring organizations ranging from the AFL-CIO to Corporate Voices for Working Families joined together to create a group called Takecarenet[22] to share information and ideas on work-family policies. During the presidential campaign, Takecarenet collected signatures for a letter to national candidates saying that voters want paid leave for parents and early education for children. In the letter, Takecarenet cited the results from a California poll showing a majority of voters without children approved of the state's new paid leave law (described in box 2.8). In a recent national poll, a majority of voters without children claimed that child-care programs are an "absolute necessity" in their community.

Also of interest in this mix of organizations is Corporate Voices for Working Families. This group is a cross-firm network created by Donna Klein, the former head of work and family policies at the Marriott Corporation, a firm recognized as a leader in this area. She created Corporate Voices in recognition of the point emphasized in this chapter, namely, that the solution to work-family challenges requires a coordinated effort that goes beyond the boundaries and capabilities of any single firm. Her group's mission is to bring "private sector voices to public discussions on issues affecting working families."[23] This is a step in the right direction.

Work and family advocacy groups and organizations seem to be growing by the day. They are making innovative use of websites, email lists, networking, coalition building, and other modern means of communicating and mobilizing. Their voices will be heard in future policy debates on these issues and increasingly they are becoming resources and participants in community and firm level discussions on issues of interest to working families. One of the most longstanding and effective of these groups, the National Partnership for Women and Families, is described in box 2.7. The National Partnership and other groups like it will be valuable resources in moving forward and sustaining support for a working families' agenda.

Toward a National Work-Family Policy: Paid Leave as a First Step

Of all the work and family issues that are gaining attention, none is more visible and more likely, in my estimation, to see action at some point soon than provision for paid family leave. Indeed, all Americans should be embarrassed by the fact that the United States joins Australia as the only two advanced economies that lack a paid family leave policy.

Only since 1993 has the United States had an unpaid family leave policy. The first bill signed by President Clinton was the Family and Medical Leave Act. This law provides workers the right to up to 12 weeks unpaid leave per year to care for a newborn or adopted child or for an ill relative. Since its passage, a number of women, family, and labor groups have been lobbying for both expansion of coverage and improvements in the unpaid leave bill and for a paid leave plan, either at the national level or, failing there, at state levels.

Box 2.7
The National Partnership for Women & Families

The National Partnership for Women & Families is a nonprofit, non-partisan organization that uses public education and advocacy to promote fairness in the workplace, quality health care, and policies that help women and men meet the dual demands of work and family. Founded in 1971 as the Women's Legal Defense Fund, the National Partnership has grown from a small group of volunteers into one of the nation's most powerful and effective advocates for women and families.

Work and Family

The Family and Medical Leave Act (FMLA) was drafted by the National Partnership in 1984 and was enacted in 1993. The National Partnership promises to work to increase public awareness of the need for society to better address the time pressures facing working families and will persevere to expand the FMLA and other family leave policies to cover more working people and more family needs.

Workplace Fairness

Ensuring equal opportunity, protecting civil rights, preventing discrimination, and monitoring welfare reform—these are just some of the challenges that the National Partnership battles every day in our workplace fairness program. Unfortunately, discrimination is still a factor in women's access to jobs, pay, promotions, and fair treatment. This is a critical obstacle to economic security for low-income women, women moving from welfare to work, and those living on the economic margins. The National Partnership works to educate women about their legal rights in the face of discrimination and to inform the public about the severe costs of discrimination to our families and our economy.

Health Care

The National Partnership is a voice for women in the managed care debate, promotes access to the full range of reproductive health services, and works to prevent discrimination based on genetic information. The National Partnership also works to expand health services for low-income women and children and to ensure quality care in Medicare and Medicaid.

Source: http://www.nationalpartnership.org

State-level Initiatives

In his last year in office, President Clinton approved a rule change that would allow states to use surplus funds in their unemployment insurance accounts to fund paid family leave. This idea met stiff opposition from business groups and others (myself included) who worried that the large surpluses in the unemployment funds that had built up in the booming 1990s would evaporate as soon as the next deep recession came along. The critics were right about this and so as the recession of 2000–2001 began to bite into these funds, political support for this funding approach evaporated. It didn't matter, however, because the Bush administration rescinded the rule change when it came into office.

The upshot of this short political story is that there is considerable discussion underway in various states over the need for some form of paid family leave. Some states have acted. The Massachusetts legislature passed a paid leave plan in 2002, but the governor vetoed it. A broad-based coalition of labor, education, and community leaders was more successful in California (see box 2.8). That state passed the first comprehensive paid leave bill in 2002, which took effect on July 1, 2004. It is funded through payroll deductions, not through the unemployment insurance system. Several other states have limited paid leave programs for new parents or specific illnesses, some of which are funded through their Temporary Disability Insurance programs. Senator Joseph Lieberman has put forward a specific proposal for a national plan, calling for minimum national standards of four weeks paid leave (out of the 12 unpaid) and financed with employee payroll deductions. States could augment these minimum standards if they so choose and could experiment with alternative financing arrangements.

There is some risk in legislating a single uniform paid leave policy. First, many firms already provide some form of paid leave

Box 2.8
The Coalition Behind California's Paid Family Leave Bill

In September 2002, California passed the nation's first paid family leave legislation. The grassroots organizing and lobbying for the bill was mounted by the Paid Family Leave Coalition, a broad coalition of advocates and unions. One of the coalition's founding members, the California Labor Federation also became the bill's lead sponsor in August 2001. As the bill gained momentum, labor played a key role through testimony, lobbying, and grassroots mobilization, using its political clout at crucial points throughout the campaign.

The California Labor Federation, which is the state-level AFL-CIO, recognized the organizing potential of work-family benefits and was interested in issues that resonated with women and low-wage workers. A strong, progressive, and politically powerful organization, the Labor Federation saw improving state safety-net benefits, such as disability insurance, as the best way to help working Californians. The Labor Federation was a member of the Paid Family Leave Coalition and had a successful track record on related legislation, including CFRA, pregnancy disability leave, and family sick leave. In 1999, a labor bill raised the State Disability Insurance (SDI) benefit. The first benefit increase in many years, it cleared the path for labor leaders to consider expanding SDI to cover family leave. The same bill directed the state to study the potential costs of providing paid family leave through SDI.

As the bill moved successfully through the state legislature and gained support, it became a high priority for the Labor Federation. The coalition, along with the federation, mobilized thousands of union members to send postcards, call legislators, speak to the press, and generate support for paid leave. When the bill was on the governor's desk, labor drove home the national significance of the decision facing the governor. Using any and all connections, they generated calls and letters to the governor from national political figures, celebrities, and the head of the AFL-CIO.

Though there were many factors that helped paid family leave to pass in California, labor's central role was absolutely critical to its passage. Today, they have a new bumper sticker in California: "Paid Family Leave—Union Made."

Source: Excerpted from "Putting Families First, How California Won the Fight for Paid Family Leave," by Labor Project for Working Families, 2003.

---

to some of their employees—mostly to professional and manager-ial and other salaried employees. A major issue, therefore, is how do these apply? Would they be substitutes or additional benefits? Would firms now self-funding these leaves be able to off-load costs to the public program? All these issues call out for experimentation with a variety of different funding and dovetailing arrangements before enacting a one size fits all national policy.

I believe business, labor, and family advocates have a window of time to experiment with the forms of paid leave that best suit a diverse economy with a large number of firms and upper income employees that already have some form of paid leave to draw on for family needs. Working families should insist that we find ways to spread these more universally to low income workers through some combination of collective bargaining or other private sector initiatives and state-level or national policies that dovetail with these firm-specific policies. Failure to move in this direction leaves as the default solution a top-down and probably all too rigid gov-ernment mandate if and when the political forces are aligned to end America's embarrassment.

In short, working families should insist elected officials follow through by enacting a national policy that meets two key conditions:

1. Paid leave should be universal, covering all workers not just the highly paid professionals and salaried employees who are allowed to take time off without losing pay.

2. While some minimum standards should apply to all, individual firms and employees should have the flexibility to design and fund their paid leave policies in ways that dovetail with the vacation, sick leave, or other leave policies already on their books or that they negotiate or implement in the future. This would overcome the common employer criticism that government regulations are too rigid and conflict with benefits already provided by the firm.

Enacting a paid leave policy is only one piece of a comprehensive national working families' policy agenda. It would, however, not be a bad starting point, as long as politicians don't view it as the end point as well.

America has a longstanding tradition of first developing and experimenting with workforce and related social policies at the state level and, once proven, moving them to the national level. As suggested above, we are now in the early phase of this pattern with respect to paid family leave. But there is more to a state-level effort than just passing paid leave. Our MIT Workplace Center has called for development of state-level Work-Family Councils that would bring together the various stakeholders to develop a private and public policy agenda for working family issues. A summary of a bill introduced into the state legislature establishing the Council is provided in box 2.9. Time will tell whether these stakeholders will be willing and able to work together for the common good. Working families in Massachusetts and elsewhere should insist they do so.

Summary

The first step for working families to regain control of their destiny is to start talking and thinking about work and family as tightly coupled. This reframing does several things. First, it eliminates any ability for opponents of change to argue that this is simply "special interest" politics at work. How can efforts to address the needs of 130 million workers and their families be a "special" interest when it encompasses nearly all Americans? Second, this framing of the issue broadens the array of parties who should have a voice on these issues, thereby taking workplace policy and practice debates out of the old and stalemated labor-management divide and opening up the possibility of building new cross-group coalitions and partnerships to pursue a working family agenda.

Box 2.9
Bill Establishing a Massachusetts Work-Family Council

There shall be a Work-Family Council in the Executive Office of Economic Development. The mission of the Work-Family Council shall be to develop broadly shared understandings of critical work-family issues in the Commonwealth, and to promote, through privately funded research, experimentation, and education both.

The Governor, the Speaker of the House of Representatives, the Senate President, and the Caucus of Women Legislators shall each appoint three members in total. Each appointee must be from one of the following categories.

(1) A member of a legislative committee or administrative agency with responsibility for issues of economic development or working family support;

(2) An employee or manager of a business representing a key sector of the Massachusetts economy;

(3) An official of an AFL-CIO member union representing public sector or private sector workers;

(4) A member of a professional association or women's organization; and

(5) A member of low-income advocacy groups or community-based service organizations including both secular and faith-based institutions.

The duties of the Council shall include but not be limited to:

(1) holding hearings to identify major work-family issues in the Commonwealth;

(2) identifying representatives of all groups with important stakes in resolving specific work-family issues and devising processes for bringing the groups together to promote mutual understanding as the basis for coordinated problem-solving;

(3) using dialogue and negotiation among stakeholders with differing interests in work-family conflicts to advance the potential for problem solving that supports both workplace productivity and family care;

(4) designing and implementing pilot projects as requested in workplaces;

(5) proposing public policy solutions to work-family issues;

(6) promoting successful policies and practices in both public and private sectors and creating a repository of best practices;

(7) providing public education on work-family issues as matters of public as well as individual concern, and on the need for public policies and private workplace practices that support the well-being of both employers and families.

Third, it takes family policy issues out of the purely personal and private realm and puts them squarely in front of business, labor, and community leaders.

In short, to put this reframing to work for them, working families need to:

• Insist that work and family issues are treated as linked and legitimate concerns in business decisions and national workforce/workplace policies. This is a cultural issue—a shift from an assumption that grew up during the industrial age that work and family were separate and should be viewed as individual choices outside the scope of business concerns. Overcoming this engrained view will require constant reminders by workers and family members themselves that these issues need to be on workplace agendas.

• Promote individually and collectively the adoption of formal organizational policies at work that allow for flexibility and collaborative engagement at the workplace to make it happen. Then employees need to work with their peers in their firms and in their professional associations to go beyond the formal policies to help change the culture that has inhibited use of these formal policies.

• Advocate changes in the internal cultures of unions and professional associations, perhaps by electing and/or appointing more women to key offices, and by putting work-family benefits and flexibility at the top of their priority lists.

• Build and participate in broad-based, community networks and coalitions that invent solutions to specific work and family challenges by engaging the stakeholders who are normally silent or that otherwise are locked in adversarial or arms-length battles.

• Hold elected officials' feet to the fire by supporting national policies providing paid family leave policies/experiments that dovetail with firm policies; flexibility in work hours that rest on a foundation of worker control; and a return to the long-run objective of reducing working hours rather than relying on longer hours as the engine of America's productivity.

• Work with other stakeholders in their communities and states to foster coordinated attacks on problems of work and family integration.

3 Contributing and Prospering in a Knowledge Economy

My father began working full time on our family farm in Wisconsin after only eight years of schooling. He knew first-hand what he missed and admonished his children to stay in school and get the most and best education we could. In his view, education was the ticket to a better, more secure, and prosperous life. He was right.

His advice is just as right for our children as it was for his. The only amendment to that advice is that our children cannot stop learning when they leave school and begin their careers. Learning has to be a life-long activity.

The cliché is we live in a "knowledge economy." Comparing who got ahead and who didn't in recent years demonstrates that this is more than a cliché. What is less well recognized, however, is how family structures and life choices interact with knowledge to shape who gets ahead.

Massachusetts comes close to the paragon of a knowledge-based economy. Over the past twenty years, its small and shrinking manufacturing sector has given way to knowledge-intensive industries such as biotechnology, health, finance, and education. As manufacturing declined from 24 percent of all jobs in the state in 1983 to 13 percent in 2000, the number of jobs requiring a college degree or more increased from 30 to 38 percent. Everyone expects this trend to continue.[1] Which families prospered in this state over the past

Table 3.1
Education, Family Structures, and Income Growth in Massachusetts, 1980–2000

	1980	2000	Absolute change	Relative change
Median income by educational attainment of both spouses				
Both less than high school	$41,340	$38,000	–$3,340	–8.1%
Both high school graduates only	51,915	56,000	4,085	7.9%
Both with some college	54,310	67,420	13,110	24.1%
Both college graduates	78,292	106,600	28,308	36.2%

Source: Paul Harrington, Neeta Fogg, and Thomas Kochan, "The State of Working Families in Massachusetts, 1980–2000," MIT Workplace Center Working Paper, 2004.

twenty years? Table 3.1 provides a clear answer; those with two highly educated parents who were both employed. Families where both the husband and wife had bachelor or higher degrees increased their family incomes by a third between 1980 and 2000, while those without a high school degree lost 8 percent and the median family's income remained stuck at about the same level it was two decades ago. As noted in chapter 2, those who gained ground did so at the price of adding more hours to paid work.

In this type of economy, knowledge is the most important source of power families have to draw on to regain control over their destiny. And because knowledge and the opportunity to apply it to paid work are the keys to value creation, they are also essential to producing mutual gains for families, their employers, and the economy. A necessary condition for turning this country around is to make sure the future workforce is well prepared to support a knowledge-based economy. That means we need to figure out how both to encourage and to help more young people get the education they need to contribute value to the economy so that they have a chance to share in its benefits. We also have to continue to reinvest in those already of working age to keep their knowledge and skills current and marketable.

The Basics

Let's start with the basics. There is no substitute for high-quality education from the earliest years of child development and preschool and beyond. We all know this and many families are doing their part to provide their children with a good start. This is true for families able to afford living in communities with well-funded public schools or who can afford to send their children to private preschool programs and elementary and high schools. These are the same families that very likely have emphasized education and child development at home from early on in their children's lives. This segment of the population is preparing for the knowledge-based economy and their investments in and commitment to education will serve them and the American economy well in years to come. The problem is that this is not the reality for enough children and families today.

A day before the normal start of the school break for the Christmas-New Year's holidays in 2003, the Attleboro school district in Massachusetts closed its doors to conserve funds.[2] Most of these kids probably saw this as an early Christmas present. I doubt they calculated the effects of losing one day of education on their future earning power or value to the economy. And no one probably bothered to estimate the costs to parents who had to juggle schedules and absorb the expense of an extra day of child care. These, however, are the long- and short-term costs of failing to adequately fund our basic educational system.

Attleboro is a small, low income, working class, immigrant community in southeastern Massachusetts. Its school district gets 55 percent of its budget from state and federal funds. Its families do not have the discretionary incomes to supplement the budgets of its schools with voluntary contributions, fund raising auctions, and in-kind contributions as is the norm in the more exclusive, high-income suburbs of Boston. Attelboro spent $6,679 per pupil in 2002 compared to between $10,000 to $12,000 per pupil in Brookline, Newton, Weston, and the other high-income districts in the state. Failure to support the children of Attleboro ensures the gaps in income between families that have access to the best and the most education and those left behind will continue to plague the state and, if replicated elsewhere, the nation.

The families of Attleboro were not alone in feeling the pain of state budget cuts. The cuts in federal funds and the decline in state revenues that followed the recession and the 2001 tax cuts caused Massachusetts to cut $500 million in state aid to local governments between 2000 and 2003. One careful study, summarized in box 3.1, reports it would take $600 million to restore spending on education in the state to its pre-2000 levels. As the Massachusetts lieutenant governor notes in box 3.2, she and the governor and state legisla-

Box 3.1
Education Budget Realities in Massachusetts

Massachusetts has the dubious honor of having cut real per-pupil spending by a larger percentage than any other state, by more than 14 percent between fiscal 2002 and 2004. . . . While cutting school aid, the state also cut aid to local governments by nearly 15 percent in its fiscal year 2004 budget. . . . Just to make up for the reduction in real education resources caused by the cuts in state aid, property taxes would have to increase by an extra 11 percent over the past two years.

For 2005, Governor Romney proposed increasing spending on education by $115 million. While this increase is welcome, it would take an increase of over $300 million just to make up for the nominal cuts in state education spending over the past two years and an increase of about $600 million to restore the level of real per-pupil state education spending that Massachusetts enjoyed just two years ago.

Source: Andrew Reschovsky, "Mass. Fiscal Crises Hit Education Hard," *Boston Globe*, January 31, 2004.

Box 3.2
Investing in Education versus Revenue and Budget Realities

When Governor Romney and I came into office one year ago, we were confronted with a stubborn recession that showed no signs of abating. Our administration resolved to avoid short-term fixes, like raising taxes, which would hurt small businesses and hinder our competitiveness in the long term. This year's budget . . . reflects an ongoing commitment to fiscal discipline and reform as well as new investments in education intended to lay the groundwork for long-term economic growth in Massachusetts. A key factor contributing to future economic growth will be the quality of our public schools and graduates. While we still have economic challenges, this year's budget demonstrates the administration's deep commitment to investing in quality education for all children, in building a high educated workforce and the belief that public education should extend from kindergarten through employment: "K through Job."

Source: Lt. Governor Kerry Healy, "Rebuilding Bay State's Educated Workforce," *Boston Globe*, January 31, 2004, p. A15.

tors recognize the need to restore these funds, but they simply do not have the funds to match the need.

For some, the task of gaining a good education cannot be separated from the challenges encountered in meeting other basic health, family, and parenting needs and responsibilities. Consider the enormous challenges some children and families in our most impoverished communities face on a daily basis. Box 3.3 illustrates the stark reality and depth of these challenges by walking through a day in the life of a community nurse practitioner whom I happen to know quite well.

Business leaders, both as citizens and self-interested employers, should be up in arms over the disparity between the high- and low-income communities and school systems. Assuming the economy grows at even a moderate rate over the next decade, business will once again face shortages of knowledge workers. The biggest pool

Box 3.3
The Children Being Left Behind

Kathy Kochan is a nurse practitioner for a community-based health-care organization that specializes in serving patients with HIV and other chronic illnesses.

I started a recent conversation over dinner with that seemingly innocuous question: "How was your day?"

My first stop today was to see one of my long-term patients, a single mother aged 41 with three teenage children living at home. The oldest is 17 and should be in the eleventh grade. He wasn't doing well in school; there were discipline issues; mom was at school every week for something or other. Finally, he left school and went into a GED program. In my view, when you go into a GED Program, you are left behind.

Another stop. As I walked in to see a 42-year-old mother with multiple physical and emotional problems I was greeted by her 16-year-old son. He is the father of a six-month-old baby who lives with the baby's mom in another city close by. The father is involved in caring for his child and holds down a job that brings in about $400 every two weeks. I asked him why he was at home and not at school. He had been doing fairly well in school but had a significant absenteeism problem. Because of this he was told to leave school. His mother said this had been going on for some time and was more than she could handle. This young man had previously been remanded to the custody of the Department of Youth Services by his mother for discipline problems. Another child left behind, this time with another generation to care for. . . .

A third stop. This was to visit a 39-year-old patient whose health has been deteriorating for some time and needs badly to conserve her strength. She has four biological children ranging in age from 17 to 13 (including a set of twins) and two adopted children, ages three and eight, whose mother (her sister) is in prison. One of her 17-year-olds has a child whom he brings home to visit from time to time. The 16-year-old is also a mother with a nine-month-old baby who also lives with them. The good news is the 16-year-old mother is in school but the baby could not get into day care at school and so is left home in the care of my patient. If she is too weak to take care of the baby on a given day, the mother has to stay home from school. Another child falling behind. . . .

continued

My patient is a good advocate for these kids but sometimes just gets overwhelmed. Last week the two little girls, both of whom have attention deficit disorder, were at home when I arrived. I asked why they weren't in school. They had run out of medication and were told not to come to school until they had medication because they were too disruptive. All this is going on when my patient should be conserving her strength to deal with her own illness. In this case, two generations of a family are at risk of being left behind if my patient can't take care of herself.

of people available to fill the growing demand for knowledge workers are minorities, children of immigrants, and young women. All of these groups are underrepresented in the scientific and engineering professions. If we don't take actions to change this, yet another generation will indeed be left behind.

Recognizing the severity of this problem, the National Science Foundation commissioned a group of business and academic leaders to explore ways to encourage more young women and minorities to take up scientific and engineering degrees and careers.[3] Box 3.4 summarizes the depth and breadth of the challenge. Given what this distinguished group described as the "quiet crisis" in the talent mix America will need to remain a world leader in scientific discovery and innovation, it challenged the business community to work in partnership with the full "educational supply chain" and with leaders of minority and women's organizations to address this crisis.

There are countless government and private sector reports like this, all making the same point: Education is important; we are not doing a good job at preparing the next generation for the workforce and economy of the future; we are at best perpetuating and perhaps even widening the gap in educational opportunities between rich and poor families and children; and, therefore, thoughtful business, government, and civic leaders ought to do their part to change all of this. I have participated in enough of these types of study groups

Box 3.4
The Best Report on the Science and Engineering Workforce

The nation's aging technical workforce draws from a narrow and decreasing segment of the U.S. population. A successor generation has shown declining interest in pivotal fields, including mathematics, computer sciences, physical sciences, and engineering itself. These trends, building gradually over many years, have produced a "quiet crisis" in the development of technical talent.

America's talent imperative is to attract and academically prepare a larger share of all of our citizens for science and technology careers. White men made up almost twice as great a share of the science and engineering workforce as they do of the population, while white women represented are underrepresented in technical fields by about 50 percent. The underrepresentation of African-Americans and Hispanics remains even more pronounced. African-Americans comprised 12 percent of the U.S. population, but held only 3.4 percent of the science and engineering jobs in 1999. Hispanics made up nearly 12 percent of the U.S. population in 1999, but were only 3.4 percent of science and engineering employment. Moreover, these demographic imbalances scarcely changed during the technology boom years of the 1990s.

Women, who comprise almost half of the college-degreed workforce, make up less than 25 percent of the science and engineering workforce, regardless of ethnicity or race. They are most fully represented in the life sciences, but account for just 23 percent of physical scientists and 10 percent of engineers.

At the graduate school level, although minority enrollments have increased during the last decade, the numbers are still dismally low. For African-Americans, Hispanics, and American Indians, fewer than 100 of each group received doctorates in science and engineering fields in 2001. During a period from 1981 to 1999, the top 10 PhD-producing institutions graduated fewer than 100 African-Americans and fewer than 200 Hispanics per institution during that time period, with the majority of institutions not surpassing the 100 mark.

The outlook is somewhat more encouraging for women, who increased their share of baccalaureate degrees in almost every broad field of science and engineering during the 1990s and earned almost 40 percent of the PhDs in those fields in 2001. Still, women have stayed away from engineering and the physical sciences in droves. In the field of computer sciences, where demand is projected to grow much faster than the rate of other occupations, the number of women has actually declined from its high in the mid-1980s.

To remain on this course is perilous.

Source: *The Land of Plenty: Diversity as America's Competitive Edge in Science, Engineering, and Technology*, www.bestworkforce.org

(as I did in the group cited in box 3.4) to realize these nice words will lead nowhere. Why? Because they reflect the same top-down view of the problem, they lack the perspective and direct involvement of the precise families they target for improvement, and they leave it to the conscience of the individual leaders and organizations to drive action. Not much will be done to change until working families get involved in shaping these reports, feel personal ownership for their content and recommendations, and are in a position to hold all groups, including themselves, accountable for taking the actions called for.

If the working families of greatest concern to the report cited in box 3.4 were directly involved in its drafting, I think they would recommend stronger action in stronger language. I could imagine such a group recommending something along the following lines:

• Close the gap in funding of schools between rich and poor communities.

• Stop treating CEOs and their firms as individual fiefdoms and get the business leaders in our community and/or industry together with us and work out clear goals, timetables, and metrics for making progress by providing jobs, internships, and mentoring programs led by successful young men and women, and hold all of us collectively accountable for meeting the goals we set.

• Keep putting the families you want to target for improvement in the same room with business, government, education, labor, and civic leaders on your panel; get us all on the same page, working together for a common purpose.

However, that type of working families–business–government–academic study group has yet to be convened. It is precisely this type of coalition that is needed to achieve the results each of these parties say they want and need.

On the topic of early childhood education, a growing body of evidence has now convinced nearly everyone that the early years of life are critical to a child's potential for learning.[4] Early childhood education and development, therefore, has to be the starting point for a knowledge-based economic strategy. This was the idea behind Head Start, one of the most successful and yet under-funded programs that came out of Lyndon Johnson's War on Poverty in the 1960s. More recently, the bill called "No Child Left Behind" enacted in 2001 with the support of the president and Congress again recognized this principle.

There is one problem. We are not putting our money behind our rhetoric. The original bill authorized Congress to allocate $18 billion a year to fund the provisions of the bill. President Bush's budget proposal called for $11 billion in 2002 and slightly more in 2003 and 2004. Even if the bill had been fully funded, it would have provided only a fraction of what independent estimates suggest would be needed to fund all of its provisions for supporting early childhood education programs in poor neighborhoods, upgrade teacher quality and certifications, set and support achievement standards, and so on. No child left behind indeed!

Both candidates for president in 2004 recognized and stressed the need to increase funding for all levels of education. John Kerry had ambitious plans to promote early childhood education, to lower the costs of college tuition, etc. In his state of the union address in January 2004, President Bush called for increasing the funding of community college job training programs by $250 million. The goal is to "prepare people for the twenty-first-century workforce." This is a laudable objective and labor market and educational experts generally agree that community colleges serve a critical role in preparing the workforce for the future economy.

Putting $250 million into community colleges is a nice, symbolic gesture. It allowed the president to give a rousing speech at Owens Community College in Toledo, Ohio, in support of his initiative.

There is one problem. Investing $250 million a year will not get the funding for community colleges back to even where it was in fiscal year 1999. Indeed, the week before the president visited Owens Community College, six staff members lost their jobs because of funding cuts.[5] Perhaps they should have briefed the president on what is needed to make a real difference in the education and training programs he was talking about.

So there is no shortage of good ideas and good intentions. The challenge lies in holding elected officials accountable to their campaign promises. That is the job of the working families coalition.

The Knowledge Economy Skill Mix

There is no substitute for a good education in the basics. But what are the basics for a knowledge-based economy? Clearly, as stressed above, mathematical, technological, and scientific literacy are essential. But in today's workplace, the ability to lead and work effectively in teams, to communicate clearly, and to solve problems are equally critical. These are key skills that employers are looking for in job applicants.[6] They are the skills needed to put scientific and technical knowledge to work. So parents and employers need to insist that these skills be built into the pedagogy and curricula from elementary school to college. As Dana Mead, former CEO of Tenneco, said, "When I recruited MIT students they had great technical grounding but not a good notion of how the real world works, how to get things done, and how to deal with people!"[7]

Elementary and secondary schools may be ahead of most universities on this score. If my own family is any indication, changes are well underway in the style of teaching and learning in good public schools. Our youngest child experienced much more emphasis on team projects and a more interactive style of teaching and learning than did his older siblings.

Nothing, however, changes more slowly than college curricula. But even as traditional a place as MIT's School of Engineering is starting to give more emphasis to these skills, prodded in no small part by comments similar to Dana Mead's. Several years ago the School of Engineering developed a program called Undergraduate Practice Opportunities Program (UPOP) to give its technologically savvy students experience and training in group dynamics, decision-making, leadership, and project management. MIT is about to take a further step by introducing a new undergraduate minor in management to complement its science and engineering majors. The idea behind this initiative is to provide these talented young people a deeper understanding and mastery of the skills needed to function effectively in today's workplaces. Employers (indeed students themselves) should be demanding that students in all colleges be exposed to this type of material and experience it as part of their undergraduate education. These are the skills needed to be productive in today and tomorrow's knowledge-based workplace.

Life-Long Learning: From Rhetoric to Reality

In the farming economy of my father's youth, eight years of formal schooling was all the time his family could afford to have him away from working on the farm. Yet over the years he somehow learned the skills needed to supplement income from the farm by being a self-employed plumber and a union carpenter. When milk prices fell, he would put more time into these other trades. He seemed to believe in the value of life-long learning long before the term was coined.

Members of today and tomorrow's workforce need to have the same willingness to continue learning throughout their working lives. But there are two big differences from my father's time. First, scientific and technical advances of the last fifty years make it less possible to do this on one's own without access to formal educational programs. Second, keeping skills current is especially important and perhaps a special challenge for women (or men) who move in and out of the labor force or work part-time at different stages of their family life course. Not only might their occupational knowledge base and job opportunities change, their access to both on-the-job and employer-sponsored training and educational programs are likely to be more limited than those of full-time employees. This raises two key questions: Will there be a sufficient supply of life-long learning opportunities and will the full range of people who need to continue learning have access to them?

The American Society for Training and Development (ASTD) reports that business spends something on the order of $200 billion, or 2 percent of payroll annually, on training and development.[8] This sounds like a lot of money. Indeed it is. The problem is that most of it goes to a small fraction of the labor force and much of the training (setting aside questions of quality) is focused on what the economics profession calls *specific training*, that is, training that is relevant to the work of the firm, as opposed to the *general training* workers need to keep their skills current if they are to find a job in the external labor market.

We should not find this surprising. It has long been recognized that the American economy suffers from what the economics literature calls a *market failure* with respect to training. That is, there is less general training than what would be good for the overall economy because individual firms fear that others will not invest their fair share.[9] No rational individual firm will want to pay the costs of general training while its competitors don't; instead they lure those trained by others to come and work for them. This problem will persist as long as individual firms make training investment decisions.

Leaving training largely to individual firms may have been tolerable in the old days when firms made a commitment to provide long-term, secure jobs for those loyal employees who chose to stay with them throughout most of their careers. We know those days are over. And it is hard to trust employers who say, don't worry, we can't provide you with employment security, but we will give you the training and experience needed to be employable if you do need to leave. This promise always sounds to me a little like a husband who encourages his wife to keep in shape and stay attractive so that if things don't work about between them she will have other good options. Few of the men I know are that open-minded or willing to put their relationships in constant competition with the market!

There are two ways to overcome this type of market failure. One would be to fund education and training on a collective industry or society basis, as we do with public education. The reality, however, is that in a world of constrained budgets and large deficits, we are not likely to see the federal government reinvest or raise taxes targeted to life-long learning at any levels close to what is needed. Indeed, federal spending on employment training has declined in the last five years. In 1999, the U.S. Department of Labor's Employment and Training Administration budget for training programs was $5.7 billion; in 2004 the president's budget request for training programs in inflation adjusted dollars was $5.0 billion.[10] We should not expect a dramatic increase in funds from this source, regardless of who is in the White House or Congress.

Former secretary of labor Robert Reich learned this lesson in the early years of the Clinton administration. He and the president had campaigned hard on the notion that the new economy required more training and investment in human capital. But when the administration had to choose between cutting the federal deficit and the investments on which it campaigned, we know the choice it made. Reich captured it well in the title of his memoir as secretary: *Locked in the Cabinet*.[11] The lesson to workers and families that depend on life-long learning should not be lost: Don't wait for the federal government to provide the funding and access needed.

If working families can't expect individual employers or the federal government to provide life-long learning, what are they to do? The answer is to make continued learning a priority on our own negotiating and decision-making agendas and to build the institutions that will see it as in their organizational interests to supply life-long learning opportunities. Some workers are already doing this.

Surveys document that most young professionals are following the advice of their college placement professionals (and some of their professors) to give top priority to opportunities for learning and development in choosing a job.[12] This is the type of labor market pressure that has the best chance of getting employers to invest in continuous development.

But the longer one stays with an employer, the less individual bargaining power a person will have since the costs of leaving the firm increase. So for the long run, there is no substitute for ensuring one has the time, financial resources, and institutional opportunities to keep skills fresh and updated. That is, employees themselves, individually or collectively, need to take control over the funding and delivery of life-long learning.

Alternative Approaches to Life-Long Learning

A number of models already exist for doing so. Various professions require a certain number of hours of education and training to retain one's certification. Nurses, lawyers, and civil engineers (now even labor arbitrators) lose their "license" unless they meet the minimum hours of continuing education. Some of this is provided directly by their professional associations and some is provided by a variety of other private sector vendors, conference organizations, or universities. Box 3.5 illustrates how one professional group, the American Physical Therapists Association, does this and how it has paid off for its members. The key to making this approach work is for professions to require their members to participate in ongoing training. If they do so, a market of training suppliers will develop to meet

Box 3.5
The American Physical Therapists Association

Ann Knocke is a physical therapist working in the Boston area. When she read a draft of this chapter and my call for professional associations to take up the task of continuing education and helping members find available job opportunities, she said: "That's what our Association, the American Physical Therapists Association (ATPA), does. My supervisor and several coworkers learned of their job openings through the Association's website. And I sit on the Association's committee that creates and maintains certification exams. A special certification that came with that role helped me secure my current job."

A visit to the APTA website (www.apta.org) shows an extensive array of membership services and benefits including a long list of job openings that can be sorted by location, job title, and specialization; professional development opportunities and professional requirements; advice on how to search for a job; mentoring opportunities; information on and lobbying efforts related to potential legislative changes affecting the profession; and a variety of insurance and other discounts the association has negotiated with providers of these services.

the demand. And, many employers will, as some do now, pay part or all of the costs of this ongoing professional development.

Another model is the joint union-management training programs funded through hourly contributions negotiated in collective bargaining. Box 3.6 describes one well-developed joint program between the Boeing Corporation and the International Association of Machinists. This type of joint program has many positive design features. It is funded with regular, predetermined contributions (in this case $.14 per work hour) and so it is not subject to the vagaries of annual budget making (and cutting). The fact that it is jointly negotiated means the parties have to make their own judgments about how important investment in training is relative to putting additional money toward pay or other fringe benefits. The work-

Box 3.6
Life-Long Learning: Boeing and the Machinists' Union

The concept of a joint program was first introduced in the 1989 collective bargaining agreement between the International Association of Machinists and Aerospace Workers (IAM) and the Boeing Corporation. The contract language states: "The Union and the Company agree that workplace knowledge and skills training for bargaining unit employees will be the joint responsibility of the Union and the Company through the IAM/Boeing Quality through Training Program (QTTP)." The IAM/Boeing Joint Programs are financed by a fund that receives 14 cents per payroll hour for all bargaining unit employees. In 1999, the budget for the joint programs was approximately $25 million.

The following nine activities are supported by the joint programs with staff selected from union and management ranks.

• Career and Personal Development
• Job Combinations
• Technology Change
• High Performance Work Organization Initiatives
• Laid-off and Reemployment Training Services
• Industrial Skill Training
• Certification and Regulatory Requirements Training
• Transfer Process Improvement and Support
• Support for "The Mutual Objectives of the Union and the Company"

During layoffs, QTTP buffers the pressure on government agencies as it helps to transition people to federal funds and gets them prepared to start training under the provisions of the Worker Adjustment and Retraining Notification (WARN) Act. QTTP has responded to three major layoff events: 29,000 workers in 1993, 14,000 workers in 1999, and 17,660 workers from 2001 to late 2002. Additionally, QTTP makes projections about labor market growth areas, teaches unemployment survival skills, and offers financial and retirement planning courses.

Source: Kevin Long and Betty Barrett, "The International Association of Machinists and Boeing Joint Quality through Training Programs," *MIT Labor Aerospace Research Agenda Case Study*, 2004.

force has a direct voice in the governance and use of these funds so that the training provided is, as is the case in the Boeing program, more likely to involve general, marketable skills. Clearly, workers and the economy would benefit from having programs like Boeing's available to more workers. One way to spread these to larger numbers would be for the federal government to provide a tax credit to firms and employees who make these investments.

Even in the absence of collective bargaining, a variety of tax incentives could be devised to encourage the buildup and use of life-long learning funds. Some of these could be vested in individuals so that they would not lose them if they leave an employer. They might, for example, use their learning accounts to finance the cost of further education or refresher courses. The key to all these models is that workers and their professional associations and unions take the initiative to supply ongoing learning opportunities and have a strong voice in their design, funding, and delivery.

Nearly all of the above life-long learning models rely on being in an ongoing employment relationship. What are we to do about people who want to reenter the paid labor market after having spent extended periods of time devoted to family care duties? Of course, here I mean mostly women.

Currently there are relatively few models other than self-financing that might meet this need. So the task is to invent new options. One option might be for professional associations and unions to step into this breach by becoming the major providers of life-long learning. I will return to this idea in chapter 7 when we take up the future of unions and associations. For now it is enough to note that this is a void waiting for some inventive institution to fill it.

Summary

Working families have a major stake in translating rhetoric about the knowledge economy into reality. Without putting knowledge, skills, and scientific and technological innovations forward as the key competitive strategies of the nation, regional economies, and individual companies, America will engage in a futile and losing race to the bottom with lower-cost countries. And we will become even more of a nation divided between haves and have-nots until the cohesion of a democratic and peaceful society breaks down.

To avoid this fate, we need to make sure the next generation is equipped to build and grow a knowledge-based economy. This will require:

• Educational systems that encourage young girls and boys of all races and cultural backgrounds to develop interests in and to obtain the scientific, technical, mathematical, and behavioral knowledge and skills needed to be successful in and contribute to a knowledge-based economy.

• Regional economic development networks and strategies that bring university, industry, and workforce leaders together to promote entrepreneurship and ensure that future organizations are built to make the best use of employee knowledge and skills.

• National economic policies that fund basic education adequately and equitably and that support and reward regions and firms for investing in human capital.

• New institutions for delivering life-long learning. These may be professional associations, unions, or some other entities yet to be invented.

4   Good Jobs

The Congress hereby declares that it is the continuing policy and responsibility of the Federal Government . . . to promote maximum employment, production, and purchasing power."
—The Full Employment Act of 1946

[It is] . . . the right of all Americans able, willing, and seeking paid work to opportunities for useful paid employment at fair rates of compensation."
—The Full Employment and Balanced Growth Act of 1978

I won't be satisfied until every American who wants a job can find one.
—George W. Bush, *The 2004 Economic Report of the President*, p. 4.

The big question on everyone's mind today is: Will there be enough good jobs available for all those who want to work? In the booming economy and tight labor markets of the 1990s, this would have seemed a silly question. Then we had what the business books called a "War for Talent."[1] Today, however, slow job growth and concern that the quality of jobs available is deteriorating worry blue- and white-collar working families alike. The good news, if there is good news here, is that the nation's dismal job growth record from the end of the last recession in 2001 through most of 2004 heightened public awareness and elevated this issue to the top of the political and policy-making agenda. Working families have a major stake in keeping it there.

It may come as news to most Americans, but since 1946 "full employment" has been the stated policy of our country. This policy was reinforced in 1978 when Congress passed "The Full Employment and Balanced Growth Act," or as it is better known, the Humphrey-Hawkins Bill. As the quote from President Bush illustrates, politicians nearly always couch their arguments for their favorite economic policy as one that will provide jobs for all Americans who want to work. Yet the reality is that historically job creation has taken a back seat to other policy objectives like fighting inflation, cutting taxes, and balancing the budget. So the challenge to working families lies in figuring out how to hold elected official and private sector decision-makers to their promise to translate their rhetoric about creating and sustaining good jobs into reality for "all those who wish to work."

Will There be Enough Knowledge-Based Jobs in America?

The term "jobless recovery," first coined following the recession of 1990, resurfaced again recently in light of the fact that America had 2.2 million fewer jobs in February 2004 than three years earlier, even though the last recession ended in November 2001. Job growth picked up in starts and stops later in the year, but the Bush administration's first term still ended with fewer jobs in the economy than we had when it began. This record would be bad enough on its own. It is made worse by the lack of agreement among experts over why job growth is so slow. The leading suspects are rapid productivity growth that makes it less necessary to hire workers to increase output, reluctance to add new workers given rising health-care and other costs, loss of manufacturing jobs to low-wage countries that fail to respect basic human and labor rights, global competition to keep prices down, loss of jobs to "offshoring," and general business uncertainty given concerns over how we will pay for the budget deficits the federal government has built up. Most likely all of these factors play some role; and so attacking each has to be part of a national strategy to create good, sustainable jobs in America. The key question is, where should working families urge policy makers and organizational decision-makers to focus their energies in creating and sustaining jobs in America?

Starting Points: Job Focused Macroeconomic Policies

Because job creation is such a visible political concern, federal policy makers often make overly optimistic predictions of job growth. Figure 4.1 illustrates the point in stark terms. It charts the projections of future job growth offered by the Council of Economic Advisors (CEA) against the actual record. Each year since 2002, the CEA predicted the country would create over 200,000 jobs per month. The tax cuts enacted in 2001 and again in 2003 were supposed to do the trick but did not, in large part because they went to the

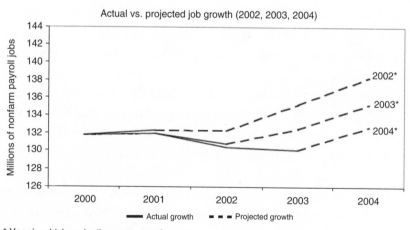

* Year in which projections were made.
Source: *Economic Report of the President*, 2002, 2003, 2004.

Figure 4.1
Job Creation: Predictions and Results. Source: Jared Bernstein, Lee Price, and Isaac Shapiro, "Missing the Moving Target," Economic Policy Institute and Center on Budget and Policy Priorities, February 12, 2004.

people at the top of the income ladder, who are more likely to save than spend significant portions of their tax cuts.

American working families deserve better. They are tired of having to wait three or more years for indirect strategies for job growth to have an effect. A more direct job creation strategy is needed. Numerous more direct options are available. If tax cuts are to be used again in the future, they need to be targeted to lower- and middle-income families that can be depended on to spend all or most of the monies received. Another option that has appeal for reasons mentioned in the previous chapter would be federal grants to states to make up for the cuts in state and local budgets. A favorite suggestion is to invest in infrastructure projects such as school repairs and renovations. Another option with dual benefits for the economy and the environment would be to invest in the infra-structure needed to reduce dependence on oil as an energy source. The point here is not to advocate a specific spending target. There are lots of worthy options. Instead, working families should simply insist that the supposed national commitment to full employment be taken at face value and hold elected officials accountable by adopting tax and spending strategies that are focused directly on job creation.

Obviously, there are limits to how much direct tax cuts and stimulus packages can do, if for no other reason than that the country has this enormous deficit to contend with. The next option, therefore, is to encourage existing firms to create new jobs. Public policy can help with this task as well. From time to time Congress and both Republican and Democratic administrations have provided tax credits to companies for investing in physical capital or research and development. This type of policy is often criticized for giving firms tax breaks to do what their business strategies would lead them to do with or without the incentive. Economists label this the "deadweight losses" associated with tax incentives. This is a real concern. But it has not stopped Congress from turning to these options before. If it does so again, there is no reason the same tax credits or other suitable incentives should not be used to encourage and reward investments in human capital. So perhaps the basic rule here should be that if federal policy makers are willing to absorb the deadweight losses associated with incentives to invest in physical capital or research and development, they should be willing to do so for investments in human capital or actual jobs as well.

Recently, I had a conversation about tax incentives with the CEO of one of America's largest global communications companies. He recalled that just before the Berlin Wall fell his company invested significantly in a European country—lured there by significant tax breaks. The tax break became part of history as soon as the wall came down and the government changed. The economic calculus of his firm's investment no longer made sense.

He used this story not to make a point about international affairs, but to illustrate why most business leaders, for good reasons, dislike the uncertainty associated with temporary tax incentives. They need to make long-term investments based on certain cost and rate of return estimates. This CEO vowed never to make the same mistake again. Yet he noted that government can influence business decision-making with permanent features of the tax code. This is one of the country's most effective tools for better aligning the goals of business with the goals of national policy and the interests of workers and their families. Providing permanent tax credits for job creation or for education and training investments would go a long way to aligning business decision making with the stated goals of national policy.

Inventing the Next Generation's Knowledge Work

Sound macroeconomic policy is only a necessary starting point. A proactive approach is needed to ensure American industry stays on and pushes out the frontiers of science and technology to discover and create the next-generation products, entrepreneurial companies, and jobs.

At MIT we know something about how to do this. Over the past thirty years, MIT has spawned over 4,000 companies that in turn have created over one million jobs.[2] Many other progressive and innovative private and public universities can make similar claims. The University of Wisconsin prides itself in nurturing many of the biotech and medical instruments businesses growing up around Madison and for its reach to industries across the state through its network of state universities centers. The University of Texas has helped Austin become a leading high-tech center rivaling Silicon Valley and Boston; so have the public and private universities in the "research triangle" in the Raleigh-Durham, North Carolina, region. Like many others, these universities put a high priority on linking their scientific and technological research to industry and to entre-preneurial networks. The hope is that out of these university labo-ratories and networks will emerge the future generation of Intels, Microsofts, Biogens, and Starbuckses.

Something important, however, is missing in these networks. They tend to be enclaves of engineering and scientific inventors huddled with venture capitalists and other potential investors. As such, they focus mainly on the technical and financial requirements for creating and building new firms, carrying over the legacy and organizational design ideas of the past industrial age. They have not yet come to grips with the role that knowledge and human resources need to play in organizations today.

A Stanford research group has studied the origins and evolution of these entrepreneurial firms in Silicon Valley, the West Coast's paragon of innovation. They found that only a little over half (57 percent) of the founders of these firms built organizations around individual "star" knowledge and talent or gave primary focus to strategies for gaining competitive advantage through teamwork and employee commitment. The rest carried over the inherited organizational practices of autocratic, top down, and highly bureau-cratic firms of the industrial age.[3] So the transformation in organizational design and practice will not come about by osmosis. To get this other half of the distribution to come into the modern era, we need to teach these would-be entrepreneurs what it takes to create, build, and manage knowledge-driven, innovative organizations.

The best way to teach this is to involve the professional workforce in these networks. The absence of their voice means that the investments in education and life-long learning are not keeping up with changing technologies and skill requirements. So perhaps it is time to bring knowledge workers together with leaders in their industries and with the academic institutions that will be producing the next generation of knowledge workers. As noted above, this networking and dialogue happens in some of the community clusters with universities that see it as their mission to foster new enterprises and engage entrepreneurs. We should be expanding the number of such university networks and ensure that we bring the workforce into these discussions.

Government's role in this process is to provide the support needed to keep American universities the crown jewels of our educational system and in return target sufficient portions of support to the development of these regional networks. In the early 1990s, Congress authorized funds to support "Manufacturing Extension Centers" that built on the legacy of the highly successful Agricultural Extension programs of an earlier era. Now is the time to apply this same model by creating Technical and Human Resource Development Centers that spread an understanding of how to integrate these complementary strategic assets in ways that foster the innovations needed to support a knowledge-based economy.

The Offshoring Scare

Can we still say to our children, as our parents said to us, "get as much education as you can and you will be sure to do well?" It used to be that knowledge-intensive, professional and technical jobs were among the most stable. Now, however, increasing numbers of knowledge workers have unstable, "contingent" jobs as consultants. These jobs also seem to be just as much at risk of being shipped offshore as lower skilled production jobs.

Not long ago, a team of IBM executives was overheard to say that the company will need to offshore more jobs in the future because "our competitors are doing it and so we have to do it." Several months later, the company followed through.[4] This herding instinct has led Forrester Research, an information-technology consulting and research firm, to estimate that America could lose 3.3 million information-technology jobs in the next decade.[5] This sends a chill down the spine of all professionals who wonder, "Is my job next?" And, if it prevails, it becomes a self-fulfilling prophecy resulting in a race to the bottom among companies seeking to minimize short-term labor costs. In doing so, they erode a strategic resource, not just for their company, but for the overall economy. So what appears to be good for any individual company may not, in the end, be good for the future of the economy.[6]

The debate over offshoring involves, in part, whether the industrial era view of labor as a cost to be controlled will continue to dominate in organizational decision-making or whether business decision-makers will begin seeing knowledge and those who hold it as strategic assets. As will be argued in the next chapter, this debate is being played out in decisions made every day in organizations, yet the voices of those who would speak for knowledge workers are sorely absent or at best weakly represented in these debates. Before we can assess how working families might get their voices heard in these debates, however, we first need to understand how much of knowledge work is at risk of being outsourced or offshored and how decisions about where and how to do it are being made.

Much of professional and technical work is organized and conducted in projects. Some of these involve cross-disciplinary teams.
A product development team, for example, might include scientists,
design engineers, manufacturing engineers, marketing specialists,
and a team leader responsible for integrating the different components of the development process. Within specialized fields, such as
information technology (IT), a team may consist of specialists in
areas such as hardware, software, specific domain or process specialists (e.g, experts at building systems for tracking trades through
a financial market), and so on.

In addition to using regular employees, firms often use outside
consultants on these projects, individuals who are either working
on a temporary basis for the firm or as independent contractors.
Some of the work may also be done outside the organization, either
in the United States or abroad. Hence that new word we are all
learning: "offshoring." This variety in employment relationships
clearly has important implications for workers and for the managers and organizations that supervise and employ them. Matthew
Bidwell, a recent graduate of our program, has been studying this
question intensively in the context of IT projects in the financial services industry.[7] He finds that many projects do indeed mix together
regular employees and outside consultants and contractors
working side by side under very different terms and conditions of
employment. Often, the mix is driven by senior management's
desire to increase workforce flexibility by reducing the number of
regular employees that they hire.

On the face of it, firms go to great lengths to differentiate the
various groups of workers on their projects. Wages, fringe benefits,
and promotion opportunities obviously vary. But so do more subtle
aspects of work such as the nature of supervision. Managers are
cautioned by company lawyers to avoid supervising contractors
directly for fear of being labeled "coemployers" under the nation's

labor and employment laws. For the same reason, supervisors are cautioned to avoid training contractors. Some firms even exclude contractors from social functions and company communications so that, if called upon to do so, their lawyers can point to a clear line between employees and contractors. Human resource departments in some firms try to limit the tenure of contractors to further protect the firm from coemployment liabilities.

In the reality of everyday project work, however, this line of demarcation gets blurred, often to the point of becoming invisible. Why? It all comes back to the role of knowledge. While sometimes outside contractors are hired simply to reduce labor costs and/or to avoid making a "permanent" commitment to new hires, many contractors are hired because they bring specialized professional or technical knowledge that the organization does not have in-house. Bidwell's work shows, however, that as contractors do their work they often acquire highly specialized knowledge that is critical to the firm. So, if the company has to downsize its workforce, lo and behold, front-line project managers sometimes resist following the stated human resource policy of dismissing all contractors before they dismiss regular employees. Why? Often the knowledge that these "outsiders" possess is as critical to the company as the knowledge of regular employees, if not more. Given the growing importance of knowledge as an asset, such considerations can dominate the more traditional questions of who is a regular employee and who is a consultant.

This scenario captures the reality of knowledge work and raises a number of questions that get right to the heart of the debate over how employment is changing in knowledge-intensive organizations. In particular, while senior management may focus on questions of relative labor costs and flexibility, the "real" nature of employment relationships are being driven by the nature of firms' work systems and the knowledge that they require. There is a real risk that these requirements will be ignored if decisions on outsourcing and offshoring are made solely on the basis of relative labor costs rather than on the current and future value of the knowledge these workers carry. Thinking only short-term about relative labor costs risks throwing the baby out with the bathwater. Companies may be saving dollars today but dissipating the knowledge assets needed to be competitive in the future.

These are tough strategic issues and choices for companies, especially in a hypercompetitive global marketplace. It is hard, given the immediacy and intensity of the cost pressures facing managers, for them to give appropriate weight to considerations of whether the organization is protecting and developing its knowledge base for the future. After all, from the point of view of any specific manager, "the future is someone else's problem; my budget constraints hit me today!"

There is a voice missing from these debates: the knowledge workers themselves. Giving them a voice would help hold decision-makers' feet to the fire and encourage them to make decisions that are in the longer-term interests of their company and the economy. They would help to explore important questions such as:

• What are the cost differences between doing this work inside or outside, in the United States or abroad?

• Are the total costs or only hourly labor rates being considered in making this decision, or, even worse, is just some headcount reduction or algorithm driving it?

• Is the knowledge that project team members bring to the task central and strategic to the firm today and in the future and therefore a capacity that needs to be developed in-house, or is it so routine and based on standard knowledge that it can be purchased outside at the lowest total cost (including the management and coordination costs associated with integrating the work into the company's core activities)?

Too often only the first question in this list is asked. And because these decisions are made separately, one organization or even one project at a time, we are not asking these questions at an industry, occupation, regional, or even national level. Creating a broader dialogue on these topics would help to ensure that these hard questions are properly addressed and give us a better chance of maintaining and building the skills and capabilities our firms and the overall economy will need to stay on the cutting edge of technology and innovation.

Engineers at Boeing have begun to raise this question about their company's decision to offshore big components of engineering work to competitors in other countries. This is known in the aerospace industry as "offsets." That is, Boeing feels it has to place portions of work for products it wants to sell to foreign customers in their country. Sometimes this is an explicit condition of getting foreign contracts. Sometimes it is implicit. Sometimes, it is little more than an outright bribe to secure the support of foreign governments or customers. But the engineers' concern, in addition to their obvious concern about job security, is that offsets are increasingly giving away Boeing's proprietary technologies and knowledge that heretofore were part of the company's competitive advantage.

Whether or not this is the case cannot be determined without much more detailed information and analysis. But this is precisely the type of strategic analysis that should be going on inside Boeing and any other company when it considers whether work should be done inside or outside the company's boundaries, by company employees, independent contractors, or outside suppliers. If Boeing engineers had access to this type of information, they could both challenge human resources executives to make rational decisions and, even more important, work with managers to figure out what changes could be made in how the work was organized, to make it competitive with outside options. This is the difficult, company-by-company work needed to make sensible decisions that find the right balance between controlling costs and protecting and further developing the strategic knowledge assets of the organization.

Anagram Corporation is a company in Minnesota that makes metal balloons for parades and other festive occasions. This innovative company decides what work to do in the United States and what to do elsewhere with a conscious eye for conserving its knowledge assets. In box 4.1, its COO summarizes why and how they make decisions about what work to do in the United States, Mexico, and China. America needs more companies to follow Amalgam's example!

Just as important, though, including the voice of the workers can ensure that these decisions will take the interests of the workforce into account alongside those of shareholders. Involving them would lead to questions such as:

• Am I treated and paid fairly regardless of whether I am employed as a "regular" employee or as a "contractor?"

• Does this work allow me to learn the skills and develop knowledge that will keep me marketable within this organization and in the external labor market?

• Has my employer made implicit promises to me that if I invest my skills, assuming the company continues to survive and prosper, I will continue to have a job?

There are good reasons to be asking these questions. Isabel Fernandez-Mateo, another of our recent graduates, has studied the wages paid to highly skilled contract workers.[8] She finds significant variations in wage rates for comparable workers that vary in part based on how close the relationship is between the temporary help agency and the host employer. Clearly, these temporary agencies know who their important clients are!

My fear is that by not engaging this full set of issues, too many firms are heading unconsciously toward the default solution of

Box 4.1
Sourcing Decisions at Anagram Corporation

Paul Ansolabehere is the COO of Anagram Corporation, a maker of metallic balloons that is headquartered in Eden Prairie, Minnesota. The company's manufacturing is done in plants in Minnesota, Mexico, and China. Ansolabehere describes their manufacturing strategy and sourcing decisions as follows:

We build the body of balloons here. Then we send them to Mexico and they paste on the paper decorative elements (which are made in China) and ship them back to us. All this could be done in a week in the United States, and it takes a week and a half with shipping from Mexico. But it would cost three times more to do all of this in the United States.

We do our final manufacturing here in Minnesota because we are the cheapest and fastest producer because of our high level of automation. It doesn't make sense to move this work; we couldn't find the kind of educated workforce needed to run our equipment in China or Mexico that we have in Minnesota. We sell to a large U.S. market, and so by remaining in the United States, we reduce our shipping costs. Moreover, our product is fashion-driven, so if a Brother Bear balloon is hot today, it'll be dead in six months. Fast as they come they die. That means we need to get it out fast. Delivery time is critical in this business.

Another big reason for not moving the plant to China is intellectual property. If you do it in China, you lose it. They share the technology with everyone. Anagram's active patents are mainly in manufacturing processes, for example, putting stuff into balloons, or—our best one—valves for the balloons. But beyond the issue of patents, in any good manufacturing plant, the vital processes are not patentable, for example, our robotized system for picking up floppy flat balloons. If I patented this robot, I would have to divulge information that would allow our competitors to copy it. So there's no way of protecting trade secrets like this in China.

Source: Interview with Paul Ansolabehere conducted by Suzanne Berger, MIT Department of Political Science and Industrial Performance Center, June 2004.

outsourcing and offshoring too much work today and, in the process, dissipating knowledge assets that could help keep America competitive and provide good jobs in the future. In the process, we ignore the efficiency and equity consequences of treating people differently who work side by side doing very similar, if not equivalent, work. The old principle of "equal pay for equal work" seems to be a thing of the past.

Workers need to put this broader set of questions on the table in their organizations, in their industries and professions, and on the national stage. Answering them is critical to making the transition from the industrial view of labor as a cost to the knowledge economy view of labor as both a cost and an asset. The debate over offshoring is alive inside corporations and in society. It just needs to be reframed and opened up, for the benefit of working families and the economy.

The Future of Manufacturing Jobs

"Blue collar guys without a lot of skills were never going to be rich. We knew we'd have to work until 62 or so. And we always understood that," says Paul Soucy, president of United Steelworkers Local 2285, who put in 25 years at Wyman-Gordon, his father and his uncles more than 40 years apiece; his brother is working there still. "What I don't understand is why people don't get what's happening to us now. We're Middle America. We're what makes America go. We're the ones buying the cars, keeping the local stores afloat, trying to put our kids through college and provide for our families. We're the core of America. And it boggles my mind that we're under attack."

—Phil Primack, "Blue Collar Blues," *Commonwealth Magazine*, April 2004.

What, if anything, can be done about the loss of good manufacturing jobs? Paul Soucy had one of the two million that were lost in the last three years alone. The percentage of the workforce employed in manufacturing has declined from 17 percent in the mid-1980s to about 14 percent in 2003. With each manufacturing job lost, some semiskilled, blue-collar worker and his or her family takes a significant drop in income, living standards, and long-term financial security, in large part because the replacement jobs available to these workers in the service sector do not pay as much. Specifically, a recent look at the data indicates that 43 percent of those who lost manufacturing jobs between 2001 and 2004 did not find full-time replacement jobs. Of those that did, 73 percent took a cut in pay.[9]

We should never lose sight of the personal stories behind these numbers. The brief stories excerpted in box 4.2 from a *Washington Post* series on the loss of the middle class illustrates the anger and frustration that families feel when they are the ones who bear the costs of the transition the economy is now going through.

This was brought home to me in a very personal way one morning on my drive to work. My daily driving companion, National Public Radio, came on with a story about the closing of Mirro Aluminum, a mainstay manufacturing company in Manitowoc, Wisconsin, where I grew up and where many in my family still live. A partial transcript of the report is provided in box 4.3.

This all sounded much too familiar. I closed my eyes and heard my father's voice some 50 years ago saying: "Don't depend on farming—there is no future in it for you. Go to school and go where the jobs are."

Are we in the same place today in manufacturing as we were in farming 50 years ago? Yes and no. The percentage of jobs in manufacturing will probably continue to decline gradually, but probably not to the 3 percent level as is the case in farming today. And, if we continue to invest in new technologies, the manufacturing jobs that will remain in the economy will be more productive and therefore higher paying, safer, and less physically arduous than the jobs lost.

The big difference between the loss of farming jobs and the loss of manufacturing jobs is that the generation that moved off the farms to other occupations could look forward to wage and income

Box 4.2
Those Who Bear the Costs

[Scott] Clark is nearly two hours into a workday that won't end for another 13, delivering interoffice mail around the state for four companies—none of which offers him health care, vacation, a pension or even a promise that today's job will be there tomorrow. His meticulously laid plans to retire by his mid-fifties are dead. At 51, he's left with only a vague hope of getting off the road sometime in the next 20 years.

Until three years ago, Clark lived a fairly typical American life—high school, marriage, house in the suburbs, three kids, and steady work at the local circuit-board factory for a quarter-century. Then in 2001 the plant closed, taking his $17-an-hour job [offshore], and Clark found himself among a segment of workers who have learned the middle of the road is more dangerous than it used to be. If they want to keep their piece of the American dream, they're going to have to improvise.

Kathy Clark [his wife, who also worked at the factory], meanwhile, got a full-time job this summer after two years of temp work. But they still have a lot of ground to make up. . . . The Clarks know they have it better than many of their friends from the plant. They have frequent, impromptu reunions at Wal-Mart, where the talk inevitably turns to who has found work and who hasn't.

Raffael Toskes Sr. has, but only for $11 an hour. . . . Lawrence Provo has given up on trying to find a job. He was out of work for nearly two years after the plant closed. Provo and his wife cut back on expenses and sold their car, furniture and jewelry. They even sold their home, and moved in with Provo's mother-in-law. But it was not enough. They declared bankruptcy, joining a record 1.6 million who filed last year.

Robert Boyer retrained in computers after the plant closed. But tech companies told him they wanted five years' experience, not a certificate from a six-month course. So he works for $11.50 an hour at Home Depot, using the wisdom of four decades as plant electrician to help customers pick light bulbs for their remodeled kitchens.

Boyer turns angry at any suggestion that the jobs picture is not that bad. "When these guys get on the boob tube and say there's jobs out there, you just gotta go out there and get them, it makes me want to go out there and grab them by the throat and say, 'Where? Where are the jobs at?' "

Source: Griff Witte, "As Income Gap Widens, Uncertainty Spreads," *Washington Post*, September 20, 2004, p. A1.

Box 4.3
Job Losses in Manitowoc, Wisconsin

On the second floor of a century-old office building in downtown Manitowoc, Wisconsin, in what was the office of United Steelworkers Local 6499, former president Gary Miller is packing up some mementos.

SCHAPER: In September, the Newell Rubbermaid Corporation shut down its subsidiary Mirro Company's aluminum cookware factory in Manitowoc, shifting production to a new plant in Mexico and putting close to 900 Wisconsinites out of work. After 30 years in a good-paying job he figured he'd have until he retired, the 49-year-old Miller, along with hundreds of others, is out of work.

Miller says he and his wife, who also worked at the plant, prepared for unemployment by saving up and cutting back on things like new clothes and eating out, but he says other displaced workers have faired far worse.

MR. MILLER: You see in the papers lately, you see a lot of homes foreclosing.

SCHAPER: The Mirro plant closing has had a ripple effect through this picturesque area on the Lake Michigan shore south of Green Bay. Jobs have been lost at local suppliers and other businesses.

In this, the first week of classes at Lakeshore Technical College, just south of Manitowoc, scores of displaced workers from Mirro and other shuttered plants in the area are taking classes in accounting, nursing, and other fields that are more in demand.

Manitowoc County, with a 10-percent unemployment rate, has been so hard hit by manufacturing job losses that enrollment at Lake Shore has already increased almost 20 percent over last year. The job cuts are also sparking new interest in the presidential campaigns. Sitting just outside the campus library, 33-year-old nursing student Todd Jewel says he didn't bother to vote four years ago.

Jewel and his classmates say they'll pay close attention to what the candidates say about health care, jobs, and the economy. Those are neglected issues for 40-year-old Lori Krazinski, who worked for 12 years at the Mirro plant.

MS. LORI KRAZINSKI: They keep talking about the economy's getting better. Well, where is it getting better? I don't see it getting better around here.

continued

SCHAPER: Krazinski and other displaced workers say they want more than just lip service and campaign promises to create good-paying, new jobs. Ironically, a few new jobs are being created right inside Manitowoc's old Mirro aluminum cookware factory that has just restarted limited production of aluminum coil as a start-up called Koenig & Vits. Company president Tim Martinez says what might have been marginal profits for Newell Rubbermaid might be just right for his smaller corporation.

Martinez says there are similar opportunities in the remnants of other Midwest factories and that politicians should do more to support entrepreneurial efforts like this. He hopes to gradually reopen more and more of the plant as a niche and contract manufacturer, with a goal of hiring close to 300 employees within two years. But that's still just a fraction of the number of jobs lost when the plant shut down, meaning many former factory workers here in Manitowoc and across the country still face very uncertain futures as they consider who deserves their votes.

Source: "Analysis: Anxiety Still a Big Issue in 2004," National Public Radio, January 15, 2004.

improvements in making the transition. The reason was that the economy and its working families were jointly prospering from having in place that old social contract. Displaced farmers could go to work in good paying jobs like the ones lost when Mirro shut its doors. And the farmers' children could go to excellent public high schools and public universities to get the education needed to make a better life for themselves and their future families. It is this virtuous intergenerational cycle that must now be replicated as we make the transition from the industrial to the knowledge-based economy.

Some of the components of a transition strategy are mentioned in the Manitowoc story—a good community college that provides training in health-care jobs in high demand; an entrepreneurial start-up by local people to recapture parts of the lost business (even better if in markets that are growing and sustainable), and a determination to evaluate candidates for the job-creation programs they offer.

But more is needed. One concern I have had for years about my home town is that it did little to bring business, labor, community, and education leaders together to adjust to what has been a twenty-year decline of good manufacturing jobs in the region. This has to be a key part of the strategy.

Sean Safford, one of our PhD graduates, has studied how once-thriving industrial communities that hit on hard times as their industries declined have reacted. His tale of two cities, Allentown, Pennsylvania, and Youngstown, Ohio, is summarized in box 4.4. The key point in his story is that in Allentown, a rich and diverse network of community, civic, business, labor, and government leaders worked together to encourage new business investment, accept new industries, and move on together. In contrast, similar networklike efforts were tried in Youngstown, but those involved tended to be from more narrow and closed groups tightly tied to the old elite and the old industries. They spent more time trying to rearrange the chairs on the deck of a sinking ship rather than look outward for new opportunities. As a result, Allentown adjusted successfully; Youngstown did not. The lesson here should not be lost: If we want to look to and plan for the future, we need to engage and involve directly all those who will inherit the future.

Needed: A Realistic *Family* Adjustment Policy

But doesn't this sound insensitive to the current workers and families who are now losing the good manufacturing jobs? What can be done to help them? This is a tough problem with no easy answers. Neither my ideas nor anybody else's are going to eradicate the wage and benefit losses these workers experience. But if some of these costs are the inevitable price we pay for the benefits of a global economy, then those of us who benefit have an obligation to assist those families that bear the costs. Rather than offer

Box 4.4
A Tale of Two Cities: Allentown and Youngstown

Allentown, Pennsylvania, and Youngstown, Ohio, both prospered as centers of manufacturing in the mid-twentieth century. But in the last several decades, they have been forced to undergo painful transformations as large manufacturing operations pulled up stakes and moved south. Allentown has been successful in making this transition. Youngstown has not. In 2003, Allentown's unemployment rate was 4.8 percent compared to 6.8 percent in Youngstown. Average wages in Allentown were 10 percent higher than Youngstown's. Thirty-one entrepreneurial companies in Allentown had garnered $1.8 billion in venture-capital funds compared to 15 firms and just $280 million in Youngstown. Allentown's population grew by 35 percent since 1980 while Youngstown's declined. In the recent economic downturn, Allentown has retained many lucrative jobs as firms have consolidated operations into the region while Youngstown has suffered further job losses as more production has slipped away to the American South, Mexico and more recently, China. What accounts for the difference?

Ask anyone in the city to cite one of the reasons for Allentown's success and they are likely to point to the Ben Franklin program, a collaboration between universities and local industry to spur innovation, entrepreneurship, and new company formation. The program has produced 23 such companies since its inception contributing over 5,000 high-end jobs to the local economy. However, my research shows an even more important role Ben Franklin has played is as a focal point for community building among local companies, government officials, universities and labor leaders.

Why did Youngstown fare poorly in its efforts to make a post-industrial transition? The main thing I found lacking there was the ability to bridge across major divisions within the community. When steel manufacturing—the city's core industry—declined, non-steel related companies were not included in the process of looking for solutions. Neither was labor, nor many of the city's major suburban leaders. Each of these constituencies ended up developing their own plan of action in the wake of the city's decline and competed with each other to achieve their own narrow goals. There was no mechanism for them to engage each other's interests; no way for them to forge new relationships to the rest of the community.

The key lesson seems to be that to adapt to the changing economy, civic leaders have to overcome the divisions between large and small companies, between various ethnic groups, between suburbs and inner cities, and between labor and management, all of which reflect their industrial legacy.

Source: Sean Safford, *Why the Garden Club Couldn't Save Youngstown: Social Capital and the Transformation of the Rust Belt*, PhD dissertation, MIT Sloan School of Management, 2004.

false hopes of saving all manufacturing jobs we should do whatever we can to keep those high value-added and knowledge-
critical jobs that are sustainable in America and then support families bearing the costs of the transition to a knowledge economy. For
starters this would require:

• Continuing their health-care coverage;

• Protecting their pension investments;

• Providing tuition and other financial assistance to their children
so that they can (to use my father's words) "get the education they
need" to achieve a better life;

• Making sure that the displaced workers can negotiate the types of
severance and adjustment packages that leading companies offer to
some of their employees or that the strongest unions and companies have negotiated in collective bargaining, and;

• Ensuring that these displaced workers can carry some of these
benefits to their new jobs and continue their union representation
or form new unions to begin the process of negotiating gradual
improvements in wages, benefits, and conditions on these jobs.

This is a realistic plan for working families caught in the transition
from the declining industrial to the growing knowledge-based
economy.

Globalization and Trade: Scapegoat or Savior?

As I was drafting this chapter, I got a call from a former student
now working for a leading consulting firm. He wanted suggestions
for how to advise his client, a midsized manufacturing firm in the
Midwest, on how to approach its employees and union to negotiate wage and work-rule concessions as an alternative to moving the
plant and jobs to Mexico.

The good news in this example is that the parties are now talking about whether and how these jobs can be saved. The bad news is that these types of discussions are happening so frequently.

No discussion about jobs can be complete today without engaging the questions the public has about the effects of international trade on jobs. Economists of all persuasions used to take as an article of faith that unfettered free trade is good for all economies, including ours. In the long run this may still be true. Recently, however, highly respected economists such as Paul Samuelson, Lester Thurow, William Baumol, Ralph Gomory, and Paul Krugman have questioned this blind faith. They note that high-wage economies are at considerable risk of losing jobs and experiencing downward pressure on living standards in a world where knowledge and skills can travel across borders to countries with vastly different labor costs. They continue to agree that in the long run the world is likely to be better off with more rather than less international trade, but they also note that, as Thurow put it, "we all live in the short run."[10]

Most workers don't need high-powered economists to tell them this. They see it playing out as they watch good jobs around them, or their own jobs, go abroad. More and more, both workers and the experts who study trade recognize that the gap between the theoretical macroeconomic benefits and the real costs trade imposes on individuals and communities has to be closed if we are to avoid a negative political backlash to free or fair trade.

The type of family adjustment policy outlined above for coping with the loss of manufacturing jobs is a starting point. Ensuring that basic human rights are protected in trade agreements and enforced is a second step. Box 4.5 lists the core human rights the United Nations' International Labor Organization says should be present in all workplaces. These will not close the labor cost differences between high- and low-wage countries. But including them in trade

Box 4.5
Declaration of Fundamental Principles and Rights at Work

• Freedom of association and effective recognition of the right to collective bargaining
• The elimination of all forms of forced or compulsory labor
• The effective elimination of child labor
• The elimination of discrimination in respect to employment and occupations.

Adopted by the International Labor Organization of the United Nations, June, 1998.

Source: Anthony G. Freeman, "The ILO Labor Standards and U.S. Compliance," *Perspectives on Work* 3, no. 1 (1999): 28–31.

---

agreements and developing meaningful ways of enforcing them will ensure that jobs that move to lower-cost countries serve as a means of improving the human rights and the standard of living of the global labor force.

A third step is to hold companies accountable for the employment standards of contractors in their global supply chains. Nike and other apparel companies learned the hard lessons that come from being singled out for violating basic human rights and employment standards. As Phil Knight, Nike's CEO, once complained, "the Nike product has become synonymous with slave wages, forced overtime, and arbitrary abuse."[11] By using newspapers, TV, and the Internet to expose abusive practices in contractor shops in Pakistan, Vietnam, and other countries, a coalition of nongovernmental organizations (NGOs), student groups, and labor activists succeeded in convincing Nike to take responsibility for the employment standards and working conditions of contractors across its full supply chain.[12] This is an example of what can be done not to stop or block world trade, but to make sure that its full costs are absorbed by those who benefit from it and that the benefits are shared by all who help produce them.

A Fair Day's Work for a Fair Day's Pay

It is not enough to create a sufficient number of jobs so that all who want to work are able to do so. There is equal concern in society about the quality of the jobs we produce. Have we abandoned the simple notion that a fair day's work should produce a fair day's pay? That principle was solidly grounded in the old social contract that now seems to have broken down. The notion of a "living wage" is also deeply rooted in our religious doctrines. Pope Leo XIII first endorsed the concept of a living wage in his famous 1891 encyclical *Rerum Novarum* (on the conditions of labor) when he wrote that all people who work should be paid at a level "required in order to live."[13]

This principle that workers' wages should grow in tandem with productivity and firm profits became generally accepted in collective bargaining following what *Fortune Magazine* called "The Treaty of Detroit" in 1950 in which General Motors agreed to a 3 percent "annual improvement factor" to match the trend in productivity growth plus a formula that increased wages in relationship to changes in the cost of living.[14] That basic principle then guided the parties for many years in the auto industry and other industries that followed the auto industry's wage-setting pattern.

Future historians will very likely look back on the last two decades of the twentieth century as the time that America lost sight of these basic wage-setting norms and principles. Three things will stand out when this history is recorded:

• Wages for median workers stopped growing, and except for the final years of the booming 1990s, had actually declined.

• Income inequality grew throughout the 1980s and even in the booming 1990s to the point that by the year 2000, the top 5 percent of families in America earned 21 percent of the nation's income and the bottom 20 percent earned only 5 percent of total income.

• In 2000, young families started out with about $1,700 less real income than did their counterparts in 1979 and, if the trend of the past two decades continues, could expect their incomes and living standards to improve much more slowly than families of prior generations.[15]

Given these trends, it is surprising that there has not yet been an explosion of pressure to increase wages. That explosion is likely to come soon, when young families realize they are working harder today for less than what their parents achieved. We can wait for this explosion or working families can call on basic moral principles and demand a living wage and gradual improvement in their standards of living.

Like the other problems facing working families, there is no single strategy or solution for how to get wages moving in the right direction again. But the starting points of a strategy have already been identified in the last chapter—building a knowledge-based workforce and using knowledge as both a source of power and a means of adding value to the economy. Using this and other sources of power that will be discussed in later chapters will require workers across the full occupational spectrum to gain a new voice at work and to demand a new transparency in organizations so that all decisions, including compensation decisions, can stand up to the simple norms of fairness. Americans continue to hold the same expectations for fairness in wages, layoffs, and other employment practices. It is the young, mobile, and well-educated employees and their families that will have to be in the vanguard of this movement, since they have so much at stake.

What about Low-wage America?

A century ago Upton Sinclair's novel *The Jungle* made Americans aware of the unsafe and unsanitary work and inhumane treatment of workers in the emerging industrial economy. His classic novel about Chicago meatpackers and their family and community lives brought their appalling condition to the attention of the public. It was then up to the social reformers of the day—the earlier industrial relations researchers and leaders of the Progressive Movement—to invent the institutions and policies eventually embodied in many of the New Deal reforms.

Today we find ourselves with a similar challenge with respect to the low-end jobs in the service sector. We even have several modern day Upton Sinclairs, although this time the books bringing to life the harsh conditions of low-wage work in America are not novels but are based on real people doing real jobs.

Barbara Ehrenreich's *Nickeled and Dimed* reports the experiences of a middle-class woman who tried to live off earnings of low-wage service jobs. She chronicles her experiences in moving from town to town, taking jobs in housecleaning, restaurants, retail stores, and nursing homes, each time comparing her temporary and self-inflicted indignities and frustrations with those stuck in these jobs. She ends her account by noting our responsibility to the working poor:

When someone works for less pay than she can live on—when she, for example, goes hungry so that you can eat more cheaply and conveniently—then she has made a great sacrifice for you, she has made you a gift of some part of her abilities, her health, and her life. The "working poor," as they are approvingly termed, are in fact the major philanthropists of our society.[16]

Beth Shulman's *The Betrayal of Work* reports the stories of low-wage workers with the experienced eye of a former union leader who represented people in many of the types of jobs held by the people she interviewed. She calls for society to agree on a new set of principles—a compact with working Americans that, in her words, has a clear and simple purpose: "Workers should be treated fairly and have the resources to provide for themselves and their families."[17]

David Shipler uses his reporter's ability in *The Working Poor* to tell the stories of workers and families who cannot seem to escape their poverty even by putting in long hours, often working multiple jobs, and battling all the health, housing, safety, and other family problems that go along with being poor in America. He notes that eliminating the need for the term "working poor" will take a coordinated private- and public-sector effort that treats these problems together rather than as separate or isolated issues. *"The term 'working poor' should be an oxymoron. Nobody who works hard should be poor in America."*[18]

Katherine Newman's *No Shame in My Game*[19] brings an anthropologist's perspective to the family struggles of the working poor in Harlem and shows vividly that most of the people living and working in our inner cities aspire to and are willing to work hard for the same things as middle-lass families. They want a living wage, education for their children, and the dignity and respect we all expect as the just reward for working hard.

In *Low Wage America*,[20] Eileen Appelbaum, Annette Bernhardt, Richard Murnane, and a team of researchers assembled by the Rockefeller and Russell Sage Foundations document the fact that 34 million people work full time for less than $8.70 an hour, the hourly wage rate needed for a family of four to reach the poverty level in America today. Their industry-by-industry analyses show that there is variation in how work is organized and how employees are managed and treated, even in "low-wage" service and manufacturing industries. This gives us some hope that managers can learn and adapt practices that can make a difference in these jobs and the lives of workers.

Together these books should not just awaken but also embarrass Americans, just as much as Upton Sinclair and his fellow muckrakers embarrassed early industrial America. The question is, what can be done about jobs that currently do not pay a living wage or that treat workers in ways that violate our basic values of dignity and fairness, and that seem to leave those who are stuck in these jobs with little hope for the future?

There are no immediate fixes or easy answers here any more than there are easy solutions to the loss of good paying manufacturing jobs. But neither are we without options or strategies. Many of the manufacturing jobs of Sinclair's time were transformed by the passage of minimum wage, industrial safety and health, wage and hour, and collective bargaining laws and by progressive managers and labor leaders determined to do better. Can we not imagine and mobilize a similar combination of sensible public policies and private sector leaders and innovations to do the same for today's low-wage workers?

The mix of tools that need to be brought to bear on this task is readily apparent:

• Sustained macroeconomic growth is the starting point. It took years of strong economic growth and tightening labor markets, from 1992 through 1995, before wages at the bottom of the labor market began to rise. Over the next five years, while the boom lasted, wages grew more rapidly for those at the bottom than they had in years and more rapidly than for most higher-wage workers. So a strong economy is the best friend, indeed, a necessary ally, in the effort to upgrade low-wage jobs. But, while necessary, it is far from sufficient since, as we have seen, the economy is not immune from business cycles. Wage growth at the bottom stalled again in recent years. Something more is needed to continue the momentum for upgrading low-end jobs during bad times as well as good.

• The experiences of moving people from welfare to work in the late 1990s shed some light on what else is needed. The evidence, mentioned briefly in the previous chapter, shows that the chances that single parents who go to work will move their families out of poverty are greatest when job opportunities are combined with education and training and with family and child support. So once again, the link between family and work is brought home.

• Two policy instruments are clearly central: minimum wage legislation and a provision of tax law called the Earned Income Tax Credit (EITC). Both of these have key roles to play in setting a floor on wages and on family income.

• The traditional economic view of service work is that it is destined to be low wage because it is so labor intensive and requires few skills. While there is considerable truth to this view, some jobs are being transformed by creative integration of advances in information technology, employee training and education, and changes in the way work is organized. Farm work changed as it became more capital intensive and informed by better information and management methods (compare the behemoth tractors, combines, and plows and the modern mechanized processes used for feeding and milking cattle used in farming today with the miniature, noisy, and more dangerous machinery and laborious chores of my youth). Advances in information technology and work design now offer the same potential for upgrading many low-wage service and manufacturing jobs.

• The craft unions of Sinclair's day thought it was not possible to organize and upgrade the jobs of unskilled production workers. Today, several unions are hard at work trying to organize and represent low-wage workers, both in traditional ways and by working in coalition with community, religious, and family advocates. These efforts will need to be successful if the campaign to eliminate the worst labor conditions in America is to be sustained through good and bad times.

The mix of managerial, community, labor-management, and public-policy instruments that need to come together to upgrade low-wage jobs will be outlined individually in subsequent chapters and brought together in chapter 8 when we outline a working families' agenda for government policy. For now it is sufficient to note that none of these private or public policy initiatives will take place unless working families across the full spectrum of occupational and income distribution recognize that we have a common stake and a moral responsibility to take up this challenge. Our modern day Sinclairs—Barbara Ehrenreich, Beth Shulman, David Shipler, Katherine Newman, and Eileen Appelbaum and colleagues—are doing their job in bringing these conditions to our attention. Now it is our turn to act.

Summary

What would a comprehensive working families' agenda to create and sustain good jobs for "all Americans who want to work" include? Here is a set of elements to consider.

• Macroeconomic policies that are directed at achieving the full employment goals enshrined in our national policies, but too often traded off for other seemingly higher priority economic objectives. The specific tax, fiscal, and other human resource policy instruments chosen need to reflect the economy as we find it at any time. The key is to keep job creation at the top of the public agenda and hold policy makers accountable for delivering on this objective.

• Permanent changes to the tax code to reward job creation and investment in education and training.

• Investment in research and development and basic research in our universities and in building inclusive networks that link those generating new ideas to the entrepreneurs who will build the next generation of organizations and the professional employees who will staff them.

• Going beyond the current rhetorical debates over offshoring by engaging business decision-makers in a dialogue over whether we are preserving or giving away our future knowledge assets and sources of competitive advantage in pursuit of short-term cost savings. This will require professional employees to raise their voices on these issues in organizations!

• Adjustment and transition strategies focused on helping working families caught in the transition from the industrial to the knowledge economy by focusing on meeting their ongoing health insurance, retirement, and educational needs.

• Integrated private and public efforts to upgrade conditions in low-wage jobs to ensure they provide a living wage, dignity, and opportunities to learn and advance—the features all Americans expect and deserve from work.

Building Knowledge-Based Organizations

Suppose American young people, parents, and citizens do their part and provide the business community and economy with the knowledge-based workforce both need. Can workers be assured their knowledge and skills will be translated into good, sustainable jobs and careers in the organizations of the future? Not necessarily. It all depends on the outcome of a largely invisible and often only implicit debate underway within American corporations. The battle is over whether or not companies will make the transition from industrial era, finance dominated, command and control, and shareholder maximizing corporations of the twentieth century, to knowledge-based and human capital centered corporations of the twenty-first. Or to state the two polar positions in the debate: Are workers to be viewed and treated as costs to be controlled or as strategic assets in which firms invest, develop, and protect?

This debate has both a soft and a hard side. Both are real and must be engaged directly by working families if they are to trust, prosper, and use their knowledge and skills to add value to the organizations that employ them.

MIT professor Douglas McGregor perhaps best described the soft side challenge nearly 50 years ago in his classic study of *The Human Side of the Enterprise*.[1] By comparing what he called Theory X and Theory Y perspectives on employee motivation, he challenged managers to reexamine their assumptions about the motivations employees bring to their jobs. The question was: Could employees be trusted and empowered to do good work or did they have to be closely directed, monitored, and controlled to act in the interests of the firm?

The recent corporate scandals, and their root causes, illustrate what is at stake on the hard side of the debate, namely the issues of the underlying purposes of the modern corporation, who has a voice in its governance, and how the risks and rewards generated by the organization should be shared among shareholders, employees, and other stakeholders.

The Soft Side Challenge: Rebuilding Trust

McGregor's question is perhaps even more relevant today than half a century ago. Trust is an essential, necessary feature for the full potential of a knowledge-based organization to be realized. Without it employees will neither use their energies nor share their knowledge and experience with others or with the organization, which limits the ability of firms and the overall economy to push out the frontiers of discovery and innovation. Unfortunately, many of the principles of the twentieth-century industrial corporation were designed using Theory X assumptions that make the workplace a low trust zone.

Management principles stemming from the era of Frederick Taylor's scientific management and then embodied in labor laws of the 1930s separated people at work into two distinct classes: production workers, mostly paid on an hourly or piecework basis; and supervisors and managers, who were paid on a salaried basis. These two groups were assumed to have separate loyalties—workers would be loyal to themselves and their families, peers, and union; and supervisors and managers would owe their loyalty and allegiance to the company. With this division came different legal rights and status—workers were covered by wage and hour laws, particularly overtime protections and their rights to join a union and engage in collective bargaining. Supervisors and managers were "exempt" from overtime coverage and from collective bargaining rights. The adversarial assumptions built into these distinctions further reinforced the tendency for a low trust–high conflict cycle to become the norm in organizations.

Anyone working today will recognize how dysfunctional, and in some cases out of touch with how work is really done, these twentieth-century organizational and legal principles are. But they persist, both as the law of the land and, in some cases, organizational practice.

Now consider the rhetoric in the contemporary literature on organizational behavior and management practice. As the list of attributes cited in box 5.1 suggests, the twenty-first century organization should be highly networked—that is, people should be interacting with each other in cross-function teams to speed the process of innovation. Decision-making authority should be delegated to front-line employees to empower them to solve problems and foster continuous improvement in operations and delivery of services to customers. Employees should be encouraged to use their discretion to solve problems and generate ideas. Supervisors should be mentors, coaches, and resources; those closest to the actual work know best how to do their jobs. And as Arlie Hochschild[2] pointed out, when workers come to work they want a positive social environment where they can develop friendships, engage others constructively, and perhaps even escape some of the tensions and hassles felt in their family lives. One need not agree with all of her views on this, but her main point resonates with most of us. We want a hassle-free work environment where we are trusted, treated with respect, valued for our ideas, and given an opportunity to contribute to the success of our organizations.

Is this just rhetoric, an idyllic and unrealistic view of work today? If we are to gain value from human and social capital, this

Box 5.1

Organizational Design Principles for Twenty-First-Century Organizations

- Organize around cross-functional core processes, not tasks or functions
- Install process owners or managers who will take responsibility for the core process in its entirety
- Make teams, not individuals, the cornerstone of organizational design and performance
- Decrease hierarchy by eliminating non-value-added work and by giving team members who are not necessarily senior managers the authority to make decisions directly related to their activities within the process flow
- Integrate with customers and suppliers
- Empower people by giving them the tools, skills, motivation, and authority to make decisions essential to the team's performance
- Use information technology (IT) to help people reach performance objectives and deliver the value proposition to the customer
- Emphasize multiple competencies and train people to handle issues and work productively in cross-functional areas within the new organization
- Promote multiskilling, the ability to think creatively and respond flexibly to new challenges that arise in the work that teams do
- Redesign function departments or areas to work as "partners in process performance" with the core process groups
- Measure for end-of-process performance objectives (which are driven by the value proposition), as well as customer satisfaction, employee satisfaction, and financial contribution
- Build a corporate culture of openness, cooperation, and collaboration, a culture that focuses on continuous improvement and values employee empowerment, responsibility, and well being.

Source: Frank Ostroff, *The Horizontal Organization* (New York: Oxford University Press, 1999), pp. 10–11.

idealistic and rhetorical view has to be translated into the reality of everyday organizational life. As McGregor and the host of organizational behavior scholars who came after him stress, it all rests on trust. But to build and sustain trust requires more than just enlightened management.

Trust is a two-way street. Employees have to do their part. The old (maybe outdated) phrase of giving a "fair day's work for a fair day's pay" still holds, only today we might revise this adage a bit to note that knowledge workers need to share ideas and expertise with others at work and be willing to work effectively in teams. In return, organizations and their managers have to be willing to respect employees and reward them for the contributions they make to the goals of the enterprise.

Perhaps no organization better illustrates the low-trust, command and cost-control mentality in America today better than Wal-Mart. It is all the more instructive because Wal-Mart has been so highly successful, now reaching the distinction as the country's largest private employer. But there is growing recognition, and some increasing public outcry, over how Wal-Mart treats its employees. Over the past several years, newspaper stories have exposed the company for shorting employees of overtime pay, discriminating against women, firing workers who attempt to organize a union, and incredibly, locking the doors at night to keep employees from stealing products (or getting out if they need to for good reason).[3] Box 5.2 contains several letters to the editor of the *New York Times* after the newspaper ran a front-page story exposing this. One reader goes so far as to suggest this story sounded like something out of the nineteenth, not the twentieth, century. Command and control is alive and well in at least one of America's most "successful" enterprises!

We must and can do better than Wal-Mart. The starting point for a new social contract in a knowledge-based organization has to be that employees commit to using and applying the knowledge they

Box 5.2
Locked in at Wal-Mart

To the Editor:
Re: "Workers Assail Night Lock-ins by Wal-Mart" (front page, Jan. 18): Because of Wal-Mart's policy of locking up employees at night, jeopardizing their health and safety, and politics that thwart the right to organize, I have yet to walk through those same doors, when they are open.
—John Armelagos, Ann Arbor Michigan

To the Editor:
"Workers Assail Night Lock-Ins by Wal-Mart" read almost as if it had been out of a 19th-century novel about the Industrial Revolution, rather than a 21st-century newspaper. It shocked and embarrassed me to think that such incidents could occur in this great country.

Congress should pass a bill that bans overnight lock-ins of workers. After all, we live in the 21st century, not the 19th. Such situations should never occur in this day and age.
—Josh Isralowitz, Rutherford, N.J.

To the Editor:
One night a few years ago I was working on a computer program for a retail chain store. At 10 o'clock, I started to leave the building, which was busy with people getting the store ready for the next day. "You can't leave until 6 A.M.," I was told. "The doors are locked, and no one here has the key."

The person who had the key was called at home and asked to unlock the door, but only after I said I would call the police.

Smart leaders and business people should recognize that the push to cut wages and benefits and human dignity is building up to a social or political explosion. They must ease greatly the pressure working people are under.

Besides, workers with low wages cannot buy goods to support our economy.
—Frank Stoppenbach, Red Hook, N.Y.

Source: *New York Times*, January 25, 2004.

bring to work by working collaboratively in modern-day teams and networks; and in return supervisors and executives trust employees to get the work done in ways employees decide are best suited to meeting the needs of their organization and their personal and family lives. This would be a good foundation to build on indeed. But it is only a starting point. Next we need to organize work in ways that use and combine the knowledge people bring to their respective jobs. Let's look at what it takes to do so both for front-line employees and for those in professional and technical jobs.

Knowledge Work Systems on the Front Lines

In today's global world all citizens must become the next generation's intellectuals.
—Kim Dae Jung, former president of South Korea

Too often the term *knowledge worker* is viewed as limited to only our most elite professionals. President Kim Dae Jung got it right. The reality is that all workers in advanced nations are at risk from lower wage competition so all workers, from technicians and professionals to front line manufacturing and service employees, need to use their knowledge and skills to full advantage. To do this, organizations need to build what are called "knowledge-based work systems."[4]

American industry is learning how to do this, largely by trial and error and from a generation of academic-industry research on workplace innovations for front-line employees and project-based management. We'll start with the front line story.

It all started in the auto industry in the early 1980s, when Toyota, GM, and the United Auto Workers transformed one of GM's most inefficient, conflict-ridden plants and labor management relationships into the most productive, high quality, and model labor management partnership in the industry. They did so by matching the

Toyota Production System with a no-nonsense, but high trust, team-based and flexible work environment that empowered workers to use their knowledge and skills to improve operations and then rewarded them with good paying, secure jobs. The plant they call NUMMI (New United Motors Manufacturing Inc.) set the standard and became the icon for innovative manufacturing that integrated technology, human resources, and organizational policies. As a result, NUMMI reemployed over 2,000 workers in 1982 who were laid off when GM closed the Fremont, California, plant and has sustained this level of employment (and plant performance) for more than twenty years.[5] This set the standard for the rest of the auto industry and became a learning laboratory for similar innovations in other industries.

What NUMMI was to autos and manufacturing in general, Southwest Airlines is to the airline industry and the service sector.[6] Like NUMMI, Southwest has performed as the nation's most consistently profitable carrier and most highly acclaimed company to work for because it focuses like a laser on the task of turning its planes around quickly in airports. To do this successfully, it needs a highly motivated, knowledgeable, committed, and coordinated workforce.

A visit to Southwest's corporate headquarters will take you down a hall with pictures of family events, picnics, and other celebrations. The symbolism is backed up in practice. Southwest values families and tries to make its workplace resemble a family atmosphere and be a fun place to work. This is a key part of its business strategy. Southwest could not succeed if people did not trust each other or the company and were constantly in fear of losing their jobs or being forced to take deep wage and benefit cuts, as have workers at most other major airlines.

Both NUMMI and Southwest are highly unionized organizations. They break the stereotyped argument that unions are dinosaurs of a bygone industrial era that have no future in a knowledge-based economy. But they also demonstrate that traditional, adversarial union management relations are no longer viable. Both cases illustrate the potential power labor and management have when they work together in partnership and apply what we know is needed to build state-of-the-art production, service, and labor management systems. I will have more to say about this later when we discuss how to build the next generation of labor unions.

Will Industry Learn from NUMMI and Southwest?

The good news is that American industry has leading examples like NUMMI and Southwest to learn from. The bad news is that many companies have been slow learners. Part of the reason for this slowness is that employees have not raised their individual or collective voices to insist that these state-of-the-art approaches be adopted at their workplaces. Their voice needs to be heard on this—both in pressing managers and, where present, union leaders to get on with the job—their jobs and their company's survival may depend on it!

Consider airlines. Southwest has been successful for twenty years in an industry that has been plagued with some of the worst labor relations in the country. Given this, one might think other companies would learn from Southwest. Some have, but most have not, at least not yet. Continental has, but only after two bouts with trying to compete by slashing labor costs and decertifying its employees' unions. That was the strategy that Frank Lorenzo brought to Continental in the early 1980s and that failed so miserably. Lorenzo was eventually banned from the industry by court order (he had been found to be cooking the books as he took over and ran into the ground former airlines like Eastern, People Express, and Frontier, as well as Continental).

In 1994, following a second round in bankruptcy court, a new management team decided to try a different strategy at

Continental, one that was based on a very simple notion: rebuild trust with the workforce on a day-to-day basis, carry over these same open and honest approaches to collective bargaining and labor relations, and the people side of the company will add value to airline operations and the bottom line. At the same time, Continental has sought to avoid falling into old traditional labor relations patterns with rigid work rules that add costs and make it difficult to serve customers well. It also has increased wages gradually over the years and has avoided the big swings in compensation of its pilots and other employee groups that we have seen at competitors such as United, US Airways, Delta, and Northwest.

Continental, like other large network carriers, continues to struggle to survive and prosper in this turbulent and uncertain industry. But, at least for the past decade, it has served as a poster child for a firm determined to find the appropriate balance between treating employees as valued assets and partners in growing the business while still recognizing that costs need to be kept under some reasonable control. While not immune from the perilous state of the airline industry since the 9/11 attacks, Continental has become profitable again and has joined Southwest as the only other airline to be listed by Fortune Magazine among the "top 100 places to work." It has made the high-trust model work in a very difficult industry environment largely by being honest and straightforward with its employees and the union leaders who represent them.

Meanwhile, the other major network carriers continue to have highly adversarial labor-management relations, even as some of them and their union counterparts march like lemmings toward liquidation or dissolution. Only recently have companies, unions, and industry more broadly begun to discuss what needs to be done to turn around labor-management and employee relations to support the survival and recovery efforts.

JetBlue's strategy was to combine common sense with innovation and technology to "bring humanity back to air travel." . . . [David] Neeleman wanted to set up a new kind of airline; one that would leverage technology for safety and efficiency and with a commitment to people.[7]

JetBlue Airways has learned from Southwest. JetBlue was founded in 1999 by a team that included several former Southwest executives and has built a rapid-growing, low-cost airline around many of the business and employee relations strategies used at Southwest. Since it began operations with lower wage and benefit costs than older and larger airlines, it has a double advantage. This serves to intensify the need for existing airlines both to cut costs and to accelerate the pace of change and improvement in employee and labor relations.

My colleagues and I are working with an industry-wide labor-management-government group to accelerate the process of learning and change. Box 5.3 summarizes some of the lessons these leaders have learned from their experiences in trying to adjust to the harsh economic climate they face. But progress is slow, and perhaps too incremental and limited to make a difference. Let's hope it is not too late for them to apply these lessons.

Adversarial traditions built on an experience of low trust and broken promises are hard to overcome. Some of these big network carriers may not be around by the time you read this unless they find a way to change and engage their workforce in a more constructive fashion and unless their employees and unions likewise recognize the need to change. Our case studies of Southwest, JetBlue, and Continental; our quantitative research on the links between labor relations, financial performance, and customer service; and our work with labor and management leaders all lead to a clear conclusion. The flying public, company shareholders, and employees will not get the service, financial returns, or job security each expects and needs until we turn employee and labor relations around in this industry.[8]

NUMMI and Southwest are not isolated examples. A large and growing body of research has documented the fact that

Box 5.3
Lessons from Experience: The Airlines

Among the key lessons industry and labor leaders indicated they took away from recent restructuring negotiations were:

1. Open, honest communications and information sharing were critical to successfully concluding recent crisis negotiations. The same will be true going forward in future negotiations.

2. Agreement on a costing methodology facilitated negotiations where it was present and held up negotiations where it was not. Pre-negotiation agreements on a common approach to costing proposals and options should become a standard bargaining practice.

3. Reaching agreement with any single employee group was contingent on negotiating or implementing agreements that called for shared sacrifices from other employee groups, including non-represented employees, managers, and executives. Where this principle was violated, agreements were either held up or rejected by employees. This suggests that any future compensation adjustments will likely receive the same cross-occupation, within-company scrutiny and have to meet the same test of fairness.

4. In times of extreme crisis, it is important for a firm to have a clear and single target for what reductions in costs are needed while being flexible and responsive to input from union representatives in how different elements of cost reductions are arranged. Having to return for more than one round of cuts because the initial target is not sufficient reduces credibility of the management and labor leaders involved and makes acceptance/ratification extremely difficult.

5. Bargaining in the age of the Internet is an open and public process with information, false or accurate, often communicated to employees almost immediately. Future bargaining processes will need to have an agreed upon strategy for how to communicate with constituents and other interested parties to keep them accurately informed.

6. Improving labor relations requires a consistent approach to how people are treated on a day-to-day basis and in the negotiations process. Effective and timely negotiations will not be realized unless a culture of high trust has been achieved at the workplace.

Source: *Options for Improving Negotiations and Dispute Resolution. A Report of the Working Group on Airline Labor Relations*, March 2004.

---

knowledge-based work systems can help companies achieve high levels of performance in industries as diverse as apparel, semiconductors, computers, steel, telecommunications, and health care.[9] So it is important for both working families and the economy to encourage more firms to transform their work systems and employment relationships. This is, however, a slow, difficult, and hard-to-sustain process, not just in airlines, but in other industries as well.

Diffusing Knowledge-Based Work Systems

It is perhaps this legacy of low trust that explains why the diffusion of knowledge-based work systems is proceeding at such a slow pace in airlines and in other industries. My colleague Paul Osterman estimates that perhaps one-third of American workplaces have transformed their practices and relationships from the traditional command and control approach to what we are calling here the knowledge-based model.[10]

What can be done to facilitate and speed up the diffusion of knowledge-based work systems and high-trust organizational strategies? One lesson from past efforts is clear: Government cannot dictate to or cajole firms and employees to do so from on high. This was tried in the 1970s and 1980s with various governmental initiatives such as the National Commission on Productivity and the Quality of Work, an effort started under President Nixon that limped along through the Ford administration and up to the Carter years. It failed because business and labor did not share a sense of urgency or ownership of the problem or the proposed solutions. Similar efforts and similar results were experienced by the Reagan, Bush (the first one), and Clinton administrations, each of which tried different approaches to convincing business and labor to work together in a more cooperative and innovative fashion. None succeeded and each administration disbanded its efforts before leaving office.

There is another model that works better and that should be expanded in the future. Diffusion of the types of transformations in employee and labor management relations and of knowledge-based work systems is best achieved in industries where management, labor, and academic groups create networks for sharing data, evidence of what works, and experiences in adapting innovative practices and models to different settings. Over the past ten years, the Alfred P. Sloan Foundation has sponsored efforts to build such collaborative projects in twenty-five industries.[11] Like the airline project just mentioned, each of these is led by a university team that works directly with industry, union, and professional association leaders in carrying out and disseminating research on what is needed to compete successfully in the industry. This industry-labor-academic network model has supported the innovation and diffusion process very effectively in industries as different as autos, semiconductors, apparel, food processing, pharmaceuticals, aerospace, and steel.

This is a model worth continuing, expanding to other sectors, and using as part of a national strategy for transforming workplace practices to support diffusion of knowledge-based work systems. It is exactly the type of broad-based network and coalition needed to promote both innovations in work organization and the family-centered workplace policies called for here. Note that the key is to get companies, employee representatives, and university educators and researchers collaborating on diffusion of these innovations, just the way the old Agricultural Extension Services taught and convinced farmers like my father how to adopt, for example, new hybrid seeds and better fertilizers (than the natural stuff cows produce). They did it by getting out into fields and experimenting with lead farmers who then showed their peers the bottom-line results that could be generated by changing deeply engrained ideas and practices. They knew about learning organizations before the term was invented!

Integrating Technology and Human Capital

Dr. Hammer points out a flaw. He and others in the $4 billion reengineering indus-try forgot about people. "I wasn't smart enough about that . . . and was not suffi-ciently appreciative of the human dimension. I've learned that's essential."
—*The Wall Street Journal,* November 20, 1996, p. 1

Some MBA programs are based on the dubious premise that their graduates can manage any organization, in any sector, effectively regardless of the scientific or technical knowledge needed to bring its products or services to life. This is reinforced by the gigantic and lucrative business consulting industry that employs so many of our MBA graduates. These general experts flitter from company to company offering seemingly wise strategic advice to managers often without first learning how the underlying technologies and human capacities that produce the products and services fit together. Failure to understand these things can prove disastrous, for the companies, their employees, and customers. Michael Hammer's quote at the beginning of this paragraph says it all. He made this statement after his "business process reengineering" con-sulting business had destroyed jobs of thousands of workers only to fall short of realizing the promised benefits of relying on new technologies and "reengineered" business processes to improve efficiency. MIT knows this first hand. It has very little in the way of process improvements to show for the $40 million it invested in reengineering efforts under the consulting tutelage of Dr. Hammer.

Today there is growing recognition that general management skills or a consultant's standard remedy by themselves will not be enough to diagnose or manage a large firm. Decision makers need to have a deep understanding of the scientific and technical under-pinnings of their products and services and have an equally strong understanding of how these technical features intersect with the knowledge and human capabilities of the workforce. Researchers have a name for this: sociotechnical integration. Japanese scholars have a nice phrase to capture this point: "Workers give wisdom to their machines." Whatever we call it, the key is to have sufficient technical and human organizational literacy to ask the right questions.

Employees, especially scientists, engineers, and technical specialists, should be asking these questions—are we using our technologies and scientific capabilities wisely and to produce products and services that meet a business need and add value to society? Neither solely technical nor solely managerial knowledge is sufficient in organizations today. The real payoffs come from integrating these different knowledge bases and applying them in creative ways to new problems.

So a high level of trust, knowledge-based work systems for front line workers, knowledge-based strategies for professional and technical work, and a well-informed integrated strategy for using advanced technologies are all essential building blocks of a knowledge-based organization. These then are the soft side of the debate over how to transform our legacy of industrial-era enterprises. Now, on to the hard part of the debate.

Knowledge and Governance in the Twenty-First-Century Corporations

One would think that in the wake of Enron, Tyco, WorldCom, and their progeny, America would be engaged in a broad-based debate over how to reform corporations to guard against a repeat performance in the future. There was a debate, albeit limited in duration and scope, but it skirted the real issue. The root cause of the scandals, and the breakdown in the social contract governing employment relationships in large American corporations that preceded them, is the increased, almost singular focus on maximizing shareholder value that dominated corporate affairs in the latter part of the twentieth century. Without changing this trend, America will not transform to a knowledge-based economy.

The duty of executives and members of corporate boards to pursue shareholder value is obviously nothing new. The modern public corporation had emerged as the dominant business organizational form by the beginning of the twentieth century when amassing large pools of financial capital was essential to build the transcontinental railroads and other large industrial companies. By putting their capital at risk, investors earned a property right to the assets of the firm and with that came the financial duty of management to use these assets in a prudent fashion on behalf of owners. But this was not the sole or exclusive force shaping management behavior. In the aftermath of the Great Depression and World War II, large industrial firms had to contend with another force—industrial unions.

John Kenneth Galbraith captured the essence of the unions' role in this era. They served as a source of countervailing power to large firms.[12] Gradually, as the postwar economy grew and labor and management developed the basic principles and practices of collective bargaining and modern personnel management, an implicit social contract evolved in which management remained free to make strategic decisions governing how to allocate the firm's assets and other resources, subject to honoring some implicit norms for how to treat employees, some of which became explicit obligations negotiated into collective bargaining agreements. Productivity growth would be shared in some combination of wages and benefits and/or reduction in working hours. And employee loyalty and good performance would be rewarded with job and financial security that grew with tenure. Layoffs would be used as a strategy of last resort, and when they were necessary, tenure would decide the order of layoffs.

Over the past two decades, a series of interrelated forces weakened and then produced a breakdown in this implicit contract.

Unions began their long and steady decline from the mid-1950s through the 1970s and then went into a more precipitous fall in the 1980s. Deregulation of key industries such as trucking, airlines, and financial services increased domestic competition as the rising value of the dollar and improving capabilities of foreign firms heightened competitive pressures on American firms. The 1980s witnessed, for the first time since the depression, widespread wage and benefit concessions and rollbacks and job cuts in industries most affected by these pressures.

At the same time, new financial instruments were becoming available that created what got labeled as "the market for corporate control." Takeover artists could amass resources and use junk bonds to threaten or in fact take over firms that appeared to have opportunities for returning more to shareholders by either selling off parts of the enterprise and/or by restructuring their finances and taking on greater debt.

The restructuring of corporations that resulted from the confluence of these developments led to large-scale layoffs of blue collar workers in the 1981–83 recession and then to layoffs and dismissals of white-collar managers and other salaried professionals in the 1991–92 recession. These differed from prior layoffs in two respects. First, more of them were permanent, not temporary layoffs. Second, the stigma and norms associated with announcing layoffs under the old social contract gave way. Suddenly, executives realized that they could lay people off permanently without experiencing a workforce, public, or stock market backlash. Layoff and restructuring announcements even were rewarded by Wall Street with a bump up in stock prices, albeit temporary.[13] Once they realized this, some firms turned to downsizing as a preemptive strike to position the company better for the future rather than as a strategy of last resort.

As pressures from Wall Street grew, executives turned more and more of their attention to meeting Wall Street analysts' short-term earnings' expectations and to restructuring operations to boost

earnings. Board committees and compensation consultants restruc-
tured executive contracts to better align management incentives
with investor interests. Boards likewise turned to CEOs who could
best manage relations with the financial community and project an
image of confidence.

The era of the charismatic CEO was born. Wall Street, the business media and press, and business school case writers alike reinforced these trends by committing a classic attribution error—they
attributed the successes of organizations to the leadership and
vision of the CEO and his (mostly his) top executive team.[14] Leadership in organizations became equated with the "transformational" CEO. These visionary leaders could be entrusted with the
task of revitalizing both their firms and the American economy. The
booming stock market and resurgent economy of the 1990s reinforced this view and the perceived value of CEOs. The self-
reinforcing escalation of executive compensation that ensued
eventually led to a 400 to 1 ratio of CEO compensation to the
average worker. Power became highly concentrated at the top of
organizations and Lord Acton's adage that "power corrupts and
absolute power corrupts absolutely" once again proved to be true.

As the dot-com bubble grew, a new class of younger entrepreneurs and professionals followed the lead of CEOs by taking big
portions of their compensation in the form of stock or stock options.
It may have been, as Alan Greenspan put it, "irrational exuberance"
that fueled the rise in stock prices beyond their real values, but the
result was a further loss of proportion and balance or sense of
responsibility to employees. Clearly, by the end of this era, the pen-
dulum had swung to view employees as costs to be controlled more
than strategic assets to be developed and valued.

It took the bursting of the market bubble and the litany of corporate scandals and the outing of how stock analysts were under
constant pressure to make overly optimistic projections to finally
generate a response. One response was a series of modest reforms

in corporate governance designed to provide more transparency and more accurate information to investors. Congress passed the Sarbanes Oxley bill that, among other things, holds CEOs and CFOs accountable for certifying the accuracy of their financial reports and builds more protections to ensure the independence of auditors. Another response came more quietly as labor unions and other groups representing shareholders became more active in sponsoring shareholder resolutions to protest excessive executive compensation or to overturn management actions such as reincorporating the firm in Bermuda or some other tax haven.

These are useful steps, but they all miss diagnosing the root cause of the problem. They seek to increase the accountability of management to shareholders and their Wall Street agents rather than ask whether the singular focus on shareholder wealth has gone too far and left behind the workers, families, and communities that depend on responsible behavior from corporations.

The scandals served a sobering and somewhat humbling function for some CEOs and business leaders. For a while, the view that corporations need to find ways to be more accountable to shareholders and to their employees, customers, and communities seemed to be gaining broader support. Still, the question is how to make this happen. The answer I propose is that employees have at least as much at stake in their corporations as do financial investors, and if we give them a direct voice in corporate governance they can both bring about the independence corporate governance reformers are calling for and safeguard their human capital investments. I suggest a simple new principle: *Employees who invest and put at risk their human capital should have the same rights to information and voice in governance as do investors who put at risk their financial capital.*

The principle that those who invest and risk their human capital should be treated just like financial investors is consistent with what corporate governance theorists Margaret Blair and Lynn Stout call a team production view of the modern firm.[15] They suggest that the modern firm is best thought of as a team in which shareholders and employees contribute necessary assets and share risks. Members of the board of directors should make decisions that are in the interests of the team, not just in the interests of maximizing the investments of one player (shareholders or employees). In their view, the movement toward maximizing shareholder value that dominated corporations in recent years was the result of a shift in power—from employees to financial investors—rather than some preordained rule of economics or law. So the debate over the future of the corporation is alive and well, at least in the high-level world of economics, legal, and organizational scholarship. The task is to move this debate from these rarified academic circles to the real world of organizational life.

Employee Voice in Corporate Governance

Do workers really need a voice in governance? What would it accomplish? For workers? For the economy?

For a number of years, Wayne Horvitz, former director of the Federal Mediation and Conciliation Service, and I sat on the board of directors of a large trucking company. We were nominated by the Teamsters' Union as part of an Employee Stock Ownership (ESOP) arrangement they had negotiated with the company. Although we were nominated by the union, our job was to serve as any other board member. But obviously, we were also there to safeguard the investments (15 percent of their wages) employees made to help this company survive in this highly competitive, deregulated industry.

At one board meeting, the CEO announced that management was considering a merger offer (we all knew at some point a merger would be necessary and the question was with whom) from a company that neither Wayne nor I recognized as a significant player in the industry. The CEO recommended accepting the merger offer since the offer price would provide a handsome premium over the current price of our stock. (Since the CEO owned a big piece of the company, the immediate cash benefits of this offer to him were quite substantial.) Wayne and I asked: "What is this company's business plan? What will happen to our employees?" We got no clear answer. After doing some homework on our own, with the help of the union, we discovered why there was no good answer to our question. This "company" was essentially a small number of speculators and financial wizards who specialized in buying companies, selling off physical assets, declaring bankruptcy, dissolving pensions, and making money from the proceeds!

At the next board meeting we opposed the merger, but were about to be outvoted when we proposed a short delay. "Let's hear about this company from people who have dealt with them directly," we suggested. Reluctantly the CEO and several board members agreed.

What took place next was one of the more surreal experiences of my professional life. The CEO and several of us boarded a chartered jet and flew to Palm Springs to meet with Teamster leaders who were there for a meeting. After two hours of listening to top Teamster officers and their lawyer tell us that we were about to deal with a bunch of crooks, we got back on our plane and the deal was scuttled. I felt we had just been part of a bad movie!

This vignette is perhaps just one rather colorful example of why, in crucial strategic situations, having an employee voice in governance can make sure that bad or even unethical (note this would have been perfectly legal and would have fulfilled our "fiduciary responsibilities" to maximize shareholder value) actions are blocked. Had Wayne and I not been there, this transaction would have been consummated and all employees would have lost their jobs and perhaps their pensions.

This is a "watchdog" example of why employees should have a voice. But there are equally powerful positive examples where by being in these decision processes, human capital (employee) considerations are raised that lead to positive value-added outcomes.

At least once a year the top twenty or so executives and physician leaders of Kaiser Permanente hold a day-long retreat with the labor leaders who represent their employees. These meetings are part of the most comprehensive labor-management partnership in the country today. The partnership at Kaiser provides employee representatives access to the information and the ability to participate in decisions that affect the viability of the organization and the long-term job and financial security of their members. One of these recent meetings illustrated the value of having worker voice at this high level of management strategy making.

The group was brought together to address a major problem: the decline in its customer base as companies turned to lower-cost, less comprehensive health-care plans. Earlier, a management team in one of Kaiser's biggest divisions had met on its own to discuss how to respond to this development. They proposed three immediate actions: layoffs, deferral of scheduled wage increases, and cutbacks in sick leave and absenteeism policies. Left to their own devices, this regional division of Kaiser Permanente would have implemented some mixture of these strategies as its first line of response to this problem. Doing so would, however, break the trust being built up through the labor-management partnership, not to mention fail to address the deeper strategic challenge these membership losses were signaling.

But because of the labor-management partnership, top-level leaders at Kaiser had to respond to union leaders' insistence that they work together to look for alternatives to layoffs and wage or benefit reductions. At this top-level meeting, these executives and their union partners discussed everything from how to restructure the organization to cope with rising costs, to what types of new health insurance products to develop, to the need to stay the course on their longer-run challenge and shared objective of helping to achieve universal access to health care for working families in America. At the end of the day, this group agreed to create joint task forces to tackle both the need for cost reductions and for customer growth. These task forces are now hard at work.

As I listened to and participated in this exchange of ideas, I kept wondering what America would be like if this type of dialogue were repeated in all companies around the country. That would indeed put workers on the same footing as financial investors and result in a much more balanced, and potentially more fair and transparent, corporate governance process. I bet such boards of directors would not approve CEO and executive salaries that are 400 times higher than that of their average employee!

Summary

I often begin the first session of our MBA organizational processes course with a series of questions about where the companies these students last worked are positioned on a continuum anchored on one end by the features of the prototypical industrial-era firm and on the other end by the knowledge-driven organization described here. The vast majority of students place their organizations somewhere near the middle of the continuum. Their companies are farther along on some components of the transformation process such as networking and use of teams. They are closest to the industrial era prototype when it comes to the goals of the firm: Most are seen as continuing to give primacy to maximizing shareholder value over managing the organization for the benefits of shareholders, employees, and customers. While most of our students feel their companies are trying to move in the knowledge-based direction, many are skeptical of their companies' commitment to this effort and even more worry there are strong countervailing pressures pulling management in the other direction.

The students almost universally agree on one thing, however. They clearly would rather work for companies closer to the knowledge-based end of the continuum. And, after some discussion, the majority agrees that neither extreme would be good for the economy (after all, costs still do matter). But they see the greatest potential for achieving joint gains for workers, families, communities, and the society in firms that stay the course and continue to move toward the knowledge-based end of the spectrum.

I suspect these students speak for all working families and indeed for most informed citizens. But they also signal a warning: There is no invisible hand of market forces, nor is there any confidence that simply enlightened management will get us where we need to go. These students recognize that the debate is underway and that they as managers in the organizations of the future will be in positions of power to influence these debates.

I am encouraged by our students' views. They will be better equipped to move this transformation along than prior cohorts, in part because they feel the same pressures on working families as the rest of us. But, these decisions are too important to leave to management alone. Remember Jack Welch's line: "Control your own destiny or somebody else will." Working families need to engage these debates directly in their organizations. They need to evaluate organizations that want to employ them against what they believe would be a fair and productive social contract.

Here are some of the key elements they might want to check on in evaluating prospective employers, and then advocate once employed:

• Does management believe in a theory X or theory Y? Do they trust employees to be self-motivated or see them as costs to be controlled?

• Is work organized in ways that allow employees to use their knowledge and skills effectively, to learn and deepen them, and to build the social capital with others needed to add value to the firm?

• Are there processes in place that provide employees with a voice on how to do their job, how to integrate their professional and personal/family responsibilities, and how high-level strategic and governance decisions affect their human capital investments and the future of the organization?

These are some of the elements of a new social contract that are needed to create and sustain knowledge-based organizations that could work for working families, their companies, and the economy. But how can working families gain this voice and exert this influence? We turn to this challenge a bit later. First, we need to take note of the limits to what we can expect from individual firms in today's uncertain economy.

6   Portable Benefits

Polaroid was one of the best corporate citizens in Massachusetts for the first 40 years of its history. Dr. Edwin Land founded the company in 1937 and guided it up until his retirement in 1980 to become the world's recognized leader in instant photography. Polaroid provided lifetime employment security, encouraged husbands and wives to come to work for the company, introduced profit sharing for all employees, created an elected employee council to provide workers with a voice in decision-making, and contributed time, money, and leadership to community affairs.

The beginning of the end for Polaroid started in 1982 when it announced the need to do what it hoped would be a one-time-only "voluntary severance" program. It was, unfortunately, not to be a one-time adjustment, but the first of many to come over the next twenty years as the company slowly declined. In 1988, in an effort to fend off a hostile takeover, Polaroid made its employees part owners in the company by cutting wages 5 percent and investing these funds in company shares. It even put an "employee," in this case, a high-level marketing executive, on its board of directors.

The downward spiral continued in the 1990s. More layoffs occurred, but this time they were no longer "voluntary." A new CEO and top management team was brought in from outside to try to turn the company around. Unfortunately, he and his team did just the opposite. The end came in 2002 when the company stock became essentially worthless and there was no way to survive without going through a bankruptcy and reorganization as essentially a new company. As it went through this process, the same top management team awarded itself (with board approval of course) "retention bonuses" so that the company would not lose its talented leadership in this time of crisis!

When a new set of buyers finally purchased the assets of the company for a bargain price, it canceled retiree health care and dropped the salary payments promised to those on long-term disability. Several of the top executives who had taken the company into bankruptcy got jobs and a stake in the new firm.

The tragic effects of this saga were brought home to me with a letter that arrived in my mailbox following a comment I made in a local newspaper about the use of executive retention bonuses. The letter was from a husband and wife who both had worked for Polaroid for over twenty years. They pointed out that they had lost their jobs, life savings, future retirement income, and the wherewithal to help their children pay for college tuitions.

Stories like this remind us that there are real people and real families behind every corporate failure. We simply have to do better for working families as we think about how to design, fund, and deliver health-care, pension, and other benefits in the future.

Few firms today can make a credible promise of long-term careers or employment security. Nor do many employees stay with a single employer over their full careers. This is likely to be even truer in the future. Young and old workers alike have learned from the sad experiences of their parents, or through their own personal experiences, that it is too risky to "put all your eggs in one basket."

America has a long-term task ahead of it—to gradually wean ourselves from depending on individual firms to provide health insurance, pensions, and other benefits and services such as family leave and life-long learning. This will not be easy. Taking up this challenge puts us right in the heart of debates over the U.S. health-care system, social security, and the absence of any national policy for paid family leave. Yet addressing these issues is critical to meeting the needs of working families and to supporting the transformation to a knowledge-based economy.

America's Historical Legacy: Do It through the Employers

Understanding why this is such a big challenge for America requires that we take a step back in time, to the 1930s. When Franklin Roosevelt and his advisors crafted social security, unemployment insurance, and other labor-market policies that govern employment relations today, they chose to use employers as the funding and delivery vehicle for these and other benefits and services. Then, as industrial unions grew in size and power, unions reinforced this pattern by negotiating health insurance, private pensions, various forms of leave, and other benefits with individual firms. Most of these benefits improved with seniority. Some further rewarded loyalty and long service with "back-loaded" benefits such as defined benefit pension funds that had payoff formulas that increased with length of service or were based on wages earned in the years immediately prior to retirement. This approach made sense in an economy of stable jobs, where employers encouraged and rewarded loyalty and long service, and employees could trust firms to keep their implied promises.

The first signs of a crack in this system came in the 1980s when a number of firms figured out that, according to the government's actuarial calculations, their pension plans were "overfunded." Then some crafty lawyers realized that firms could grab the overfunded amounts from their pension funds and use them for other purposes. The fear (real in some cases, probably imagined in others) was that if the firm didn't reappropriate these funds, a hostile buyer would see an opportunity to take over the firm and take the money and run.

Another crack in the dike came when employers observed in the mid-1980s and early 1990s that they could lay off large numbers of blue- and even white-collar workers, not, as in the past, as a strategy of last resort in times of economic difficulty, but in good times as well. As noted in the preceding chapter, maybe, with the right spin for the analysts, they could even get a little bump up in their stock price.

A third weakening of the firm-centered model came as firms shifted from defined benefit to defined contribution, cash balance, and/or 401(k) pension plans. Instead of guaranteeing retirees a fixed amount of monthly income at retirement age and funding the pension plan adequately to cover these future liabilities, the new plans shifted the risk to employees by making a specific contribution to a fund that would accrue until retirement age. Rather than getting a certain amount, retirees would get whatever the invested funds generated up to that point.

The final straw came in more recent years as health-care costs went into their second upward spiral in less than a decade. The gradual growth in health-care coverage that had been achieved from the 1940s onward stopped by 1980 and pressures to share more of the costs with employees increased. More recently, as box 6.1 reports, policies promised retirees were cut back or canceled as their costs and numbers covered increased. As a result, health care is now the number one issue in collective bargaining and human resource budgeting in companies across the country.

By 2004, thoughtful leaders in business, labor, and government finally began to recognize what workers already knew: the firm-centered model for financing and delivering benefits no longer makes sense. But the unanswered question is how to change to something better suited to today's more mobile workforce and uncertain labor market.

Some steps in the right direction can be taken.

Box 6.1
Cutbacks in Retiree Health Insurance

Employers have unleashed a new wave of cutbacks in company-paid health benefits for retirees, with a growing number of companies saying that retirees can retain coverage only if they are willing to bear the full cost themselves.

Scores of companies in the last two years, including the telecommunications equipment giants Lucent Technologies and Alcatel and a big electronic utility, TXU, have ended medical benefits for some or all of their retirees and instead offer to let them buy coverage through a group plan. This coverage is often more expensive than many retirees can afford. . . .

Many companies, especially retailers with high turnover and low-paid workforces, and technology companies with relatively young workers, do not provide retirees any health benefits. [See table below.]

Many retirees are bitter about such changes. "I took the offer to retire in 2001 mainly because they were protecting health care benefits," said Edward Beltram, 58, a former Lucent human resources manager [who] must now pay $375 more a month to maintain coverage for himself and his wife.

Mr. Beltram, who worked for Lucent and for units of a predecessor company for 31 years, added, "I feel they have reneged on their promises."

Leaving a Job, Losing Coverage

Number of employees	Percentage of companies promising retiree health benefits to current employees
10–499	5%
500–999	24%
1,000–4,999	30%
5,000–9,999	41%
10,000–19,999	45%
20,000 or more	51%

Source: Milt Freudenheim, "Companies Limit Health Care Coverage of Many Retirees," *New York Times*, February 3, 2004.

One big step would be to adopt a new design principle for all future labor-market services, benefits, and social-insurance policies: Do not tie them to employment with a specific employer and, by all means, do not make them graduated benefits linked to weeks, months, or years of service with a specific employer. All future benefits and funding formulas should be one hundred percent portable.

In this regard, social security is the model to follow; unemployment insurance is the model to avoid. Social security benefits are not tied to tenure with a specific employer and part-time work is covered. Unemployment insurance requires a minimum length of service with a specific employer before a worker becomes eligible. So while social security covers nearly all workers, today only about one-third of those out of work receive unemployment benefits. Some are not covered because they are new labor-force entrants who can't find jobs, some have not worked full time for a specific employer long enough to gain eligibility, and others have exhausted their benefits (normally lasting 26 weeks unless extended by Congress or state legislatures during periods of high unemployment).

Health Insurance

Employer-provided health insurance got an initial boost during World War II when the War Labor Board, the agency overseeing collective bargaining, allowed unions and companies to introduce this benefit in return for holding down wages. This quickly became a popular bargaining issue because employees do not pay income taxes on money they or employers put to health insurance (or pensions). Figure 6.1 shows the gradual growth in health insurance coverage that this development set off. As the chart shows, growth in coverage peaked in 1979 at just under 70 percent of the workforce and had declined to approximately 64 percent by 2000. Today an estimated 45 million Americans do not have health-insurance coverage.[1]

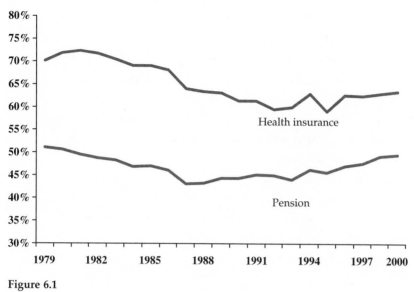

Figure 6.1
Health Insurance and Pension Coverage, 1979–2000. Source: Lawrence Mishel et al.,
The State of Working America 2000–2001 (Economic Policy Institute, 2000).

The problem is deeper. Costs once again are escalating, rising
between 13 and 15 percent in recent years. Firms providing health
insurance are desperately trying to contain and lower their costs by
increasing employee insurance premiums and copayments for
office visits, drugs, and other services, eliminating or raising the
costs of health-care coverage previously promised retirees, or shifting to lower cost, less comprehensive plans. New firms are less
likely to provide health insurance today than did start ups in the
past and those new or small employers that do provide coverage
are turning to the bargain basement priced plans. Some temporary
help firms provide what are now known as "access only" plans to
people they place. That is, they are available if the temporary
workers pay most or all of the premiums. Few can afford to do so.

In the past several years, many employees either accepted in collective bargaining or had imposed on them increases in copayments
for their health insurance. Retirees were especially hard hit. The

Medicare Reform Bill passed by Congress in 2003 has a provision to subsidize firms so that they do not drop their retiree health-care and drug coverage. So the question might be asked: Who should get this subsidy? Should it go into the general coffers of the company or should it be transferred to employees or retirees who made concessions in this area already? This is an interesting question, but not one that will even be asked unless employees have the opportunity to voice it.

The widespread recognition of these problems has sparked a host of proposals for reform, some of which would continue to rely on employers as the funding and delivery channel, some of which rely more on government funding, and some of which allow for individual medical savings plans similar to 401(k) pension plans. Some

Box 6.2
State Level Initiatives to Address the Uninsured

In a sign of a growing political consensus, Senate President Robert E. Traveglini and Governor Mitt Romney said yesterday ... that they want to focus next year's legislative session on dramatically cutting the number of people in Massachusetts without health insurance.

Traveglini set a goal of providing healthcare coverage to at least half of the 500,000 uninsured Massachusetts residents by the end of 2006, pledging to make what he called "an economic and a moral failing" the centerpiece of the legislative session.

Source: Scott S. Greenberger, "State Leaders Aim at Healthcare Gap," *Boston Globe*, November 16, 2004, p. A1.

****

"Next year I am committed to working with the Legislature to pass a comprehensive, market-based reform program for healthcare."

Source: Mitt Romney, "My Plan for Massachusetts Health Insurance Reform," *Boston Globe*, November 21, 2004, p. K11.

companies and unions are working together with their health-care providers to improve quality and lower costs. Others have agreed to work together to find a national solution to this crisis. To date, however, there have been more words than actions. In 2004 both major presidential candidates and several congressional leaders put forward plans for reform. And because the costs of providing health care to the uninsured are borne most directly by state taxpayers, I believe the most innovative solutions to this problem are likely to come from this level of government. As the newspaper excerpts in box 6.2 show, there is already considerable bipartisan dialogue over how (not whether) to tackle this problem in Massachusetts. Look for similar efforts in other states in the near future.

This is not the place to propose a solution to this complex problem. If American history is any guide, a "solution" is more likely to evolve out of a series of incremental steps, each dealing with a piece of the problem, rather than in one big comprehensive reform. So what is most important for working families is that they be a part of this process of reform and that they have a clear focus on their interests and goals. Among these should be:

Universal and continuous coverage All family members need to be covered by health insurance whether or not parents are working in paid jobs, moving between jobs, or out of the paid labor force.

Fairness If employees have to bear higher costs of health insurance, they should also share in any cost relief provided to employers if and when transition programs are introduced that offer options for moving from employer-sponsored to publicly-funded plans or to individual medical savings accounts.

Pooling Continuation of broad pooling principles is essential if we are to avoid creating even more of a divide between young healthy people and the elderly or otherwise higher risk and higher cost populations.

Weaning from reliance on individual employers While it may be neither necessary nor wise to absolve employers from all responsibility to provide health-care benefits, a gradual, perhaps step by step, process of moving to other funding arrangements is critical. Otherwise, we will continue to penalize the most progressive and mature firms that are doing their best to meet their responsibilities to employees and retirees and reward those that would undercut them by breaking prior promises or starting up new firms unencumbered by any of these legacy costs.

Pensions

The growth in coverage of private pensions can also be traced to collective bargaining developments back in the 1940s. Like health insurance, pension bargaining got started during World War II, but it really took off after a 1949 Supreme Court decision ruled that pensions were included in the list of mandatory subjects in collective bargaining. That is, employers and unions had to negotiate over pensions if the other side introduced a proposal on this issue. As shown in figure 6.1, like health insurance, pension coverage gradually expanded up until the late 1970s and has stayed at about 50 percent of the workforce since then.

This simple chart masks a major change in the nature of pensions. In the past two decades there has been a massive shift in pensions from defined benefit plans to various types of defined contribution plans. Between 1992 and 1998 among all the households with pension plan coverage, the share covered by only a defined benefit plan dropped from 40 percent to 20 percent while the share of households covered only by a defined contribution plan grew from 37 percent to 57 percent. About 17 percent were covered by some mixture of the two plans. Whether measured by total assets, contributions, or members, defined contribution plans are now about twice as large as are defined benefit plans.[2]

Coverage is also highly unequal. Over 80 percent of households in the top 20 percent of the income distribution have some type of pension plan compared to less than 30 percent of households in the bottom 20 percent. Young workers, part-time workers, short-tenure employees (less than one year of service), and those not represented by a union are less likely to have a pension plan.

Recently a friend of mine who was a high-level labor relations executive in one of the country's most successful firms described how he protested to no avail the company's decision in the mid-1980s to shift certain salaried employees' annual bonuses from cash awards into investment in company stock that could not be redeemed until their retirement date. He thought it both unfair and unwise to require this amount of their compensation to go into company stock. He believed that this was ill advised even when a company is doing well and likely to continue to do well. Neither employees nor, as it turned out, this executive had a voice in this decision. The CEO decided this was the way to go. Like most others, the CEO's decision looked great in the go-go 1990s as the company's stock more than doubled. But then it fell to about one-third its peak value when the stock market went bust. My friend will not be scraping to make ends meet now that he is about to retire. But he and I share a concern for the thousands of less well paid salaried employees. They are left with much less than would have been the case had the company continued a defined benefit plan or listened to his plea to put less of their deferred compensation into the company's stock.

We will never know how much American workers actually lost in future retirement savings as companies made a host of decisions to change pension, deferred compensation, and retirement policies over the course of the last decade. Some was lost as companies took back portions of "over-funded" plans, some was lost through the shift in risk to employees, and some was lost because employers are contributing fewer dollars into retirement savings in the new defined contribution arrangements than would have been the case if the defined benefit plans had been maintained.

These are complicated decisions requiring technical expertise and involve choices that often trade off company and employee interests. It is unfair and indeed, undemocratic, to exclude employees from having a voice in deciding how these choices are made. It is, after all, their money and their future retirement security that is at stake.

Another concern I have is that Americans are not saving enough to prepare for their retirement. A 2001 Federal Reserve study found, for example, that among households with retirement accounts that were approaching retirement, half had savings of $55,000 or less and one-fourth had savings of less than $13,000.[3] Clearly, this will only provide a meager supplement to whatever social security income these families will receive. Unless something changes, the next generation of retirees will not come close to having the level of retirement security as did their parents who retired in the era of defined benefit plans.

The movement to defined contribution and 401(k) plans does increase portability, since these funds can be rolled over to a new plan if an individual changes jobs. Most of these, however, are still under the control of employers, many require significant amounts (although less post-Enron than before) to be invested in the company's stock, and very few have any employee role in their oversight and governance. When we add the shift in risk of these plans to employees and their families and the reality that the dollars flowing into these plans will fall far short of the amounts needed for financial security for most retirees, it is obvious that further reforms and improvements are needed.

This issue will be high on the national agenda and will be a major policy issue within private corporations for years to come. It will be closely tied to debates over how to address the coming shortfall in funding of social security. Once again, working families have a major stake in the choices made in both the public and private forums where options are debated. They need to be there to give voice to the following goals:

Expanding pension coverage America needs to break out of the twenty-year lull in growth in pension coverage, particularly among lower-income workers and families.

Higher contributions More money needs to be saved and invested, both by employers and employees. To do otherwise ensures that America will return to having many retired households living below the poverty line rather than having the dignity of financial security that most of today's elderly enjoy.

Portability We need to continue to move toward the ultimate goal of 100 percent portability of pensions.

Employee choice Employees should have the choice over where to invest their funds and not be required to invest specific amounts in their employer's stock. This is just as simple and sensible as the commonsense advice not to "put all your eggs in one basket."

Expanded options for 401(k) plans Today only employers can offer and administer 401(k) programs. This constraint should be lifted to allow professional associations, unions, and others to do so as well.

Employee representation on all pension funds It seems unconscionable to exclude employees from voting their own representatives to serve as trustees of their own money.

Funding social security Private pensions can only be supplements to and not replacements for a solid and safe social security system. Addressing the problems in both programs is essential to providing a dignified and secure retirement for all working families in America.

Other Benefits and Services

How can we move away from dependence on individual firms for other benefits and services? There is no single or easy answer here either. Some new ideas and solutions will need to be invented. We have already suggested the need for a national paid family-leave policy and for individual pretax savings accounts that could be used for life-long learning or to meet other personal or family needs when moving between jobs. Flexible and portable accounts like this might be part of the solution.

What, If Not Employers?

Ultimately we will need to create new institutions that take up the role that single employers played in funding and administering benefits when they were bound by the old social contract. One option is to encourage unions and professional associations to step into this void, an idea we will take up in earnest next.

Restoring Voice at Work
and in Society

By now it should be clear why working families need to restore their voice at work and in society. The question is, what forms should this voice take and how can we get there? Will this come in the form of a resurgent and revitalized labor movement? Or will some new instruments of worker voice and organization emerge that replace unions as we knew them in the industrial age? Which option would better serve the interests of working families?

Lessons from History

In the heat of a debate at the 1935 convention of the American Federation of Labor (AFL) over how to organize the growing number of unskilled and semiskilled production workers in the rising industrial economy, John L. Lewis, head of the Mineworkers Union, punched "Big" Bill Hutchinson of the Carpenters Union in the eye and stormed out of the hall with his industrial union supporters. What was to become the Congress of Industrial Organizations (CIO) was born. Over the next three decades, the CIO organized ten million production workers in steel, autos, rubber, electrical, and other manufacturing industries. Through collective bargaining, jobs that had been given up as inherently low wage, unsafe, and unskilled and that were held by workers destined to remain poor, were transformed into jobs that allowed these workers to move their families into the middle class, send their children to college, and retire with dignity and security.

Union representation has risen and fallen in long cycles in the United States. Declines tend to be gradual and extended; rebirths and resurgence, like the rise of the CIO, tend to come in abrupt and unpredictable bursts. Each time, labor's resurgence tends to coincide with three things: (1) a shift in the nature of the economy and the organization of work and production, (2) an economic, social, or political crisis that shocks America into recognizing the need to change the direction of the country, and (3) the emergence of a new vision and strategy for how to rebuild unions that is more in tune with the needs of the contemporary workforce, organization of work and production, and economic realities.

The American labor movement may be approaching another of these historic turning points. Union membership has fallen to below its predepression numbers. Today less than 9 percent of private-sector workers is represented by unions. American workers once again have lost their voice at work and in society. Incremental efforts of unions to organize in the same ways they did in the heyday of the industrial economy will not work. Something new is needed. The shift from the industrial to the knowledge-based economy calls for new models of worker voice and representation at work, in corporate enterprises, and in community, state, and national affairs. What is needed is a new vision and strategy for mobilizing and giving voice to modern working families.

The good news is that many progressive leaders in the labor movement and outside of it recognize this. There is an active debate underway over what shape the "next-generation unions" will look like, as Amy Dean, former CEO of the South Bay Labor Council and one of the creative voices for change, puts it. Andrew Stern, president of the Service Employees International Union (SEIU), and leaders of several other AFL-CIO unions have opened a highly public debate with their peers over the future of the labor movement. They see the need for a more streamlined structure in which existing unions would merge and specialize in specific sectors and focus on organizing strategic companies and communities. He and many others within the labor movement also recognize the need for a new approach to organizing and representing workers, one that is better matched to the contemporary labor force and economy and one that reaches out to build alliances with other progressive forces (see box 7.1).

The elements of a new model are emerging at the grassroots level, as in the past, through a combination of innovations within existing unions and associations and the development of new, complementary efforts of groups outside the labor movement. So, if history is a guide, out of the ashes of the current labor movement will emerge new agents and models of worker voice and mobilization that, together with the legacy unions that change and adapt, will constitute the "next-generation" instruments for worker voice.

Before taking up how working families might help shape and be served by these next-generation institutions, we first have to address the negative image some Americans have of unions and union leaders. Americans have always had a dual image of unions. The majority value and approve of unions because they know fairness dictates and workers and their families need a voice in a democratic society. Yet many Americans also harbor a negative image of the leaders who represent "Big Labor." Only by acknowledging the existence of both these images can we begin to think creatively about the forms of worker voice and organization that are needed and can be built.

The Best and Worst of Labor Unions

In October 1991, I stood in a corridor at the Omni Shoreham Hotel in Washington, D.C., waiting for Polish president Lech Wałesa to finish speaking to the AFL-CIO convention. I was there to meet with

Box 7.1
Andy Stern's View of the Twenty-First-Century Labor Movement

American workers improved their lives over the course of the twentieth century by uniting their own strength with the strength of other workers through unions. In the twenty-first century we need a labor movement that has the strength to deal with *this century's* challenges.

We aren't going to rebuild the labor movement to what it was—that workforce and economy no longer exist. We need to transform unions, not try to return to the old model.

We need an agenda—a clear economic agenda for working families—not just a hodge-podge of ideas—but one that clearly defines what we stand for. Too often we have come across as a movement or a political force that is intent on defending the New Deal, not one that is creating the new economy. The New Deal was very important in its time but we have to build on this and look forward, not just lament how current policies are taking us backward.

When we talk about changing the AFL-CIO or building something stronger, we have in mind the need for alliances. We learned about the power of alliances in this past election from the examples of our relationships with organizations such as Americans Coming Together (ACT) and community organizations that worked with us on voter registrations. Our role should be to unite many different organizations that share our commitment to working families in ways that allow each to maximize its effectiveness.

If the government or business wanted to promote a new model of unions—less worksite focused and more skilled and industry based—there are lots of things we could do. We could promote efficiency and opportunities for individual workers. Unions have the potential to be that kind of intermediary here, as they are in other countries.

Source: Personal interview, November 2004.

Billy McCarthy, the president of the Teamsters' Union, to discuss a problem with a trucking company his union represented (a different problem than the merger example in chapter 5). I was thrilled when Mr. Wałesa walked by and we shook hands and exchanged greetings. Then, as I sat down across the table from McCarthy in the Teamster's suite, it dawned on me that within minutes I had seen about the best and the worst leaders the world's labor movements had to offer.

The Teamsters have since instituted a series of internal and government-mandated reforms in an effort to root out the corruption McCarthy inherited from his predecessors. And there have always been many dedicated and honest local Teamster leaders and staff who have served their members well. But this negative "Big Labor" image comes to mind whenever I find myself explaining to students and other skeptical audiences why a free, independent, strong, and innovative labor movement is both in their interest and essential to the future of our economy and democracy. Yes, unions carry considerable baggage. They are overly bureaucratic and slow to change. Some do have long histories of corruption. And yet, warts and all, unions have served as the most important instrument of economic and social progress for working families of the twentieth century. As one union bumper sticker puts it: "Remember who brought you the weekend." One could add to that, middle-class wages and lifestyles for millions of blue collar workers and families, private pensions, health insurance, vacation pay, grievance procedures, and most other elements that we now associate with a "good job."

Workers agree. Some might find it ironic that as union membership and power declined over the years, a growing majority of Americans "approve" of and see a need for unions. Americans are leery of letting unions get too powerful, but evidently a growing number now worry that they have lost too much power and believe some rebalancing is needed. National polls reported in 1980 that 55 percent of Americans approved of unions compared to 67 percent in 1999.[1] Today, nearly 50 percent of the workforce would join a union if given the chance compared to 30 percent in 1976.[2] And over 70 percent want a more flexible and cooperative voice in workplace and corporate affairs. So the majority of Americans recognize the continuing need for a voice at work and want to see a new generation of unions and some new forms of more direct worker voice and participation develop and be available to them.

Out of the Ashes: Reinventing Unions and Professional Associations

John Sweeney won the first-ever contested election for the presidency of the AFL-CIO in 1995, promising to renew the labor movement's commitment to organizing. Indeed he has done so and has reinvigorated organizing efforts by expanding and strengthening the AFL-CIO's Organizing Institute, recruiting talented and dedicated young people to the labor movement, and urging national unions to put more resources into organizing. But these efforts have not produced a resurgence in membership, in large part because the traditional organizing model is incapable of turning the labor movement around.

The traditional organizing model is governed by the National Labor Relations Act (NLRA), first passed as part of the New Deal in 1935. For years, independent researchers, government commissions, and participants in union organizing drives have known that this law no longer protects workers or fulfills its promise of providing them with a voice at work. We will discuss how the law needs to be reformed and modernized in chapter 8. For now, we simply need to understand why, even with proper reforms, the current law and the organizing model it supports will not provide modern working families with the voice they need.

Following the traditional organizing model under the NLRA, it takes a majority of workers in a given location or bargaining unit to vote to join and be represented by a union for collective bargaining. If a majority is not achieved, none of those who preferred to be represented gain representation. It is an all or nothing, high risk venture. To get a majority to vote for a union, the evidence shows that workers must be deeply dissatisfied with and distrust their employer, risk their jobs or career prospects, and hold on for two to three years before any benefits are likely to be realized. Their chances of winning an election are on average about 50 percent, and are considerably lower if employers resist or delay the process (as they are counseled to do by their lawyers and consultants). And even if they gain certification, these workers face another 30 percent chance that their union will not be able to achieve a first contract or sustain a relationship with the employer.[3]

These threshold conditions for gaining access to representation via the traditional organizing model are simply too high and too risky for all but the most desperate workers. Moreover, the ultimate irony is that by following this traditional organizing approach, it is largely American *managers and their consultants*, not American workers or unions, who decide who will be organized. From a working families' standpoint, this is ludicrous. Aren't workers supposed to be the ones to decide whether or not they want and get representation? An alternative approach is needed to take management out of the process.

What Needs to Be Done?

We have to make a cultural change in how we approach and organize workers. I don't think you can just organize from the top down through employers or depend on finding workers who are mistreated anymore. You have to organize from the bottom up. You have to change the culture in which organizing takes place.

Workers don't have to be against the employer to be for the union. We can make the employer much stronger by partnering and helping the employer face the global economy. It's time we change, not to catch up but to get ahead.

—Richard Trumka, secretary treasurer, AFL-CIO, November 2004

Richard Trumka captures a growing sense among labor leaders that a new organizing model is needed. They recognize that a new model must be based on what workers and their families want and need from work and must convey a positive vision and credible strategy for representing and meeting the changing needs of workers and families. A way to start is to recognize how these needs change as people move through different stages of their careers and family lives.

Table 7.1 summarizes this point vividly by showing the common and different priorities workers of different ages and family situations bring to work. These data come from surveys of over 8,000 workers conducted by Towers Perrin, a leading human resource consulting firm. They report one obvious fact: Good wages and benefits remain as important as ever to today's workers. Regardless of age, these are expected to be part of any good job and, therefore, the first responsibility of any institution that seeks to represent

Table 7.1
What Attracts Employees by Age

Top Attractors	U.S. Overall	18–29	30–44	45–54	55+
Competitive base pay/salary	✸	✸	✸	✸	✸
Competitive health care benefits package	✸	✸	✸	✸	✸
Opportunities for advancement	1	1	2		3
Work/life balance	2	2	1	2	
Competitive retirement benefits package	3			1	1
Pay raises linked to individual performance	3		3	3	2
Learning and development opportunities		3			

Source: *Towers Perrin Talent Report 2001: New Realities in Today's Workforce*
Key: ✸ Core rewards that rank at the top for all groups
1–3 Top differentiators in rank order

workers is to address these needs. But that is not enough. As noted earlier, young workers are especially concerned about gaining access to opportunities to learn and advance on their job. Balancing work and family life is a high priority throughout normal child-bearing and -raising ages and rises to the top priority as people move through middle age. Retirement security rises in priority as people advance in age and approach the later stages of their working years.

Positive Vision and Strategy

To interest and mobilize these modern workers, the next-generation unions will need a positive vision and strategy that addresses these common and varied needs. That means going beyond the traditional organizing model that relies on deep dissatisfaction, frustration, and distrust of one's employer before turning to collective representation. Unions must offer a hopeful, positive vision of how workers themselves can realize their aspirations over the course of their careers and family life stages. This is what Trumka means when he suggests that the entire culture of organizing needs to change. Some unions are already doing so.

The Harvard Union of Clerical and Technical Workers' (HUCTW) organizing slogans illustrate this approach quite nicely: "You don't have to be anti-Harvard to be pro-Union" and "Harvard works because we do."[4] The union backs up these slogans with an organizing strategy that emphasizes building a supportive community and network among employees before seeking collective bargaining certification.

This same approach has been successful in organizing predominantly female health-care workers in Massachusetts, Minnesota, and elsewhere. The fact that women respond well to such an organizing strategy should not be surprising. For many years, women have expressed significantly greater interest in joining unions than their white male counterparts. In fact, women account for nearly three-fourths of all new union members in the 1990s. So addressing the needs of women is clearly a necessary condition for restoring voice at work and meeting the needs of working families. Strategies such as those followed by the HUCTW and other unions that have been successful in organizing large numbers of women need to be pursued more extensively.

While work-family balance and integration are not solely women's issues, the reality is that women have been in the forefront of this movement and are likely to respond with more enthusiasm to organizations that champion this cause, put it high on their agenda, and provide leadership to such efforts. Women are a prime constituency and potential source not only of new union members, but of creative new ideas, energy, and leadership.

Some critics of the HUCTW approach say it is too expensive and takes too long to achieve majority representation status. One respected labor law scholar has proposed a solution to this problem. In *The Blue Eagle at Work* Charles Morris suggests labor law permits and protects workers' right to be represented by a union even before it demonstrates it has majority support.[5] So perhaps the National Labor Relations Act is not as rigid and difficult to use to organize workers as conventional wisdom and practice would have us believe. The conventional view is that in the absence of a majority workers lack the power to get an employer to take them seriously and are exposed to retaliation. This may be true in some settings but, then, sometimes the only way to prove conventional wisdom to be wrong is to try out alternatives like this.

Lifetime Individual and Family Memberships

Under the standard industrial organizing model, union membership and representation are linked to a specific job or bargaining unit. Once a worker leaves the job, representation is lost. Given this, it is not surprising that today there are twice as many former union members in the country as there are current members!

An alternative approach, better suited to today's mobile workforce, would be to recruit individual workers and family members independent of their workplace and employer and outside of the process built into labor law. Once recruited, the relationship with members could be maintained for life by providing the labor market and educational services and benefits individuals and families need as they move through different stages of their careers and family lives. Consistent with the history of the way many unions began, these types of organizations might serve as mutual benefit societies by providing workers with health insurance, savings programs that build retirement security, life-long education, work-family supports, and the social networks and information needed to find jobs when required. They would also provide quick and effective advice and representation to solve problems and if necessary represent workers in trouble, individually and collectively. As noted earlier, this is the void that needs to be filled if America is to wean itself away from reliance on individual firms to fund and deliver these key benefits and labor market services. Let's build the type of worker-led organizations needed to fill this void!

A good deal of experimentation is already underway with this approach. Both the National Education Association and the American Federation of Teachers recruit and provide an array of representational services and benefits to teachers under collective bargaining contracts and those not able to obtain formal bargaining recognition. Working Today, an innovative organization described in box 7.2, follows this approach in providing an array of health benefits, networking, and other benefits and services to independent contractors in New York's media industries. The Communications Workers of America (CWA) has experiments underway such as Washtech, the Alliance at IBM, and an internal organizing effort called WAGE at General Electric.

Box 7.2
Working Today

Working Today is a national nonprofit (501[c][3]) organization that represents the needs and concerns of America's growing independent workforce through advocacy, information, and service. These independent workers—freelancers, consultants, independent contractors, temps, part-timers, contingent employees, and the self-employed—currently make up about 30 percent of the nation's workforce.

To make sure that independent workers have access to key protections such as health insurance and other benefits, Working Today has built links with professional associations, membership- and community-based organizations, unions, and companies. That way, they are able to reach large numbers of independent workers, enabling them to gain access to services and essential products previously available only to the traditional workforce of full-time, long-term employees.

In September 2001, Working Today launched the Portable Benefits Network (PBN), an innovative project to deliver benefits to independent workers in New York City's Silicon Alley. In May 2003, the PBN was renamed Freelancers Union to better reflect the ideas that guide this organization and all of the services they offer—benefits, resources, and advocacy.

Working Today also educates policymakers and the public about the needs of this new workforce. They advocate for policy changes, calling upon lawmakers to create a pragmatic safety net of laws and protections, services, and benefits that people can rely on as they move from job to job or assignment to assignment.

Founded in New York City in 1995, Working Today has received grants and other support from both the state and city of New York, as well as from leading foundations, including the Ford Foundation, the John D. and Catherine T. MacArthur Foundation, J. P. Morgan Chase, the New York Community Trust, United Hospital Fund, the Rockefeller Family Fund, and others.

Source: www.workingtoday.org

Box 7.3 describes Working America, another approach to recruiting individuals developed by the AFL-CIO. Approximately 800,000 individuals have joined this organization in its first year of operation, largely in response to door to door canvassing in selected states and communities. According to Karen Nussbaum, Working America's executive director:

The key to our success so far is that we tap into the central economic concerns of working families both nationally and in the communities we target. We have been especially active on overtime pay and the exporting of jobs. Our members delivered 35,000 letters to President Bush protesting his new overtime rules. Our "ask a lawyer" page on our website got 50,000 inquiries on the new rules. Our "job tracker" feature—where anyone can enter a zip code and find out who is exporting jobs in their community— has had 500,000 visits in the past three months. The long run goal of Working America is to provide a political voice for people who do not have a collective bargaining relationship. We want to create a new source of

Box 7.3
Working America

WORKING AMERICA is people like you—working women and men, retirees, people who want to set America's priorities straight.

WORKING AMERICA, a community affiliate of the AFL-CIO, is a powerful force for working people. With the combined strength of 13 million union men and women and millions of nonunion workers who share common challenges and goals, we fight in communities, states and nationally for what really matters—good jobs, affordable health care, world-class education, secure retirements, real homeland security and more.

And we work against wrong-headed priorities favoring the rich and corporate special interests over America's well-being.

WORKING AMERICA uses professional research, communication, education, canvassing, lobbying and community organizing to demand that politicians address the priorities that matter most to working people—not just wealthy special interests. Make a difference for your community, for America and for your working family.

Source: www.workingamerica.org

worker power that is geographically based and that makes full use of the Web to activate workers and encourages them to get involved in electoral and legislative affairs and to hold elected officials accountable.

Direct Participation

Today's workers want a direct voice. They no more want to be told how they are being represented by a centralized bureaucratic union or association than they want to be told to trust that management will take care of their interests. Having a direct voice in how to do one's job, how to improve the flow of work, and how to build a collaborative, high-trust work environment increases job satisfaction, dignity, and self worth.[6] As discussed in chapter 5, studies have shown that worker participation, combined with other appropriate workplace innovations and investments in technology, increase product and service quality and productivity. So any modern system of worker voice and representation must be based on a foundation of employee participation in the day-to-day affairs and decisions that affect how they do their jobs and how they can better contribute to the success of the enterprise.

American industry has developed lots of ways to do this, from the quality circle movement of the early 1980s to more on-line organization of workers into teams that take responsibility for some of the duties traditionally assigned to first or second line supervisors. The challenge with these processes lies in sustaining them through turnover of managers and others who championed their creation or through the first budget crunch, layoff, or other normal crises that one can expect to occur. Employee participation is often the first thing to go when crises arise, either because it is viewed as nice but not essential or because a new executive takes over who carries a command and control managerial style that should have been left behind in the last century. The key, therefore, is to give workers the ability to initiate and sustain a direct voice in the workplace with or without managerial champions.

On this score, Europe is ahead of America by several decades. Most European countries, and now most recently the European Union, provide all employees in an enterprise the right to elect representatives to a "works council," a representative body that meets, consults, and works with management on workplace and workforce issues. I will come back to discuss the public policy changes needed to support this type of workplace representation in the next chapter.

Collective Bargaining: Past, Present, and Future

So far the examples mentioned are all geared to situations where it is not yet possible to achieve the majority support needed for gaining collective bargaining status. This does not mean that unions should give up on the goal of achieving a collective bargaining relationship. America still needs a forum where hard decisions are made over how to balance worker and employer interests. But even in collective bargaining, new approaches are needed, and in many cases they are emerging in practice.

Throughout the twentieth century, collective bargaining served as the main tool both for determining union members' wages and for advancing union and nonunion workers' wages, benefits, and working conditions. Traditionally, collective bargaining has been most successful in advancing worker interests when two conditions were present: (1) unions organized, or served as a credible threat to organize, a sufficient part of the relevant labor and product market to "take wages out of competition" and (2) unions could mount a credible strike threat as their key source of power.

Today, both of these conditions are problematic. Global competition and the rise of domestic nonunion competition in all but a few industries and some large cities make it difficult to take wages out of competition. Moreover, since 1980, the strike, with some notable exceptions, has largely turned into a defensive weapon used only as a very last resort to ward off employer demands for concessions.[7]

A four-month strike by grocery workers in California is a recent case in point. The workers went on strike to oppose employer demands to cut their health-care plans in anticipation of Wal-Mart opening stores and paying lower wages and benefits. In the end, the union was able to hold the line for its current, but not for its future, members. The strike ended only when the union agreed to allow the companies to pay lower wages and benefits to all employees hired in the future.[8]

The most visible exceptions to this shift in the effects of the strike are examples like the Teamsters-UPS strike in 1997 and the Justice for Janitors' campaigns in Los Angeles, Boston, and several other large cities in recent years. These illustrate how the role of the strike has changed from an economic action aimed at stopping production to a more public and political action designed to mobilize public support. While these strikes imposed economic costs on their target employers, their real source of power came from the support these unions gained from the public and the coalition partners the unions mobilized in support of their demands.

Nobody likes strikes. Yet a deadline does focus the mind and motivate parties to make hard decisions. The right to withhold one's labor individually or collectively is something that most people see as an essential safety valve that workers should have to draw on if necessary, as long as it does not pose significant risks to the safety or welfare of the public or other bystanders. The implication is that the public would like to see collective bargaining do its work without having to rely on strikes to get the job done.

The good news is that there is a range of tools that parties can use to improve the effectiveness of negotiations and dispute resolution that reduce reliance on strikes.

Today a growing number of union and management negotiators are learning and applying the techniques of modern "interest-based" negotiations. At its core, this is simply the application of standard problem-solving techniques to bargaining problems—

focusing on identifying each party's interests, brainstorming and exploring multiple options, sharing and using information, using mutually agreed upon criteria to choose among options, and communicating actively and jointly with constituents and other concerned stakeholders throughout the process and when an agreement is reached. This does not mean that differences in interest are eliminated or all conflicts are avoided. Instead they are addressed and engaged in a more constructive fashion.

Variants in interest-based negotiations now occur in nearly half of labor negotiations in the country.[9] In reality, as the processes unfold, most tend to be some combination of interest-based and more traditional negotiations. So the modern tools of the trade for labor negotiations are at hand and can be used in ways that are consistent with finding innovative and effective and equitable solutions to today's problems. Working families should insist that these new tools be used by the union and management teams that negotiate contracts on their behalf.

One other feature of labor relations needs to change—the notion that bargaining occurs on fixed schedules of two, three, or more years. Today's markets, technologies, and workplace conditions change too rapidly for things to remain fixed for long periods. That is why many of us in the field have long advocated more continuous interactions and consultations in what have been called labor-management partnerships. We have already referred to several different examples of such partnerships, ranging from the most extensive and far-reaching one found at Kaiser Permanente,[10] to more limited but focused partnerships such as at NUMMI, or even more informal ones such as at Continental or Southwest Airlines. As noted in chapter 2, unions such as the UAW and SEIU's Local 1199 of Hospital and Health Care Workers jointly administer programs that provide a wide array of family, child care, immigration, training and development, and other services and benefits suited to the needs of their constituents and families.

Not all of these partnerships last forever. One of the most ambitious partnerships ever designed was used to create and manage the Saturn Corporation.[11] In the early years of Saturn it helped achieve the vision of building a "new kind of company and a new kind of car." Within two years of its startup, Saturn achieved the highest customer satisfaction ratings among all cars built in the United States. But, alas, as the initial champions of the Saturn partnership retired, the partners fell back into more traditional ways. Indeed, the history of labor-management partnerships is that they come and go as the need arises. Partnerships are not a panacea, but they continue to be an option that parties can turn to if they develop sufficient trust and confidence in each other to make them realize their full potential.

The lesson here is that partnerships or broader transformations in labor-management relations can and do serve important functions and work when labor and management are well matched in strength and share a pragmatic judgment that by working together each can serve its constituents better than by other more traditional or arms-length means. They have an important role to play in labor management relations today and in the future, and they could have a stronger role if supported by public policy, as they were in the federal sector from 1992 to 2000.

Voice in Strategic Decisions and Corporate Governance

Over the past two decades, union leaders have come to recognize the need to go beyond collective bargaining to get access to where the real power lies in corporations and where the key decisions are made that shape workers' long-term security and welfare—in the inner circle of executive decision making and corporate governance. This level of management has traditionally been viewed as off-limits to workers and their unions. Management's right to make these strategic decisions is specifically protected under the National

Labor Relations Act. That doctrine is another holdover from the industrial-era notion that it is best to set up a clear and distinct division between management and workers. In a knowledge-based organization, this line becomes blurred and needs to be erased if the full potential of this type of organization is to be realized. Employees have important knowledge to bring to strategic decisions and have a stake in who makes them.

Recognition of the need to influence these decisions has produced a variety of different efforts. In addition to the labor-management partnerships described above, unions have also gained seats on corporate boards (steel, trucking, airlines), negotiated commitments to neutrality in organizing campaigns (telecommunications, autos, aerospace), and mounted capital strategies aimed at using the leverage of union pension funds to sponsor shareholder resolutions on specific topics and/or to pressure companies to change specific anti-worker practices (the AFL-CIO, several national unions, several state employee pension funds). All of these have had some successes and some show considerable promise. But none has penetrated more than a small fraction of the corporate world.

Thus, even more fundamental breaks will be needed from the traditional New Deal doctrine that workers and their representatives have no legitimate right to a voice in strategic business decisions or corporate governance. As noted in chapter 5, this requires challenging basic concepts regarding the goals and responsibilities of corporations and those who govern them.

Workers' Voice in Society

Two weeks after the attack on Pearl Harbor, President Roosevelt called labor and business leaders together and told them he needed their support and cooperation to win the war against America's totalitarian enemies. Roosevelt's secretary of labor, Frances Perkins, and other government officials followed up that historic meeting by working with labor and business leaders to create the War Labor Board (WLB). This tripartite body (made up of labor, business, and government appointed neutrals) oversaw labor management relations for the duration of the war.

The dividends for the war effort were immediate and obvious. American factories and workers (including the many women who filled "men's jobs") produced the goods and services needed to support American soldiers. Work stoppages were either avoided or settled quickly and fairly in ways that avoided setting off an inflationary spiral.

Six decades later, Americans are still reaping the longer-term dividends of bringing these diverse stakeholders together. Out of the deliberations of the WLB came many of the principles and benefits that guided labor management relations and personnel management for decades following World War II. Along with pensions and health insurance, cost of living allowances, grievance procedures, sick leaves, and paid vacations were among the workplace innovations endorsed by the board that went on to become accepted principles of modern human resource management and labor relations.

Imagine how America's labor and management leaders could have and would have responded had the same approach been followed after the terrorist attacks of September 11, 2001. Unfortunately, unlike Roosevelt, President Bush saw no need and has shown no interest in asking national labor and business leaders to work together with him to help pull the country through a prolonged period of national crisis and war. Nor did his secretary of labor, Elaine Chao. When a secretary of labor from a previous Republican administration suggested Chao call business and labor leaders together to discuss what they might do to help the country through this crisis, she said: "Why would I want to do that? I'm interested in the 21st century labor force, not the past."

Dialogue among top business and labor leaders has also dissipated to perhaps its lowest level since the 1930s. The few longstanding forums for business-labor dialogue that did exist, such as the National Policy Association (formerly the National Planning Association), the Collective Bargaining Forum, the Work in America Institute, and several private labor management groups, have all disbanded. The demise of these forums signal a perception on the part of business, labor, and government leaders that it is no longer necessary to build and maintain communications and personal relationships with each other.

A small personal anecdote illustrates the void left in national discourse when business leaders discuss issues of significant importance with and then without well-informed, articulate, and independent representatives of workers and their families.

In 1984, former undersecretary of labor Malcolm Lovell created a national level labor management group called the Collective Bargaining Forum. For the next fourteen years, CEOs of some of America's largest companies, such as General Motors, Xerox, Alcoa, Kaiser Permanente, and American Airlines, met to discuss labor management issues with leaders of the AFL-CIO and presidents of the major unions representing workers in industries such as steel, paper, clothing, health care, communications, and autos.

My colleague Bob McKersie and I helped Lovell facilitate these meetings. At one meeting, in the midst of a discussion of the need for corporations and unions to do more to help local communities affected by plant closings, a new CEO who just joined the group that day leaned over and asked me "who's that guy talking?" I told him it was Jack Sheinkman, president of the Amalgamated Clothing and Textile Workers Union. "He's really good," the CEO whispered; "I never hear this kind of thing at the Business Roundtable!"

Later that morning, all the union leaders had to leave for another meeting. The discussions among the CEOs who stayed for lunch turned to the issue of corporate philanthropy. One highly influential CEO argued strongly and eloquently for eliminating all corporate giving to community organizations on the grounds that this amounted to giving away shareholders' money. None of his CEO colleagues challenged his views, or pointed out the inconsistency of this view with the discussion of a few hours earlier. I wondered whether this view would have gone unchallenged if Jack Sheinkman or his other labor colleagues had stayed for lunch.

America's democracy is weakened by the current void in national dialogue. The personal bonds so needed to pull society through crises are not being formed. Instead America's business and labor leaders are growing farther and farther apart. We can do better. One way would be to promote more community-based forums that bring labor and management together like the remarkably resilient Labor Guild of the Archdiocese of Boston that is described in box 7.4. Imagine how much better off we would all be if every American community had a similar institution devoted to building bridges and strengthening personal bonds among labor, business, and civic leaders.

Building New Sources of Power

The story of David and Goliath poses a question about which many remain intensely curious: under what conditions can the resourcefulness of an underdog overcome the institutionalized resources of the powerful?

—Marshall Ganz, *Five Smooth Stones: Strategic Capacity in the Unionization of California Agriculture*, PhD Dissertation, Harvard University, 2000

Five Smooth Stones is the creative title Marshall Ganz chose for his PhD dissertation that chronicled how Cesar Chavez and his United Farm Workers (UFW) drew on the sources of power they had available to take on the seemingly much more powerful California agribusiness industry. The UFW succeeded in getting contracts for farm workers in the 1960s because they reframed the issue from one of traditional collective bargaining to one of a social movement that drew on deep religious faith, ethnic solidarity, peaceful civil

Box 7.4
The Labor Guild of the Archdiocese of Boston

Shortly after we moved to Boston twenty-five years ago Joe O'Donnell, the jovial director of the Harvard Trade Union Program, invited me to join him at an annual gathering of Boston's labor-management community, the Cushing (later Cushing-Gavin) Award Dinner. I protested: "But I don't know any of these people." Joe was not to be deterred by such a solvable problem. "That's the point; I'll introduce you to everybody you need to know in this town." True to his word, as he saw me reluctantly walk into the reception before the dinner, Joe took me by the arm and proceeded to introduce me to "everybody I needed to get to know" using his customary Irish humor and obvious personal rapport with labor and management leaders. Before the night was over he had transformed me from being, in his words, "the newest ivory tower professor in town" to a member of the Boston labor-management community.

I recalled that story when, sixteen years later, I proudly accepted the guild's Cushing-Gavin Award at the annual dinner. In the intervening years I saw the power and good work of a community-based institution determined, against all odds, to bridge labor and management differences and to bring a soft but consistent faith-based perspective to its mission. Father Ed Boyle, the guild's leader for most of these years, is often called to offer the invocation at various conferences, dinners, luncheons, etc. One part of his invocation always includes a prayer "for those who prepare and bring us this food and serve us at this meeting."

Behind the scenes, this remarkable Jesuit has quietly brought countless of labor and management leaders in Boston together to build the personal bonds that can be drawn on to help solve problems when they arise. From time to time he has personally mediated or facilitated the resolution of difficult disputes. Throughout it all he has been the voice of the worker inside the diocese's considerable bureaucracy, reminding it of the obligation to respect its teachers, nurses, and other employees and their organizations.

Every community in America would benefit from an equivalent guild.

disobedience, personal sacrifice, and broad-based coalition building. These were the sources of power they used to overcome the
odds, just as David drew on his personal resources to defeat
Goliath—his experience in firing stones with his slingshot to herd
and safeguard his sheep.

So where will the power come from to get business (and government) to the table and to once again deliver tangible benefits to
workers and their families? The days are over where unions could
simply "take wages out of competition" and enforce standard
common rates of pay and benefits on all employers competing in
the same labor or product markets. This may have been possible
when markets were coincident with national borders, but no
American worker or his or her union can take wages out of competition with workers in China or other low-cost developing
nations. Nor will the power that is typically associated with a strike
be sufficient.

So, like David facing the prospect of going up against the seemingly more powerful Goliath, the next-generation unions will need
to draw on new sources of power. I believe there are opportunities
to be exploited.

Knowledge as Power

We have already identified the most important source of power
workers can bring to their jobs today: their knowledge, skills, and
readiness to put them to work. As noted in chapter 3, knowledge is
the necessary condition for workers to have the individual bargaining power to navigate successfully in today's labor markets.
That is why unions need to expand current efforts to provide
workers with the life-long education and training needed to keep
their skills current. Life-long educational opportunities can be one
of the key benefits and services unions offer to recruit and retain
life-long members. If unions and professional associations take up

this role, they will help society wean itself from dependence on individual firms and help overcome the market failure mentioned earlier.

Information and Communications

Consider the successful efforts of the coalition of forces that have come together to make transparent and publicize exploitation of labor in the supply chains of transnational companies. The campaigns to fight child labor and achieve fair labor standards for employees of Nike and other highly visible transnational firms came about because of the publicity given to exposés of violations of basic human rights of workers in these companies' supply chains in developing countries. The strike at UPS in 1997 and the Justice for Janitors' efforts in Los Angeles and Boston were successful in part (maybe in large part) because they were able to gain broad public understanding and support for their cause. A sustained and effective multichannel information and communications strategy is essential to any modern organization, including a modern labor movement.

The Internet is one obvious tool to support using information and transparency as a key source of power for labor. Colleagues at Harvard and Wisconsin, Richard Freeman and Joel Rogers, respectively, use the catchy term "open source unionism" to emphasize this point. They envision the next-generation unions using the Internet to get their message to workers around the world; to organize them, mobilize them in organizing campaigns, political campaigns, and collective bargaining negotiations; and to educate and represent them on a daily basis. Clearly the Internet is a tool that all modern organizations and social movements need to master and incorporate into their strategies. Labor is no exception.

More traditional media channels are equally important. Often labor leaders complain that the existing media are biased against them and only cover labor when there is a conflict and therefore miss the good things labor does on an ongoing basis. By and large this is an accurate critique of the current media. Changing this bias and increasing exposure to the concerns and perspectives of working families will require a significant investment of talent and resources on the part of the labor movement. The fact that Barbara Ehrenreich's book *Nickeled and Dimed* has been so popular and widely acclaimed suggests there is a large ready audience for this type of information about work as it is actually experienced today.

Exit

Industrial unions have urged employees who are dissatisfied with conditions on their job to stand up and fight to improve them rather than simply leave in search of a better job. That approach fit the stable workplace and long-term employment relationships of the industrial era many union members both wanted and experienced. For many this will continue to be the dominant way unions improve the working conditions and lives of their members. But for a significant portion of the workforce, particularly for more educated, mobile professionals, the ability to move from a job that does not meet their needs or expectations to a better one is equally important. And, over time, reducing the costs of mobility and making exit a more viable option serves as a key source of power not only for the individuals who move, but for those who stay. As any manager (or dean) will attest, nothing focuses the mind or generates improved conditions like a credible alternative job offer. Thus, reducing the costs of interfirm or geographic mobility by providing information on job opportunities, contacts and referrals, and portable benefits could be an increasingly important source of power for unions and professional associations.

Leveraging Labor's Capital Investments

After receiving a Morgan Stanley newsletter to clients that warned against investing in unionized companies, AFL-CIO president John Sweeney wrote Morgan's CEO a letter (with a copy to union pension funds that use Morgan's services) indicating labor's strong disagreement with this point of view. The response from Morgan's CEO was quick and decisive: a personal visit to John Sweeney, a public clarification that the article did not represent Morgan Stanley's view of unions, and a series of meetings between union leaders and Morgan Stanley analysts discussing the productive contributions unions and good labor-management relations can make to firm financial performance. Morgan Stanley understood immediately the potential power of a large, unhappy client. Clearly, pension power is labor's sleeping giant!

The AFL-CIO's Department of Corporate Affairs and several unions have been active in developing shareholder resolutions and other capital strategies. The evidence from these efforts is that they are more successful when they focus on governance issues or executive compensation rather than traditional workforce or labor-management issues and when they are done in coalition with other groups such as Institutional Shareholders Services (ISS). Specific pension funds such as CALPERS and those in strong union states like New Jersey and Wisconsin have also been supportive and active in shareholder resolution campaigns. This is a source of power for the future.[12]

Coalitions and Networks

Labor can't go it alone. Labor's biggest wins in recent years have come when labor unions in specific communities have built coalitions with community, religious, civil rights, women and family advocates, and other groups. Labor has formed coalitions with local affiliates of organizations such as the Interfaith Alliance, the Industrial Areas Foundation, and ACORN. Working together, these coalitions have passed living wage ordinances, supported "no-sweat" campaigns, implemented school reforms, and created employment and training programs. Box 7.5 describes the work of the National Council of La Raza, a Latino advocacy group, that is engaged in discussions with Tyson Foods Inc. about working conditions and employment practices in Tyson's plants. Working families will benefit enormously if these coalitions increase in number and become more visible in their communities and across the country. In return, these coalition partners will be there for labor unions in their times of struggle.

Many of these coalitions are more than just another source of power for working families and unions. They also exemplify and

Box 7.5
Latino-Labor Coalition at Tyson Foods

Tyson Foods Corporation is one of the largest chicken-processing companies in the country. Over the past decade the workforce in this industry has shifted with a significant growth of Latino immigrants. Several years ago the National Council of La Raza (NCLR), a Latino advocacy group, began examining Tyson's employment practices, and it concluded the company was taking advantage of the vulnerability of newly arrived immigrants who complained about safety conditions or tried to organize a union. NCLR expressed its concerns and the company agreed to talk about them. The media pressure ultimately led to the formation of a committee composed of company officials, La Raza, and several neutral experts in labor relations and workplace safety. The committee commissioned an independent safety audit and analysis and discussed options for implementing a corporate code of conduct covering other labor and employment practices. An agreement was reached that commits the company to address the safety issues identified in the audit while discussion of a code of conduct continues.

illustrate the moral foundation that underlies their joint efforts to give voice and bring economic justice to working families. This is especially true of the growing number of joint efforts between labor and religious groups. One such effort underway in Boston is summarized in box 7.6. Religious leaders organized under an umbrella group called the Greater Boston Interfaith Organization (GBIO) have been working with the SEIU to support and provide representation to Haitian immigrants working as aides in area nursing homes. By organizing through their church and immigrant networks, this coalition has been able to do things neither the union nor the GBIO had been able to do on its own, including gaining union recognition for these immigrants in a number of local nursing homes.

Freedom of association and support for unions lies deep in many religious traditions, dating back at least to Pope Leo XIII's 1891 encyclical *Rerum Novarum*. Many of us working in this field draw particular strength and energy from our efforts to promote values and principles that are consistent with our moral and religious traditions. So for many people, whatever power comes from building and participating in these coalitions has special meaning and force.

Passion with an Umbrella

Several years ago Maureen Scully and Amy Segal wrote a paper with the creative title of "Passion with an Umbrella."[13] They studied the growing number of informal groups arising in corporations that seek to bring about change by working within the prevailing culture of an organization. Some of these are known as "identity" groups since they form around specific racial, gender, ethnic, or other identity features. One of the earliest and most successful of these was the Black Caucus at Xerox that started as far back as the 1970s.

The catchy title of Scully and Segal's study conveys the essence of how these groups bring about change. Rather than confront or

Box 7.6
A Hybrid Organizing Model: Nursing Assistant Campaign in Boston

Haitian community leaders suggest that over 70% of the 41,000 Certified Nursing Assistants (CNAs) working in Massachusetts are Haitian. The paradox of the ethnic niche occupied by Haitians in the nursing home industry is that despite being fertile ground for traditional unionism (single industry, single occupation, relative low job mobility), union organizing in this industry has been extremely difficult (only 5 percent of Massachusetts' nursing homes are organized compared to 10 to 12 percent nationwide).

The recent nursing assistant movement took the ostensible form of a civic movement orchestrated by the Greater Boston Interfaith Organization (GBIO), a coalition of religious organizations, and the Service Employees International Union (SEIU) Local 2020, though the activities clearly supported unionization of nursing homes. For example, in addition to organizing new nursing homes, the campaign aimed to influence the negotiations in seventeen unionized nursing homes whose contracts would expire in 2004. The physical act of organizing the workers in this movement took place in the Haitian community—i.e., in church meetings, through ethnic media, and in people's homes. In the course of partnering with the Haitian community, both GBIO and SEIU learned that the ethnic identity of workers provided a cohesion that made mobilizing around it extremely potent. Despite initial difficulties in gaining buy-in from the workers, GBIO and SEIU were able to mobilize broad support from community institutions (both in the Haitian community and other communities) and ultimately pressure individual employers to sign a workers' bill of rights.

To date, in the course of less than two years, the campaign has resulted in five new nursing homes being organized under Local 2020, and led to successful settlement of all seventeen contracts that expired in 2004, rendering an average hourly wage increase of 50–70 cents for certified nursing assistants.

Source: Kyoung-Hee Yu, "Hybrid Institutions in the Labor Market: New Immigrants and Forms of Representation," Working Paper, MIT Workplace Center, 2005.

challenge the prevailing culture, values, or ways of doing things in the organization, these groups seek to use the culture to promote their group's objectives. An MIT example illustrates this approach.

In the mid-1990s, women faculty in the School of Science met with their dean to discuss their feeling of being treated unfairly and being undervalued compared to their male counterparts. The dean, in MIT fashion, said, "show me the data" behind your feelings. In response, the women did a careful study of salaries, lab space, committee assignments, and other indicators that are central to the work and careers of scientists. When shown the data, the dean, true to his word, along with the provost and the president recognized MIT had a serious and significant problem. Subsequent studies of women faculty in other departments showed similar, problematic patterns.

MIT leaders had begun to quietly take actions to address these issues when the *New York Times* and the *Boston Globe* somehow got wind of them. To MIT's pleasant surprise, the national publicity that resulted turned out to be overwhelmingly positive, in large part because MIT acknowledged its problems and demonstrated a determination to work on them.[14]

This approach will be needed in the knowledge-based organizations of the future. Informal collective action, by employees who share a commitment to the overall goals and values of their employer but are not afraid to raise tough issues that need attention, is exactly what employees want most and what will be critical to restoring workers' voice in the knowledge-based organizations of the future.

Summary

The cumulative effects of labor union decline have left a void in worker voice at work, eroded the standard of living in America, and weakened our democracy. Standard calls for union resurgence—to put more resources toward traditional union organizing, to reform labor law, or even to promote greater dialogue, cooperation, or consensus between business and labor—have not worked and will not on their own reverse the decline in worker voice.

More fundamental changes are needed that build on a vision capable of addressing the aspirations and expectations workers bring to their work, careers, and families; a strategy for recruiting individuals into life-long membership in unions; structures that support community, state, and national initiatives and coalition building; and a broadening out of the sources of power unions see as part of their toolkit.

Many of the pieces of this alternative approach are already being tried out in isolated experiments within individual unions and around the country. The time appears ripe for such an effort given the pressures on working families today, the void in political leadership and discourse on these issues, the lost confidence in corporate leaders and market forces, and the toll that is being exacted on current and future generations by the war on terror and the domestic and international tensions that will very likely be with us in its aftermath.

America is once again at a historic crossroads with respect to worker voice. We can begin by working collaboratively to fashion the next-generation organizations, institutions, groups, and forums for engaging the voice of today's workers and their families in the constructive ways that can produce mutual gains for workers, families, and the economy and society. Or we can continue to ignore and suppress efforts to restore voice at work and in society and wait for the pressures on working families to explode. The longer we wait for the crisis the more we risk recreating the adversarial culture and modes of interaction that characterized the industrial era.

Working families should not wait for others to decide their fate. Instead, here are the initiatives they might take to restore their voices at work and in society in a fashion that adds value to the economy and strengthens our democracy:

• Take the lead in organizing and building progressive and forward-looking labor organizations and professional associations that do not depend on distrust of employers as their basis for organizing.

• Maintain these memberships over the full course of their careers and family life stages. Advocate for a new array of family membership benefits ranging from early child care and development through college tuition assistance. Make these priorities in negotiations with employers to the point that they too become a part of the standard portfolio of benefits and services families get from work.

• Use exit as a source of power by insisting their unions and associations develop services and portable benefits that lower the costs of changing jobs and help to allocate the economy's human resources to their most efficient uses.

• Insist on a new transparency in organizations so that all employees have access to the information they need to decide whether to continue to invest their human capital in a firm or move it elsewhere.

• Insist on a direct voice at work that involves peers and managers in cooperative efforts to solve operational, personal, and family problems.

• Promote labor-management partnerships that add value and realize the full potential in human capital and knowledge-based organizations.

• Rekindle the dialogue at community, state, and national levels needed to restore trust, promote economic development and change, build stronger and collaborative communities, and strengthen the economy and democracy.

• Expand the range of options used to promote change at work by taking collective action consistent with the norms and culture of one's organization and profession.

Realizing this vision will require fundamental changes in public policies, if for no other reason than to restore the promise of labor law to provide all American workers who want a union or some other form of collective representation access to this fundamental human right. We now turn to how this might be done.

A Working Families' Agenda for Government

From 1993 to 1995, I served on one of the best kept secrets in government: The Commission on the Future of Worker Management Relations. Shortly after taking office, President Clinton and his secretaries of commerce and labor charged this group of former cabinet secretaries, business and labor representatives, and a few of us miscellaneous academics with the task of updating labor and employment policies. We all felt this was a worthwhile, maybe even noble, effort since academics and professionals in our field have known for some time that our policies are badly out of date and no longer deliver the results they promised when enacted as part of the New Deal.

Alas, few American citizens understood this or even knew that a commission was working on these issues. As a result, we got mired under the weight of standard business versus labor politics, lacked a public constituency demanding change, and in the end failed to get much done. But, we wrote two nice reports that are gathering dust on various shelves.[1]

The failure of this commission was only one example of the larger problem Robert Reich, President Clinton's first secretary of labor, described in *Locked in the Cabinet*.[2] Despite campaigning for the presidency around the slogan "Putting People First" and emphasizing the need to invest in America's workforce, once President Clinton was in office the pressures to reduce the budget deficit dominated any consideration of workforce issues. Sound familiar? Likely to happen again? Absolutely. In fact, things can and did get worse. In a letter to Transportation Security Administration screeners, Under Secretary Admiral J. M. Loy wrote:

[H]aving considered the security screeners' critical role in national security, I have concluded that collective bargaining would be incompatible with national security interests. I have therefore issued an order today that precludes collective bargaining on behalf of screeners.[3]

In early 2003, a staff member of the newly created Transportation Security Administration, the unit responsible for screening passengers at airports, sent me a copy of Admiral Loy's letter quoted above. (This person was struggling with the moral dilemma of having to implement this policy or resign in protest and wanted my advice. You can guess what advice I gave.) I never thought I would see the day when we let a government executive, acting with the full force of the president, unilaterally strip workers of their right to join a union and engage in collective bargaining. Couched in the Orwellian guise that worker voice would constitute a threat to national security, this action, more than anything else, signaled a disrespect for the fundamental rights of workers and disdain for what these employees could add to our national security, not to mention to customer service.

This was not an isolated action. The Bush administration has assaulted working families in other ways as well. One of its first acts, signaling the direction of things to come, was to rescind executive orders promoting labor management partnerships in the federal government and cooperative project agreements in construction. Apparently, if you can't get rid of union representation, adversarial labor relations are preferred over cooperation and partnership. Then ergonomic reforms that were under development for nearly a decade and had already been reviewed by a panel of the National Academy of Sciences were set aside "for further study." Later, ignoring a majority vote in Congress, the administration's Department of Labor revised its wage and hour rules to eliminate overtime after 40 hours of work that could affect as many as six million middle income professionals, technicians, team leaders, and office workers.

The key lesson from this history of stalemate under a Democratic administration and regressive steps under the Republican administration that followed is this: A forward-looking working families' policy agenda and actions will be taken seriously and pursued vigorously only when the American public stands up and demands its voice be heard. This is true regardless of who occupies the White House and which party controls Congress. Working families and their progressive allies in business, labor, and civil society need their own agenda, one guided by a clear vision of what needs to change.

The vision for a working families' policy agenda has been laid out throughout this book: Government policies should be geared to giving working families the tools to regain control of their future and to help transform our policies and practices from ones that fit the industrial age of the 1930s to ones that can help all the parties at the workplace build a prosperous knowledge-based economy. Let's now translate this general vision into a concrete policy agenda.

Two Americas at Work

One useful thing our commission did was to go around the country and listen to American workers, managers, and community leaders tell us about their experiences at work. Hearing people talk about their work and how it intersected with their families illustrated vividly that we have two distinct worlds of work in this country. These two worlds are best expressed in the words of some of the people who met with us and told us their stories.

The Atlanta hearings were a case in point. In the morning, we heard all about the innovative and progressive things community colleges, companies, unions, and other groups in the region were doing. Box 8.1 provides excerpts of their testimony. By the time we

Box 8.1
The Bright Side of the Morning

Excerpts from Testimony at the Southeastern Regional Hearing of the Commission on the Future of Worker Management Relations, January 11, 1994

On a state-wide Collaborative Council:

[The] Council on Competitiveness is a collaborative effort, at the state level, to develop a unified workforce development system for Georgia. . . . It involves seven agency heads, the state AFL-CIO, the state Chamber of Commerce, the Georgia Council of Vocational Education, and the Employment and Training Council. The interesting thing about the Council is that it is a voluntary collaborative.
—Amanda Hyatt, Chair, Council for Competitive Georgia

On a joint union-management training program:

Right here in Atlanta at AT&T's Atlanta Works Cable Manufacturing facility, the nearly 2,200 workers represented by the Communications Workers of America are being offered a unique approach to skill upgrading. . . . Workers volunteer for an assessment session to evaluate their strengths and skills in areas of reading, writing, decision making, goal setting computation, communication, organization, critical thinking, motivation, learning preferences, and problem solving. . . . Each participant develops an individualized learning program.
—Kathy DeLancy, The Alliance for Employee Growth and Development

On Bell South's commitment to continuous negotiations and problem solving:

As we are finding it necessary to change how management and unions deal with each other on a day-to-day basis, we are also finding that . . . the longstanding practice of negotiating a contract every "X" number of years—three years in our case—no longer is adequate to meet today's fast-changing environment. With rapidly evolving technology and ever increasing competition that constantly demands changes in the work environment, the work rules which govern that work environment must also be assessed.
—Jerry Barnes, Bell South

continued

On Delta Airlines' philosophy of employee involvement:

Corporations and employees that pursue a harmonious relationship which addresses all parties' concerns and needs will be able to perform more productively, thereby ensuring the long-term viability of the company and the job security of employees. A more proactive approach by companies and employees in encouraging employee involvement and participation would benefit everyone involved.
—Maurice Worth, Delta Airlines

broke for lunch, we were feeling pretty optimistic about what was possible, indeed what was really happening in this part of the country. A rude awakening awaited us in the afternoon.

After lunch, we turned to the dark side of labor relations in America. The tragic but all too real stories of Florence and Jimmy Hill and of Deborah Wright and her family, told in boxes 8.2 and 8.3, remind us that America has failed these working families.

These stories (and the mountains of research evidence behind them showing that these were not isolated or unrepresentative examples of today's workplace realities) convinced me that we need a two-track government workforce and workplace policy. One track should govern those progressive firms, unions, and workplaces that are moving forward to empower workers, to work together in a collaborative fashion, that respect everyone's rights and responsibilities at work, and that have structures and processes in place that provide employees an independent voice and means of resolving disputes. These workplaces are well on their way to building the type of knowledge-based economy described throughout this book. They are out in front of government policies and for them the best thing the government can do is to serve as a catalyst supporting their good works. They best know how to meet the goals and expectations society has for work and should be given considerable flexibility over how to meet these goals and expectations.

Box 8.2
The Dark Side of the Afternoon

Statement of Florence Hill, employee, Highland Yarn Mills, High Point, North Carolina

Well, after they started decertification, it started getting worse. And we did stand up; we believed in the union, we believed in fighting for the workers' rights. And so, when they couldn't get to Jimmy [Mrs. Hill's husband, who also worked in the mill], they started on me. They had a supervisor and a fellow employee that—he would say all kinds of nasty things to me, he would shimmy around me, he would take a-hold of his crotch and shake his crotch at me. And he'd tell me, "Let's you and I go out and have this freaky sex." And it was constant.

For nights I did not sleep. Jimmy and I would go home, and we would walk the floor. Jimmy would lie down about 5:00 in the morning, but my day had started all over again because of my family. And I'd have to go back in that mill again, 3:00 in the afternoon, and I didn't know what I was going to face, I didn't know what they was going to do to me next.

I was not allowed off of my little section that I worked in. When I'd go to the bathroom, the supervisor would follow me. Anywhere I went, I was being followed. I'd take my break; they'd cut me down to two 10-minute breaks and a 15-minute break. I was checked. I'd go through the mill. I'd always been a happy-go-lucky person, I could speak and I—you know, be friendly with people. But I got, as time—I'd have to hold my head down when I walked, because I didn't know what I was going to see, I didn't know what these people were going to do to me.

And it got so bad, the stress, my hair even dropped out. It just— my hair would just come out, just drop out, I was under so much stress. And then when the—these pictures, pornographic pictures, things that I had never dreamed of before. I am 60 years old, and I had never seen these type pictures before in my life. They were placed in my drawers where I could see them, and notes placed all over the mill insinuating that I was having an affair with another man, insinuating that—that I was in love with another man.

And then, the stress got so bad that I did have a heart attack.

Box 8.3
Statement of Deborah Wright, Former Employee, Minnette Mills, Grover, North Carolina

---

During the first campaign, people were really for the union until the company stepped in, and they started scaring everybody and they fired me and my husband. Well, at the time they fired us my daughter was pregnant, and she was having a lot of kidney problems. And they depended on us a lot. And after we were fired, we just couldn't do much for her.

After we were reinstated at Minnette's we thought everything would be better, because the courts were behind us. It was worse. They harassed us from the day we started back. They kept us in the office all the time. If another employee done something wrong, they took us to the office for it. And the reason the campaign started in the first place was because Minnette's is so unsafe. . . .

The second time we had our campaign, people got scared again. It was mostly older people that got scared, because they were saying that we didn't have, you know, the right to get a union and stuff. They wanted—they said they would close the doors if we got a union in, and they said that there wouldn't be a union in Minnette Mills. And they said the only right we had was to go out the door.

Well, the older people at our plant were scared because it was a lot harder for them to find a job than it would be for my age group. But to me, I felt like, you know, the law was protecting us. But the company showed us the law didn't protect us, it protected them. And I think the law should protect employees as well as employers.

Then there is the reality of workers like Florence and Jimmy Hill and Deborah Wright and their families. They work in environments that carry over the worst features of our industrial legacy. Theory X management is not harsh enough to capture the human indignities they suffer from firms that still see workers as throw-away commodities—labor costs to be controlled—and that see unions as an outside force to be avoided and suppressed at all costs, regardless of society's values or laws.

In these workplaces, government must continue to perform its historic role of protecting worker rights and enforcing vigorously the laws of the land. By targeting its enforcement efforts on the most egregious violators, and providing more flexibility for those demonstrating their ability and willingness to internalize responsibility for meeting the letter and the spirit of the law, those stuck in the old industrial, adversarial mode might begin to see the light. They will have an incentive to get on the transformational track.

To open up opportunities for this two-track approach to the design and enforcement of employment policy requires taking on the toughest of all policy challenges: breaking the twenty-five year stalemate over labor law. This will not be easy. It will require both new ideas and the energies of the coalition of working families and their progressive allies and, most important, broad public support.

Modernizing Labor Law

Fixing the Basics

The empirical evidence and details for the types of reforms needed can be found in the two reports of the commission cited earlier. It documents that 10,000 workers a year are fired for organizing. This amounts to about one out of every 20 workers who voted for union representation in the 1990s. Workers trying to organize can expect it to take two to three years to get through an election process if an employer decides to use legal delaying tactics. Then there is about a 30 percent chance that even if a majority of workers vote for union representation, they will never get a first collective bargaining contract because employer resistance shifts to the bargaining table. The data are clear. The law does not work to protect workers' right to join a union in America. This is nothing short of a national disgrace. The stark reality is that current American labor policy violates the fundamental principles of human rights and the principles of social and economic justice embedded in Catholic, Protestant, and Jewish religious traditions and doctrines.

How to fix the law's basic features is also relatively clear. The commission, and most others who have proposed changes from time to time, focused on three aspects of the law: (1) reducing time required to determine whether or not a majority of workers want to be represented by a union, (2) reducing the conflicts and risks associated with voicing one's views in support or against organizing, that is, raising the penalties imposed on those employers or unions that violate workers' rights, and (3) ensuring that if a majority support a union, they will in fact get a first contract and start their bargaining relationship off on a constructive course.

There is a variety of ideas on how to meet these criteria. Senator Edward Kennedy and others have introduced a bill that proposes the clearest approach consistent with these criteria. Their Employee Freedom of Choice Bill provides for (1) recognition of a union if a majority of workers give written authorization for a union to represent them or if a majority votes in an election, (2) stiffer penalties for labor law violations, and (3) mediation and binding arbitration in first contract negotiations if the parties cannot agree to terms on their own.

This is a good starting point. Fixing labor law in this way is essential to protect workers from employers and unions that continue their adversarial and in some cases abusive behavior reminiscent of the industrial era. Taking these overdue actions will deal with the most egregious violators of workers' basic human rights.

That's half the job. What can be done to support those firms, unions, and workforces that are on a more positive track and are ready or trying to empower employees to help build knowledge-based organizations?

Giving Workers the Cooperative Voice They Want and Need

As surveys consistently show, employees want access to information about their job and enterprise and a direct, cooperative voice in decisions that are critical to their future. Unfortunately, American labor law does not provide for this type of worker voice. That is why for many years I and others have advocated allowing all workers—hourly and salaried—in an establishment to vote to create something akin to the works councils found in Europe. These bodies consult with management on the full range of human resource and workplace policies and practices and have access to the types of information employees need to determine whether their human capital is being safeguarded and well invested. Moreover, these councils meet what the vast majority of American workers say they want at work—a cooperative form of direct employee participation with a cooperative and involved management. Equally important, it leaves it to the *employees* to decide if they want this type of forum at work. It can then serve as the umbrella that is needed to support the more decentralized involvement of groups to promote positive changes—pursue, for example, the dual work and family agenda in their respective areas as the need arises. Remember the "Passion with an Umbrella" example from chapter 7. America needs a means to foster this type of collaborative approach to meeting the needs of working families and their employers.

Voice in Corporate Governance

Earlier I proposed a simple principle for corporate governance in knowledge-based organizations: *Employees who invest and put at risk their human capital should have the same rights to information and voice in governance as do investors who put at risk their financial capital.*

The need for employee voice in corporate governance can be addressed, in part through public policy changes, but also in part through initiatives by workers themselves. One policy change that I believe is long overdue would be to require that workers be allowed to elect representatives to be trustees of their pensions. This is already the case for most state and local government employees and for those employees covered by multiemployer pension funds. But it is not the case for employees covered by firm-specific pension funds. There is no logical reason for this exception and simple fairness would dictate that the people who contribute to these funds and depend on them for their retirement security should be represented on the board that oversees them. This should be part of any modernization of labor law.

No laws bar workers from electing members to corporate boards of directors. It is just very difficult to do so unless a severe economic crisis forces firms to give employees a board seat in return for wage concessions. Congress could take an affirmative step to providing employees a voice in healthy companies by requiring public corporations to have worker-nominated directors, as is the case in Germany and several other European countries. There may, however, be better ways to do this, such as simply having the Security and Exchange Commission make it easier for employees to mount candidate slates and have them put on the shareholders' ballots rather than leave this process to corporate executives to nominate their chosen candidates and to block nominations by others. Opening up the election process and allowing employee groups, unions or otherwise, to propose their candidates would be a major step in making corporate governance more accessible to employees.

Diffusing Knowledge-Based Work Systems

Thoughtful government leaders have struck out several times in efforts aimed at supporting the diffusion of progressive workplace practices that have demonstrated their value in improving productivity, firm performance, and employee well-being. Some of these

were reviewed earlier, along with the one example of a highly successful strategy for promoting adoption of these innovations. The
successful strategy is actually not one initiated by government, but
by the Alfred P. Sloan Foundation. The industry by industry academic, business, and labor networks created over the last fifteen
years are models from which government can learn. The key to
Sloan's success, as well as the central lesson for future government
efforts of this type, is to engage these stakeholders directly in the
learning process and to provide them with the type of concrete data
and evidence that they find convincing about how to engage the
workforce and integrate new technologies, production and service
delivery processes, and human resources to build world-class organizations and industries. So in this case, government may not need
to be the driving force. Simply encouraging foundations like Sloan
to stay the course and continue their efforts might be the best policy.
At a minimum, learning from the successes of the Sloan approach
would be essential to future government initiatives to promote
workplace innovations that will support a knowledge-based
economy.

Promoting Labor-Management Partnerships

Lessons from history should also inform a working families' agenda
to promote the types of labor-management partnerships needed
in a modern economy. As noted earlier, the Bush administration
rescinded executive orders that encouraged labor-management
partnerships in the federal government and project agreements in
the construction industry. Reversing these actions would signal
support for transforming labor-management relationships from
their adversarial past to more constructive and productive
partnerships.

Beyond this, grant funds, similar to those that used to be available from the Federal Mediation and Conciliation Service to support

labor-management joint initiatives, should be made available to private sector parties. Other more proactive steps could also be considered, such as providing capacity building grants to labor organizations to develop the skills needed to construct and lead the "next-generation unions." A similar approach was followed in the 1970s to support efforts to train a cohort of industrial hygiene experts in the labor movement who went on to provide advice to unions and companies on how to implement the relatively new Occupational Safety and Health Act.

I, along with many other academies and neutrals in the labor relations field, have argued for these labor law reforms and updates for many years. Taking care of this long-overdue task will provide a foundation for addressing other challenges that require effective institutions of worker voice to be in place in American workplaces so we can experiment with new ways to address the most pressing problems facing working families and their employers and communities.

Paid Family Leave

The case for allowing states to experiment with different ways to fund and deliver paid family leave was outlined in chapter 2. Putting it at the top of a national working families' agenda as well sends three important messages. First, it signals the intent to reframe all workforce policy initiatives and thinking to conform to the dual agenda of addressing workforce and personal and family needs. It makes the analytic and political point that the times call for a truly *family-centered labor market policy*. Second, it brings together the broad coalition of forces that need to work together on the full workforce agenda—women, family advocates, labor, and the progressive forces in the business community that recognize the need for a sensible, workable, and flexible family-leave policy. Showing what can be done when these groups work collaboratively will send a powerful message—to themselves, to members of Congress, and to the American public. Third, it illustrates how we can put the two-track strategy to work and use it to accelerate the pace of workplace change and innovation.

As suggested in chapter 2, the design features of a paid leave program could be left to state-level experimentation, subject to meeting some minimum standards. If a state does not enact a program to meet these standards within a definable period of time, the federal minimums and funding arrangements would then apply. The virtue of this approach is that it would encourage dialogue at the state level to address a host of work and family policy and community issues and allow the business community to work constructively to design a paid leave policy that dovetails with what firms in their state already provide for some of their employees. These state policies could go a step further for those workplaces in which workers have a voice in deciding how to integrate paid leave into their existing employment policies and benefits by allowing them to certify that their policies meet or exceed the minimums.

What should be the minimum standards and default funding arrangement? These would undoubtedly need to be worked out with members of Congress who would serve as the sponsors and champions of the bill. Senator Lieberman has proposed the clearest set of standards and funding methods that are consistent with the approach noted here. His proposal calls for four weeks of paid leave at 50 percent of a workers' wage, funded through employee contributions of about $30 per year for the average worker. The program would be administered at the state level with flexibility over how each state designs its benefit payments. This offers a concrete way to get started and perhaps could also help jumpstart state-level discussions over how to ensure this policy dovetails with existing company and union practices and benefits. If my experiment with corporate human resource and work and family professionals described in chapter 2 is any indication, this type of collaborative and representative group and process would indeed generate creative and workable ideas no legislator or government regulators could dream up on their own.

Minimum Wage and Earned Income Tax Credit

It is an affront to our commitment to the work ethic and to the dignity of work for anyone to have to work for poverty wages. Moreover, the growing gap between the haves and have-nots in American society is an insult to our democracy and inconsistent with the moral standards of social justice and solidarity (support for the common good) embedded in our various religious traditions.

We know what the tools are for addressing these issues: an increase in the minimum wage and expansion of the Earned Income Tax Credit (EITC). These are now widely recognized as alternative and complementary instruments for raising the real incomes of low-wage workers and families. The evidence is clear. Over 34 million Americans work at wages that keep their families below the poverty level. The minimum wage has remained stuck at $5.15 per hour since 1996. Increasing it would help those at the bottom and make a small but substantive contribution to reducing the wage inequality so present in America.

The standard argument against raising minimum wages is that it reduces demand for entry-level, low-wage workers. The empirical evidence, however, has now convinced most objective analysts that moderate increases have little if any negative employment effects.[4] Obviously, if the minimum wage is pushed up too high, it will have this effect. Given that it has been nearly a decade since the last increase, a modest increase of the magnitudes used in the past would clearly not pass this threshold. Moreover, an increase of $1.50 spread over a reasonable period of time would be about what it would take to restore the minimum wage to its purchasing power level of 1970. This is why several hundred economists signed a letter in 2004 endorsing an increase in the minimum wage. Getting this many economists to agree on anything should be enough to put this endorsement into the *Guinness Book of World Records.*

The EITC has two advantages over the minimum wage. First, it has no negative employment effect because it reduces (or eliminates) income taxes on earned wages rather than increasing the wages employers pay. Second, it is linked to *family* needs by being graduated for the number of people in one's household. It is geared to helping working families. A combined proposal to complement increases in the minimum wage with increases in the EITC to ensure that working families achieve incomes that move them at least above the federally determined poverty line should be a key part of a working families' agenda.

Creating Good Jobs

Clearly, creating and sustaining good-paying, high-quality, knowledge-based jobs has to be an ongoing, top priority of any working families' agenda. As suggested earlier in this book, there is no single strategy for making this happen.

The Basics: Sensible Macroeconomic Policies

A strong jobs agenda requires a combination of efforts, starting with a strong macroeconomic policy that promotes sustained economic growth and job creation. Without this, all other micro or specific job creation or training and education initiatives are likely to fall short of their objectives. This lesson has been clear since the 1960s and is as valid today as in the past. The basic rules of economics do hold, even as we saw in the "new economy" of the 1990s, and there is no reason to believe they will be repealed in the knowledge-based economy of the future.

So attending to the basics is critical. At this moment, a strong case can be made for reallocating the tax cuts of recent years to benefit more directly lower- and middle-income families. And some federal relief to state and local government budgets could both address critical infrastructure needs and have a direct effect on job creation. But economic conditions change, and so any suggestion that priority should be given to greater stimulus or more fiscal restraint may have only at best a 50 percent chance of being right by the time you read this.

One thing is clear, however. The huge federal budget deficit must be reduced. The only way this can be done without further undercutting essential human and social services is to repeal some or all of the tax cuts that have gone to the most wealthy Americans in recent years. The prospect of a debt overhang (or should I say hangover) of $3 trillion will scare off investors, keep the economy struggling to create the jobs we need, and starve all domestic programs that serve working families. We will suffer and our children will pay the ultimate price for our irresponsibility.

Working families can also insist that federal policymakers follow through on the nation's stated commitment to full employment by keeping this issue on the front pages of newspapers so that policy makers keep it at the top of their agendas. Tax and spending policies can then be judged against their ability to deliver on this objective.

Investing in Human Capital

Can we promote job growth through more targeted tax or investment initiatives? A number of proposals have been put forward to do this. One is an investment tax credit that would apply to new jobs and/or to investment in education and training, akin to the investment tax credits sometimes made available for capital investments. In principle this sounds good; in reality these are hard to monitor and it is difficult to avoid paying organizations for what their business strategies would lead them to do even in the absence of incentives. While these are serious drawbacks of these types of incentives, they are no more problematic than incentives offered for capital investment. So the principle here might be if Congress or an administration is willing to absorb the dead-weight losses associated with capital investments, they should do so for human capital investments as well.

Earlier I emphasized the need to promote research, entrepreneurship, and regional economic development by supporting university-industry-employee networks. This should be a visible and central part of a modern job creation strategy. These networks should, however, be inclusive. The next-generation new business start-ups need to begin by building knowledge-based organizations that are committed to and attuned to meeting the needs of all their investors—financial, human, and community. By building inclusive networks up front, communities have a better chance of making the transition to a knowledge-based economy in which family and civic responsibilities are taken seriously.

These same groups can ensure that we follow a design principle of proven value for funding education and training programs. Studies of employment and training programs and community colleges consistently document the benefits of having good industry links so the skills being taught are the ones in demand in today and tomorrow's organizations.

One of the most useful things national leaders who are committed to both building and sustaining good knowledge-based jobs in America could do is to host a series of regional industry, technology, and jobs summit meetings in which university researchers and leaders of specific industries and employee associations and unions meet to discuss what it will take to stay on the frontier of science and technology and what skills will be needed to support efforts to push out this frontier. Adapting a popular sports' saying to fit this scenario, the best defense against the threat of offshoring jobs will be a good offense.

But these types of gatherings must be more than symbolic gestures. The federal government is investing less today in workforce training than it did before the Bush administration took office. Recall the irony of President Bush's speech to that community college in Ohio that had just laid off staff members. His intent to support a small increase in funding for community colleges rang hollow, given cuts in employment and training imposed during his first term in office. If we are to truly "prepare the twenty-first century workforce" we have to put our money where our mouth is.

Jobs, Trade, and International Standards

Can or should something be done to stem the loss of jobs to trading partners or other low-cost countries overseas? This is a highly contested debate, made even hotter by the visibility "offshoring" issues are getting in the press and in the minds of working family members. It is time to go beyond the platitudes or rhetoric on this issue as well.

Some have proposed tax penalties for moving jobs offshore. Others have proposed eliminating incentives in the tax code that encourage offshore investment, especially those that allow firms to avoid paying taxes on profits made by offshore operations. These are likely to be extremely hard to implement and even harder to enforce. In the end, firms intent on moving or investing outside U.S. borders are likely to find ways to work around such changes in the tax code. A more direct, sustained, and long-term strategy is needed, one that focuses on gradually upgrading the employment and living standards in developing countries and that holds American corporations accountable for contributing to this long-term objective.

The place to start is with trade agreements negotiated bilaterally with other countries, with regional country blocs, or in World Trade Organization deliberations. In such forums the United States should take the principled position that core labor standards endorsed by international business, labor, and government through the International Labor Organization must be respected, enforced, and monitored. A more proactive and collaborative step would be to endorse and urge all American firms to participate in Kofi Annan's *Global Compact*. Doing so would put the rhetoric of corporate social responsibility into action and use the power and resources of corporations to work for their own good and the common good of the world economy.

The final plank of any trade and jobs program must be to support the families that are bearing the costs of economic and technical change. This is one of the costs that society must be willing to bear if it wants to enjoy the benefits of an open and fair trade policy. Building broad-based political support for a fair trade policy will require going beyond the limited programs such as Trade Adjustment Assistance (a program that provides limited income supports for workers who can show they lost their jobs because of international trade) or even more ambitious ideas such as "wage insurance" (tax subsidies that would make up the difference between wages on a job that is lost and wages on a replacement job). These are helpful supports for the individuals who can show a direct link between trade and their job loss. A more meaningful and necessary program would focus on helping *families* adjust to permanent job losses by covering health insurance and retirement security, and, most of all, ensuring that children of those caught in the transition from the industrial to the knowledge economy have access to the educational opportunities they will need to move on to where the job opportunities beckon them.

Work Hours and the Overtime Quagmire

No set of rules is more complicated, controversial, and out of step with the way people work today than those governing who is covered and who is exempt from payment of overtime. We noted earlier that the distinction between exempt and nonexempt is at best blurred in workplaces that empower workers. The Bush administration stirred up controversy on this issue by having its Department of Labor revise the overtime rules in ways that could eliminate coverage of many middle income employees.[5]

The net result is that the working hours of these people may well increase, for less pay than they would have received in the past, precisely at the time that working families are already stretched to the limit. This makes no sense and is a direct assault on working families. The simple agenda objective would be to reverse these actions. Congress has tried to do so several times. Working families should insist it keep trying until it does so.

But the complex rules governing exempt and nonexempt distinctions that are in place also no longer work. A well-grounded, analytic, and transparent process is needed to modernize and simplify these rules.

Any effort to change these rules should be guided by a clear and simple principle: *No changes in overtime regulations should have the effect of increasing the hours of work or reducing the take home pay of employees, or reducing employees' control over their work schedules.*

Workplace Regulations

For years I have advocated providing those employers and employees who have effective institutions and forums for employee voice and representation the flexibility they need to "internalize" enforcement of regulations governing their workplaces. Here is where our two-track approach can demonstrate its greatest potential for working families, progressive businesses, and society.

Over the years, the number of employment standards and other regulations governing the workplace has increased substantially. The need for flexibility in how firms meet the goals of employment statutes increases over time as the economy and range of employment arrangements become more varied. Business leaders often voice legitimate complaints about the rigidity and complexity of government regulations of the workplace. They note, often with good reason, that today's economy is too varied for a "one size fits all" approach to regulating the workplace. All too often regulations are written to deal with the worst violators of employment law. These rules thereby impose costly and inefficient restrictions on those employers who are committed to meeting their legal obligations or to going beyond the minimum standards required by law. So the challenge lies in finding ways to allow more flexibility in how good employers meet the objectives and basic standards society sets for work and employment relationships while still safeguarding the rights of employees in settings where this commitment is lacking in their workplace.

If there was assurance that employees have an independent voice at their workplace through collective bargaining and/or through the American equivalent of a works council, a range of possibilities opens up for internalizing enforcement of things such as safety and health, family leave, working hours, and overtime arrangements. If the parties add an alternative dispute resolution system available to employees that meets the standards of due process that professionals in this field have developed, one could also encourage use of these systems, including private arbitration, to provide more prompt and less costly resolution of employment disputes.[6]

Pensions, Social Security, and Health Care

As noted in chapter 6, health-care, pensions, and social security reforms will all be front and center on the national agenda for years to come, and I laid out a working families' agenda for these issues in that chapter. The key is for working families to assert their interests on these issues and insist on having their voices heard and represented in the deliberations to come. One thing, however, should be avoided at all costs. *No more risk should be placed on the backs of workers and their families by privatizing part of social security or by allowing healthy workers with disposable incomes to further weaken the pooling principle by creating individual medical saving accounts.*

Whose Department of Labor Is This Anyway?

The purpose of the Department of Labor shall be to foster, promote, and develop the welfare of the wage earners of the United States, to improve their working conditions, and to advance their opportunities for profitable employment.
—Congressional Act creating the Department of Labor, March 4, 1913

Working families need a voice and advocate within the federal government to put this agenda to work. Theoretically, they have had one since 1913. That was the year the U.S. Department of Labor was created and given the above charge.

Since then, this cabinet-level department and its secretary have served as the primary locus of ideas, analysis, policy development, and advocacy for workforce issues.

The department has had its ups and downs, with a number of highly distinguished secretaries, such as Frances Perkins, Franklin Roosevelt's secretary (and the first woman cabinet member). "Madame Secretary," as she came to be called, led the efforts to enact the signature labor and employment policies of the New Deal. Other distinguished Secretaries have served in Republican and

Democratic administrations since then. President Kennedy appointed labor expert Arthur Goldberg, who then went on to become a Supreme Court justice. W. Willard Wirtz and Ray Marshall, both widely recognized national experts and advocates for education and training, served Presidents Johnson and Carter, respectively. President Nixon chose George Shultz as his first labor secretary and Shultz went on to serve the country as secretary of treasury and then as secretary of state during the Reagan years. John Dunlop and William Usery, two of the country's most respected and experienced experts in labor management relations, served under President Ford. Each of these people brought stature, independence, and professionally grounded ideas to this office and built staffs with the technical expertise needed to analyze and evaluate the merits of alternative proposals and programs.

But the Department of Labor has also had its low points. Sometimes it has been used as a depository for political appointees administrations were looking to place somewhere out of the way. When this happens, as it has in recent years, the department has become essentially a puppet of the White House, unable to challenge the president's political advisors or to stand up for working families.

What would it take to reestablish the department as the place where working families' voice is heard? Staffing it with respected and experienced people who have a clear agenda endorsed by the president would be a good place to start.

Frances Perkins illustrates this best. She laid out a clear agenda for Franklin Roosevelt when he asked her to serve as his secretary of labor. Box 8.4 tells her story in her own words.

The same clear agenda and means of pursuing it are needed today. Here is where the working families' coalition called for in this book comes in. The main message of this chapter, indeed of this book, is that a working families' agenda must be backed by a strong and broad-based political coalition.

Box 8.4
Frances Perkins's Vision and Agenda

Roosevelt came right to the point. "I've been thinking things over and I've decided I want you to be Secretary of Labor."

Since the call from his secretary, I had been going over arguments to convince him that he should not appoint me. . . . I said that if I accepted the position of Secretary of Labor I should want to do a great deal. I outlined a program of labor legislation and economic improvement. None of it was radical. It had all been tried in certain states and foreign countries. But I thought that Roosevelt might consider it too ambitious to be undertaken when the United States was deep in depression and unemployment.

In broad terms, I proposed immediate federal aid to the states for direct unemployment relief, an extensive program of public works, a study and an approach to the establishment by federal law of minimum wages, maximum hours, true unemployment and old-age insurance, abolition of child labor, and the creation of a federal employment service.

The program received Roosevelt's hearty endorsement, and he told me he wanted me to carry it out.

Source: Frances Perkins, *The Roosevelt I Knew* (New York: Viking Press, 1946), pp. 151–152.

In the past, the biggest political force behind the Department of Labor was the labor movement. This seems appropriate because the AFL-CIO is the largest, most representative, and most powerful voice for workers in America. But the labor movement cannot be the only constituent. When the department is viewed as only a voice for the AFL-CIO, it gets marginalized by others in the administration and targeted as a "special interest" enclave. Then the political and policy task comes down to "what do we need to give them to make them minimally happy and how do we keep them at bay on other issues we want to pursue?"

So a broader political coalition is needed to work with and complement the labor movement. Several secretaries made good use of national labor management committees or groups to advise the secretary and/or the president on key issues. As noted earlier, the 9/11 attacks provided a golden opportunity to take this course, but it was rejected. Some process is needed to build support and to explore where possible consensus might be found on how best to pursue a working families' agenda.

But as noted earlier, there is a deep ideological divide between business and labor. New voices need to be added to diversify and broaden those consulted to break the stranglehold that business and labor together hold over working families' issues.

In the heat of debates among members of the Commission on the Future of Worker Management Relations, a coalition of 21 women's organizations came together and insisted their voice be heard. They could not and would not be ignored. They asked to testify at a commission hearing. Our commission chairman, John Dunlop, agreed. They then organized a day-long conference on working women and Dunlop and I attended, listened, and spoke. I found this to be the most refreshing and innovative group of all those that presented ideas to the commission. They brought a perspective on work, labor, family, and community issues that we did not hear from other union or employer leaders. Despite their diversity, they surprised everyone (including themselves) in reaching agreement on several controversial policy issues. And this coalition worked in partnership with the labor movement and with some groups within the business community. The value they added to the discussion should not be lost on whoever takes on the task of building the political coalition needed to support a working families' agenda in the federal government.

State-Level Policy Initiatives

Finally, the potential for state-level policy making should not be ignored. Again, history offers a possible lesson. The progressives and labor reformers of the early twentieth century achieved much of what was to end up in the New Deal labor and social legislation by first getting their ideas enacted and tested at the state level. States like Wisconsin, New York, and other progressive enclaves served as the experimental testing grounds for the New Deal by enacting safety and health, unemployment insurance, and women and child labor protections. A similar effort has been underway in recent years by organizations such as the National Partnership for Women and Families in their quest to enact paid family leave statutes at the state level. So far, they have only been successful in one state—California. But given the present political stalemate in Washington, and the dim prospects for making progress on a working families' agenda in the near future, the state level may offer the best opportunity for progress.

Summary

Working families should insist that government leaders take their agenda seriously. The overriding goal needs to be kept front and center: To provide working families the tools they need to regain control of their futures and to contribute to building a knowledge-based economy.

The key tasks that lie ahead are to support those organizations and institutions that are committed to working together to realize this goal and to protect workers and families who work in environments that do not share this commitment. To do this we need to:

• Enact flexible paid family leave and other policies needed to support efforts to address the dual agenda of work and family in America's workplaces;

• Design, fund, and implement a coordinated job creation and human capital investment and development strategy;

• Make sure all working families earn incomes that move them out of poverty;

• Restore worker voice at work and in society in ways that support this overriding goal;

• Update overtime rules and other government regulations through a process of consultation with those affected by these rules, and;

• Restore the Department of Labor to its former stature, professionalism, and influence, and broaden the coalition behind it.

9   A Call to Action

The silence from American working families and their progressive allies is deafening. But if history is any guide, this will not last much longer. Nor should it. Just as we teach our children to stand up and speak out for what is right, so too should working families and their allies stand up and say "enough is enough" and speak out and demand access to the tools they need to restore the American dream and to get on with the task of building a knowledge economy that works for all of us.

The Working Families' Toolkit

What do working families need to do this? The tools that I believe they need have been laid out in prior chapters and are summarized in short form in the Working Families' Toolkit shown in box 9.1. To contribute to a modern knowledge-based economy, working families need flexibility to integrate work and family life; a good basic education and ongoing life-long learning opportunities; economic policies that, in fact, generate and sustain enough good jobs for all who want to work; organizations that use knowledge-based work systems to generate and sustain good jobs and meet their responsibilities to shareholders, employees, and communities; portable benefits to allow them to move across jobs as necessary over their careers; an independent and strong voice at work and in society;

Box 9.1
A Working Families' Toolkit for Today's Economy

- Flexibility to integrate work and family life
- Education and life-long learning
- High-quality jobs for all who want to work
- Knowledge-based workplaces and corporations that are account-able to shareholders, workers, and communities
- Portable and secure benefits
- Voice at work and in society
- Commitment of business, labor, government, and community leaders to work together to restore trust and the values Americans hold for work and family life

---

and a broadly shared commitment to work together to restore trust and the values Americans hold for work and family life.

How Do We Make This Happen?

By now you are probably saying: This may make sense, but isn't this essentially a hopeless cause at the moment, given the deep divisions now visible in American society, the indifference of the current administration to these issues, the gridlock in Congress, the weakness of the labor movement, and the reticence of progressive business leaders to break ranks with their peers and competitors? A quick look back in history to the beginning decades of the twentieth century provides both a parallel story and the motivation to stay that course.

Then, like now, the economy was in the midst of a historic transition, from an agrarian to an industrial economy. Then, like now, the policies, institutions, and practices governing work had not caught up with the changing times; and federal policy was limited by the view that only common law, the market, and perhaps states could regulate employment. It took three decades of research, social

activism, and state-level experimentation by a coalition of academics, leaders of the progressive movement, and forward-thinking
business and labor leaders to develop the ideas and new workplace
practices that eventually became the basis for the New Deal policies of the 1930s. Box 9.2 summarizes the work of one of the groups
that led this effort, John R. Commons and his students and progressive allies in the state of Wisconsin. Perhaps we are in another

Box 9.2
We've Been Here Before

From the time John R. Commons got to the University of Wisconsin
in 1904 until the mid-1930s he and his students studied how labor
markets and the nature of work were changing as the country and
workforce made the transition from an agrarian to an industrial
economy. They documented the harsh consequences of long hours
and unsafe working conditions, the hardships associated with unemployment or injury in the absence of any social insurance safety net,
and the poverty many faced in old age for lack of a pension or social
security program. They toiled for thirty years, documenting the
failure of government policies or the fledging, craft-based labor
movement to meet the needs of the changing workforce and
economy.

Over these years Commons worked with other progressives to
invent and test policies in the state of Wisconsin such as unemployment insurance, workers' compensation, child and women's labor
protections, and tripartite labor, business, and government procedures for administering these laws.

When the economic and social crisis of the Great Depression
created a national mandate for change, these ideas and state-level
innovations provided a framework for action. Commons became
known as the intellectual father of the New Deal labor and employment legislation. His students (by this time Commons was advanced
in years and in declining health) populated the Roosevelt administration and played key roles in designing and administering the
legislation and agencies that brought to life social security, unemployment insurance, minimum wage and overtime regulations, and
collective bargaining rights for private sector workers.

phase of history similar to the pre–New Deal era. Let's hope it doesn't take thirty years and a crisis as deep as the Great Depression for national leaders to act.

What can we do to speed up this process? I believe the answer to this question lies in remembering and acting on the parable of five smooth stones presented by Marshall Ganz in his study of Cesar Chavez and the California farmworkers. Individually and collectively, the potential members of a viable working families' coalition need to draw on the resources and sources of power we each bring to the table. Here is what each of us can do.

Individuals and Families

Let's start with what has to be the base of any working families' coalition. We all are members of working families. We need to identify ourselves as such and begin to see the common cause we have with other families. Change must start with a self-examination of what we want and have a right to expect out of work and our personal and family lives.

Consider doing a mental exercise similar to what I have my undergraduate students do as their first class assignment. They are to interview their parents and grandparents to find out what those generations wanted from and got from their work and careers and then ask, how similar or different am I? What do I want? What should I and can I expect from work today? The second part of the assignment is for the students to build a strategic, career development and action plan outlining what they need to do individually and collectively for themselves and their class peers to realize their goals.

The purpose of the exercise is three-fold:

1. to get students to reflect on how work has changed over three generations and to understand how their parents' experiences, in

some cases sacrifices and hardships, and in others successes, put these young people in a position to do well in life;

2. to get students to think about what they want from their careers, and life, and;

3. to emphasize their collective responsibilities and potential to work together to both change the world of work and to support each other in pursuing their aspirations and dreams.

I'll place my bets with these young people. Do you remember the quote from Mike Amati in chapter 1? Many in his generation echo his interest in achieving a better balance between work and family life than did their parents. And as keen observers of the layoffs, downsizings, loss of retirement savings, and the stresses their parents or other family members feared or endured, they are determined to keep their labor market options open. I encourage them to do so. I remind them about a basic principle of negotiations that we teach: the importance of having a good alternative. A key source of power is knowing where good alternative jobs are and being willing to move to them if their current employer is not meeting their expectations.

The toughest thing to get across to these young professionals, however, is that they cannot do this on their own. They must be collectively organized, not necessarily into traditional trade unions, but into the next-generation alumni and professional associations and networks that provide them with the information and contacts they need to know where the alternative job opportunities are and what the benchmark conditions are that they should insist their current or prospective employer meet. This is their latent source of power and they should not be hesitant to exercise it. They hold the key to change!

The last part of the discussion of this assignment is to ask the class how typical they think they are of the population of people in the labor force today or of all people their age. They quickly see the point. So I leave them with a question to discuss among themselves: What obligations do they have to others in society that perhaps lack the individual bargaining power that comes with the education and skills of a college graduate?

We all need to ask ourselves this last question. Remember the stories from the *Washington Post* about the people who are getting squeezed out of the middle class as they lose good, often union, manufacturing or information technology jobs? These people can easily become alienated or turn to reactionary causes and movements that further polarize society. Or, they can channel their frustrations constructively by joining or forming organizations that lobby for change, raise their voices, and look for collective solutions to their problems. They are precisely the individuals and families that are bearing the costs of the transition from an industrial to a global knowledge economy so the rest of us can reap its benefits in the form of lower prices and new and better services. They should demand their rightful compensation for bearing these costs. Telling their stories to the *Washington Post* or, even better, to papers in their local communities, to their local talk show hosts, and to their local, state, and federal representatives is their latent source of power. The more we bring the costs of this transition into focus, the sooner we will take actions needed to share the benefits of economic progress more fairly.

Perhaps the largest group of workers and family members is those for whom the other shoe has not (yet?) dropped. They are employed in good jobs with promising and, by and large, satisfying careers. Because they very likely have a spouse who is also working part or full time, their families are at least able to hold their own or improve their standard of living. To be sure, they have stresses and strains that come with balancing work and family responsibilities, but so do most of their peers, so they find ways to cope.

For these individuals and their families, life-long learning is still the key to keeping the other shoe from dropping in midcareer or later in life. All who now have a good job should take to heart the biblical admonition the nuns taught us in grade school: "God helps those who help themselves." The moral of this story is that we need to take advantage of every opportunity for on-the-job training, continuing education, and skill development that our employer and union or professional association offer. And if these organizations do not offer such opportunities, ask why not, get active, or find an employer, union, or professional association that does!

What about those who both lack individual labor market power and have no professional association or union available to them? This is a large and growing fraction of the labor force. It includes many immigrant workers and families, employees in the low-wage service industries and occupations, and many single parents caught in the double bind of not having a spouse's income to complement theirs or enough time to balance their work and family responsibilities, let alone seek out continuing-education opportunities. These are people who most clearly need the resources of local ethnic, religious, labor, and professional networks. Recall the examples of the Haitian immigrants who gained representation in nursing homes through the combined efforts of the Greater Boston Interfaith Organization and the Service Employees International Union.

Religious-ethnic-labor coalitions like this are forming and attempting to represent immigrant and low-wage groups all around the country. They need to continue to grow, work together, and organize. Coalitions like these that build around ethnic communities and extend their reach to the workplace, if supported and allowed to grow, will become a defining feature of the "next-generation" labor organization.

Ethnic or immigrant networks are clearly not limited to low-wage workers. Anna Lee Saxenian has documented how Chinese, Indian, and other ethnic networks in Silicon Valley provide professionals with information and access to job opportunities in the region's high-technology firms.[1] Some of these networks also help would-be entrepreneurs gain access to the venture capital they need. Fei Qin, a PhD student in our program, has documented the importance of similar networks of Chinese immigrant professionals in the Boston area.[2] She finds these networks both help in finding jobs and in improving wages. These networks apparently are quite good at steering their members not only to jobs, but to good jobs!

We cannot ignore or forget yet another group. Recall the example of the children left behind in families caught in the grip of inter-generational transfer of single parenthood, poverty, illness, little or poor education, and lack of good role models for how to get ahead. This too is a part of the American reality, just as it was in the 1960s when sociologist Michael Harrington wrote about *The Other America* and in the 1970s when Daniel Patrick Moynihan warned us about the long-term effects of broken family structures.[3] These are perhaps the most difficult problems we face and they cannot be addressed by just focusing on work or even solely on welfare to work pro-grams. Here the solution has to begin by strengthening the families themselves. Only by doing so can they break the intergenerational cycle of teen pregnancy, single parenthood, and lack of strong adult role models. Building stronger families must go hand in hand with societal efforts to provide the education, health, and related human services and job opportunities needed to break the cycle. There are no easy answers here, just a lot of hard work ahead. But the sooner we start, the more chances we have of not leaving these children and their families behind.

The point of these examples is to emphasize that there is not just one big working families' coalition that could be formed to address the challenges facing workers and families today. Instead there are multiple and different networks, coalitions, organizations, and indi-vidual opportunities that are either available to different groups or that, with some initiative, could be created. These are the types of efforts that are needed to create a working families' base, a foundation for moving forward.

Labor Organizations and Professional Associations

The life and work situations depicted above imply that there is also no single model, structure, or strategy for the "next-generation" labor unions or professional associations. Nor will traditional labor organizations be able to function independently of employers, civic and religious groups, and immigrant community leaders and networks. The reverse is also true. Employers and community-religious-immigrant networks all need the collective resources and the workplace and occupational presence and power that labor organizations and professional associations bring. So America has an enormous stake in the development of a new generation of labor organizations that are well matched to the needs of different groups and skilled in working in coalition with others.

This cannot happen without the changes in public policy and managerial opposition to collective actions called for in this book. But we clearly have a chicken-and-egg problem to overcome. Those policy and behavioral changes won't happen unless labor organizations demonstrate their ability to add value to the lives of workers and their families and to supply employers with the well-prepared, skilled workers needed to fuel a knowledge economy. Twenty-five years of failure to change labor law through inside political maneuvering should be enough to demonstrate a different approach is needed.

This is what the debate underway within the labor movement is all about. The way forward is to work in coalition with potential allies wherever they can be found or created, to demonstrate the value a forward-looking union can add to workers, families, communities, and employers, and to gradually build the public support needed to change and modernize public policies and employer behavior.

Unions will also have to learn to work effectively together. The achievements of the coalition of Kaiser Permanente unions should not be lost on others in the labor movement. By forming a coalition they not only turned around a labor-management relationship that was becoming more adversarial and mutually destructive by the day, they also built a partnership with a progressive employer that could become a model for how to deliver the coordinated high-quality health-care services the country so badly needs. Unions in the airline industry in particular, and perhaps others on the front lines of public and customer service, would do well to learn from this example.

The same degree of coordination will be needed at the community level if unions are to serve as life-long representatives of their members. Over the course of their careers, workers are likely to move across jobs that may be represented by different unions and move in and out of union-represented jobs. Coordinating the hand-offs of members from one union to another in the first instance and maintaining relationships and providing services in the second will be major challenges for unions, given their balkanized structure. This too will require changes in and further consolidation and simplification of national and local union structures.

More than anything else, however, union leaders need to redefine their organizing and representational models. As a first step this requires moving from a defensive posture that relies on unscrupulous employer behavior to one that recruits workers for life and stresses the dignity of work and the value union membership provides to workers, families, and the economy. Second, it requires development of services and benefits that fit this organizing model. Third, it requires broadening the sources of power used to improve the lives of workers and their families. Collective bargaining will continue to be a powerful tool for unions, but it may not be the exclusive or in some cases even the primary tool. Corporate-wide campaigns that make creative use of media, community coalitions, pressure of litigation and consumer education, and ease of exiting from substandard employers are all sources of power that are rising in importance relative to the traditional threat of a strike.

Progressive Business Leaders and Management Professionals

Most business leaders I know agree (privately at least) that the polarization that currently exists across these different groups today is not only bad for our democracy and society, in the long run it is also bad for business. They know a knowledge economy cannot prosper and realize its full innovative potential with a polarized, stressed, and worried workforce.

Business leaders also rightfully worry about the large number of Americans who report a lack of trust and confidence in business executives and feel that corporations are concerned mainly with short-term profits and are not giving due weight to their responsibilities to their employees or communities.

These business leaders also know from their first-hand experience that pressures are building at their workplaces. They see this most directly at the moment in the need for health-care reform. So this would be a natural place for business leaders to join others in a search for ways to address the rising costs, uneven distribution of the cost burden across firms, and the gaps in insurance coverage in America. By doing so they could take a first step toward rebuilding the personal bonds with labor, civic, and governmental leaders needed to tackle even tougher issues that separate these groups today.

There is no shortage of other issues. The task of the business community in this decade is to rebuild in a modern way the social contract that was severed by the restructuring, loss of retirement savings, and corporate scandals of the last decade. They cannot do this alone. Rebuilding trust requires reengagement. The current workforce (and if I am reading them right, particularly young workers) will not buy the top-down rhetoric that dominated the business press (and teaching in business schools) of the past. They want to be involved in shaping their own destinies and are intent on doing so. As demographics shift and labor markets tighten as they gradually will, American business will be in the fight of its life to find and to retain the human resource talent it needs to be on the cutting edge of innovation and competitiveness. So now is the time for it to invest in building that workforce and rebuilding the trust it will need to attract, motivate, and retain it.

To make this shift in approach will require senior executives to once again signal to human resource (HR) professionals that it is time to change their approach. For the past two decades, these professionals followed the lead of their CEOs and turned inward and put up stronger ideological barriers to "outsiders" or "third parties" that sought to engage them and influence the direction of workforce and workplace policies. In the past when unions were a threat this translated into aggressive "union avoidance." In recent years it took the form of a knee-jerk resistance to any new workplace regulation. Today this mentality is carrying over to work-family policy debates. Only if top executives now signal the need to reengage will these HR professionals respond in kind.

I believe progressive HR leaders are ready and able to so, at least if initial reactions to the ideas in this book are an indication. In the summer of 2004 the New America Foundation hosted a roundtable discussion of an early draft of these ideas featuring Sue Meisinger, the president of the Society for Human Resource Management, Donna Klein, the CEO of Corporate Voices for Working Families, Chris Owens, the director of the Public Policy Department of the AFL-CIO, and Beth Shulman, author and advocate for low-wage workers. The summary of the dialogue presented in box 9.3 shows

Box 9.3
Testing the Waters

What happens when you bring together thoughtful human resource professionals, work-family advocates, and labor leaders to discuss this working families' agenda? The gathering hosted by the New America Foundation illustrates both the challenges and the potential for progress that could come if this type of dialogue were continued and expanded to similar forums around the country.

Sue Meisinger is the president of the Society of Human Resource Management (SHRM), the largest association of HR professionals in the world. She noted: "There is a lot in this agenda we agree with, particularly with respect to the need for increased investment in education and life-long learning, flexibility to support work and family life, and the call for health-care reform and increased retirement savings. Our members may not be ready to endorse a revival of the labor movement or legislated paid leave, but we recognize that employers, employees, and government all have important roles to play."

Donna Klein, CEO of Corporate Voices for Working Families, indicated: "Corporate Voices was founded in recognition of one of the points emphasized here, namely, the need for businesses to work together to address work-family issues, especially for low-wage workers. We see our organization as providing a private sector voice in the public policy debate over these issues that needs to happen."

Chris Owens, the director of public policy for the AFL-CIO, agreed that "there is an important role for state level experimentation but this cannot be a substitute for strong federal standards. So as we work with different community, religious, and other groups we have to keep our eye on the ultimate task—rebuilding a social contract that meets the needs of workers and families all across the country."

Beth Shulman brought the voice of the working poor to the discussion, noting that "we all have a professional responsibility to restore dignity to work by providing jobs that support a living wage and opportunities for individuals to advance while managing their personal and family responsibilities."

By the end of the workshop, the leaders of these diverse groups had accomplished at least two important goals. First, they could see areas of agreement among them and issues where they respectfully disagree. Second, the dialogue needed to discover common ground and perhaps to eventually bridge some of their differences had begun and all agreed they were willing and interested in continuing it.

So, I say, let the dialogue continue!

that while these groups clearly bring different perspectives and interests to the table, they share considerable common ground around education, workplace flexibility, and concern for reducing family income disparities. This is exactly the type of common and separate mix of interests on which pragmatic and productive coalitions can be formed. So I say, let's get more of these conversations going and continue them until they generate results!

Community, Religious, and Identity Groups

Support for economic and social justice is deeply rooted in most of our religious traditions. The problem is that some of this legacy has been drowned out in recent years over debates about abortion, gay and lesbian rights, and clergy abuse of children. The point is not to diminish the importance of any of these issues. They all deserve attention and are legitimate topics of discussion, debate, and spiritual guidance. But we can no longer afford to let these more divisive issues push social and economic justice issues aside. Organizations such as the venerable Boston-based Labor Guild are community resources that reach out across business, labor, and governmental lines. Others, such as the Greater Boston Interfaith Organization and the Interfaith Alliance, focus their energies more directly on building coalitions that support the working poor to improve their work and family lives. These groups and others like them deserve more attention and stronger support from the religious hierarchies to which they are attached. This is both because these activist organizations are living the social doctrines that underlie these religious traditions and because doing so is the only way to reverse the loss of trust (and faith) many young people now feel. Moreover, as the examples of the coalition between Haitian immigrants and the SEIU in Boston and the La Raza committee active at Tyson Foods both illustrate, community, immigrant, and religious groups need some organization to have an ongoing relationship at work to deliver sustained benefits to their members and constituents. This may not always result in formal collective bargaining relationships. The Tyson-La Raza process calls for a corporate commitment and set of safety standards the corporation agrees to meet and a process for meeting and monitoring them. The codes of conduct Nike and other transnational companies in the apparel industry have put in place illustrate that this type of effort can even produce results on a global scale. Whether these will be effective or provide employees with sufficient voice and protection remains to be seen, but they show there are multiple ways to influence and work with corporations today.

State Policy Makers

If history is a guide, states now provide the most likely venue for innovation in work, family, and education policies. This is especially true at present in part because the prospect for progress at the federal level is bleak at best. It is also true because the prospect of competing for the presidency is a gleam in many the eye of state governors. That is why we are working to create a Massachusetts Work-Family Council with a broad mandate to engage local business, labor, community, and government leaders in a dialogue over how to find common ground on a forward-looking work-family agenda. Stay tuned—I believe we are on the cusp of a new era of innovation in states like California, Massachusetts, Wisconsin, New York, and perhaps some others that have not historically been on the forefront of social and economic policy innovation.

Federal Policy Makers

An agenda for federal policy makers was laid out in chapter 8 and need not be repeated here. But we have to face the facts. There is little taste or political will in Washington at the moment to take up this agenda. At a minimum, the agenda favored here can be viewed as a shadow government policy in the classic European tradition. But it is presented here less as an oppositional statement to current policy makers than as a vision for the longer term and to show that there is an alternative, pragmatic strategy for meeting our generation's responsibilities to the next. If current national policy makers are not willing to take responsibility for addressing these issues we will simply have to continue to work hard to replace them with leaders who are willing to do so.

The Good News: America's Innovative Character Is at Work

Will America wait until these pressures burst before being forced to change the course of this country? Maybe. Or maybe we are beginning to recognize not only that something needs to be done but that things can be done to relieve the pressures.

The good news is that true to our traditions, as these pressures were building, new creative ideas for how to address them began to emerge. Some are coming from the workers and families themselves, especially from young women and men. Some can be seen in the efforts of leading companies, unions, community groups, state governments, and even some academics. To highlight just a few of the innovative responses noted in prior chapters:

• Young professionals are increasingly asking about how work and family are viewed in the industries and firms they are about to enter. Remember Mike Amati's questions.

• The Women's Bar Association of Massachusetts took the lead in documenting the costs of long work hours and its impact on women in the profession. The persistence of their leaders got the attention of senior partners in the big law firms in the state. They continue to hold the senior partners' feet to the fire, even in a slack labor market.

• Sullivan, Weinstein & McQuay figured out how to design a successful law firm that takes advantage of the growing pool of lawyers who want to balance work and family life, each in their own way, according their varied life stages.

• Leading companies are putting in place more and more "family-friendly" policies and in some cases, like Deloitte Touche, taking steps to retain women who take external offers. These examples suggest companies might just be beginning to break out of the "ideal-worker" legacy of the industrial era.

• Companies such as Southwest Airlines are demonstrating how it is possible to be successful in a highly turbulent industry by valuing people and their families, making the company a fun place to work, and being focused on organizing work and labor management relations to ensure their human and social capital contribute to the firm's strategy.

• New theories of the firm, such as the one developed by Margaret Blair and Lynn Stout, are gaining momentum. These models see human capital, that is, the knowledge and skills of the workforce, as the critical strategic resource and asset today and thereby challenge the privileged role financial capital played in management and corporate governance during the industrial era.

• Kaiser Permanente and its coalition of unions are demonstrating how a labor-management partnership can add value and protect employee interests by working in partnership with managers and physicians. Working together they might just show us a model for delivering the high-quality health care that all Americans deserve.

• The Harvard Union of Clerical and Technical Workers may be showing us a picture of the "next-generation union" by using a positive message ("You don't have to be anti-Harvard to be prounion") to organize. This union and its leaders have demonstrated how unions today can and should treat work and family as core issues in bargaining and in day-to-day problem solving.

• The UAW and the major auto companies and Local 1199 of the Service Employees and the New York Hospital Association are working together delivering a host of family, child-development, and education and training services. These joint efforts demonstrate the power of seeing family members as a key part of the constituency of the union and the responsibility of the employers.

• New organizations like Working Today are emerging to provide health care, networking on job opportunities, and other labor-market services to meet the needs of mobile professionals in the contract workforce.

• Working America is using a combination of community mobilization and creative use of Internet communications to educate and mobilize a broad cross section of individuals and families who see common cause in a progressive working families' agenda. The full potential of this approach will likely be discovered through trial and error in years to come.

• The tale of two cities, Allentown and Youngstown, shows that diverse community networks, not just the same old crowd dominated by the business elite, are able to confront economic or other crises when they occur and help make the transition from an industrial to a knowledge-based economy.

• California has enacted the first paid family-leave program. Perhaps this is a positive example of "as California goes today, the rest of the country goes tomorrow."

• The Sloan Foundation has built successful industry-specific networks involving academic researchers, companies, and unions that support the mutual, evidence-based learning needed to spread knowledge-based principles across American industry.

• A number of academics and other writers are exposing the difficult lives of America's working poor and raising the consciousness of those who benefit from their services.

• A groundswell of concern is arising from middle-class Americans over the offshoring of knowledge-based jobs that make them worry: "Is my job next?" Politicians are now noticing and once again are putting jobs and work on the national agenda.

America's pragmatic innovative character is at work again. Piecemeal examples like these give us confidence that we can bring about real change. What remains to be done is to put the pieces together to create a picture that is so clear and compelling that it mobilizes the American public and its leaders to action.

Back to Basics: Work and Family Values

The new activism on the part of working families called for here will only be as strong and as inspiring as the moral foundation on which it rests. That is why the bottom line of box 9.1 calls for all of us to work together to restore trust and confidence in the American dream. The core values that built this country and that those of us in the baby-boom generation inherited from our parents celebrated hard work and strong families and taught us the values of cooperation, community responsibility, and solidarity. These are just as relevant today as in the past.

The agenda laid out here rests on the belief that America is ready to return and recommit to these values. If we do so, our families now and the next generation will be the beneficiaries. If we don't, future historians will look back and chastise us for standing idly by during some of the darkest days in American history.

Notes

Chapter 1

1. Muriel Siebert, "To Encourage Recovery, Encourage Investors," *New York Times*, August 6, 2002, p. A19.

2. "How Many People Lack Health Insurance and for How Long?" Congressional Budget Office Report, May 2003.

3. *Retiree Health Care Benefits Now and in the Future*. Kaiser Family Foundation, January 2004. www.kkf.org.

4. See, for example, "Is Your Job Next?," *Business Week*, February 3, 2003, pp. 50–60.

5. Richard B. Freeman and Joel Rogers, *What Do Workers Want*? (Ithaca, N.Y.: Cornell University ILR Press, 1999); Seymour Martin Lipset and Noah Meltz, *The Paradox of American Unionism* (Ithaca, N.Y.: Cornell University ILR Press, 2004).

6. Alex d'Arbeloff, Preface to Thomas A. Kochan and Richard L. Schmalensee (eds.), *Management: Inventing and Delivering the Future* (Cambridge, Mass.: MIT Press, xi).

7. Kofi Annan, "Corporate Citizenship in a Global Society," in Kochan and Schmalensee, *Management*, pp. 17–23.

8. Jack Welch lists this phrase as the first of his six business rules in Noel M. Tichy and Stratford Sherman, *Control Your Own Destiny or Someone Else Will!* (New York: Harper Collins, 1995).

Chapter 2

1. The statistics on the workforce and working hours used in this chapter come from a variety of published sources. Data from Massachusetts are reported in Neeta Fogg, Paul Harrington, and Thomas Kochan, "The State of Working Families in Massachusetts," MIT Workplace Center Working Paper, WFC #0001, 2004. The

national data are taken from the *Economic Report of the President*, 2000 and 2003, and from Lawrence Michel, Jared Bernstein, and Heather Boushey, *The State of Working America 2002/2003* (Ithaca, N.Y.: Cornell University Press, 2003).

2. Ralph Gomory and Kathleen Christensen, "Three Jobs-Two People," *Washington Post*, June 2, 1999.

3. Beth Shulman, *The Betrayal of Work* (New York: New Press, 2003), pp. 17–18.

4. Jane Waldfogel, Sandra Danzinger, Sheldon Danzinger, and Kristin Seefaldt, "Welfare Reform and Lone Mothers' Employment in the U.S.," paper presented at a conference on parents and employment, Bath, England, October 2000.

5. For a more detailed discussion of the "ideal worker," see Joan Williams, *Unbending Gender: Why Work and Family Conflict and What to Do about It* (New York: Oxford University Press, 1999).

6. Francine D. Blau and Lawrence M. Kahn, "The US Gender Pay Gap in the 1990s: Slowing Convergence," Working Paper, Cornell School of Industrial and Labor Relations, 2004.

7. Ernell Spradley, Ayah Johnson, Julie Sochalski, and William Spencer, *The Registered Nurses Population: Findings from the National Sample Survey* (Washington, D.C.: Department of Health and Human Services, March 2000).

8. Ibid.

9. "Part-time Partner Redux," Case study prepared by Thomas A. Kochan, 2002, available at http://web.mit.edu/workplacecenter/docs/TCWPC101.pdf.

10. *More Than Part-Time* (Boston: Women's Bar Association of Massachusetts, 2000).

11. Lotte Bailyn, Robert Drago, and Thomas A. Kochan, *Integrating Work and Family Life: A Holistic Approach: A Report of the Sloan Work-Family Policy Network*, 2001. Available at http://web.mit.edu/workplacecenter/docs/WorkFamily.pdf

12. Renee M. Landers, James J. Rebitzer, and Lance Taylor, "Rat Race Redux: Adverse Selection in the Determination of Work Hours," *American Economic Review* 86 (1996): 329–348.

13. Rona Rapoport, Lotte Bailyn, Joyce K. Fletcher, and Bettye H. Pruitt, *Beyond Work-Family Balance: Advancing Gender Equity and Workplace Performance* (San Francisco: Jossey Bass, 2002).

14. Paul Osterman, "Work/Family Programs and the Employment Relationship," *Administrative Science Quarterly* 40, no. 4 (December 1995): 681–700.

15. Forrest Briscoe, "Bureaucratic Flexibility: Large Organizations and the Restructuring of Physician Careers," PhD dissertation, MIT Sloan School of Management, 2003.

16. Matt Richtel, "Young Doctors and Work Lists: No Weekend Calls, No Beepers," *New York Times*, January 7, 2004.

17. Kate Kellogg, "Identity, Power, and the Profession of Surgery: A Model of Work Hours Reduction in a High Status Profession," PhD dissertation, MIT Sloan School of Management, 2005.

18. Thomas Kochan, Joel Cutcher Gershenfeld, and Wanda Orlikowski, "Beyond McGregor's Theory Y: Human Capital and Knowledge Based Work in the 21st Century Organization," in *Management: Inventing and Delivering the Future*, ed. Thomas A. Kochan and Richard L. Schmalensee (Cambridge, Mass.: MIT Press, 2003), p. 97.

19. For reviews of the evidence on the business case for work-family benefits, see Ellen Galinsky and Arlene A. Johnson, *Reframing the Business Case for Work-Life Initiatives* (New York: Families and Work Institute, 1998) or Marcie Pitt-Catsouphes, *Metrics Manual: Ten Approaches to Measuring Work/Life Initiatives* (Chestnut Hill, Mass.: Boston College Center for Work & Family, 1999).

20. A good source on the array of union initiated and negotiated work-family benefits and services is the Labor Project for Working Families http://laborproject. berkeley.edu/home.html. The specific examples cited in this section are taken from Susan Cass, "Labor-Management Partnerships for Working Families," 2003. Available at http://web.mit.edu/workplacecenter/LMP.pdf.

21. Cass, "Labor-Management Partnerships for Working Families," p. 27.

22. http://www.takecarenet.org.

23. http://cvworkingfamilies.org.

Chapter 3

1. The State of the American Dream in Massachusetts, MassInc, 2002. http://www.massinc.org.

2. "Facing Budget Crisis, Town Closes Schools," *The Boston Channel*, December 23, 2003.

3. The Quiet Crisis: Falling Short in Producing American Scientific and Technical Talent, http://bestworkforce.org.

4. J. Shonkoff and D. Phillips, eds., *From Neurons to Neighborhoods: The Science of Early Child Development*. Washington, D.C.: National Academy Press, 2000.

5. CNN News Report Summary, January 21, 2004, http://www.cnn.com.

6. Peter Cappelli, Lauri Bassi, Harry Katz, David Knoke, Paul Osterman, and Michael Useem, *Change at Work* (New York: Oxford University Press, 1997), pp. 157–158.

7. Dana Mead, former CEO of Tenneco, personal interview, November 2004.

8. Anthony P. Carnevale, Leila J. Gainer, and Janice Villet, *Training in America: The Organization and Strategic Role of Training* (San Francisco: Jossey-Bass, 1990).

9. For discussions of the under-investment in training see Michael Porter, *Capital Choices: Changing the Way America Invests in Industry* (Boston: Harvard Business School Press, 1994), or Thomas A. Kochan and Paul Osterman, *The Mutual Gains Enterprise* (Boston: Harvard Business School Press, 1994).

10. http://www.dol.gov.eta.

11. Robert B. Reich, *Locked in the Cabinet* (New York: Knopf, 1997).

12. See, for example the data in box 7.1.

Chapter 4

1. Bruce Tulgen, *Winning the Talent Wars* (New York: Norton, 2001).

2. "MIT: The Impact of Innovation," http://web.mit.edu/newsoffice/founders.

3. Michael T. Hannan, M. Diane Burton, and James N. Baron, "Inertia and Change in the Early Years: Employment Relations in Young, High Technology Firms," *Industrial and Corporate Change* 5, no. 2 (1996): 503–535.

4. Bob Herbert, "Bracing for the Blow," *New York Times*, December 26, 2003, p. A35.

5. Sharon Gaudin, "Offshoring of IT Jobs Expected to Accelerate," Forrester Research Inc., November 18, 2003, http://www.itmanagement.earthlink.com.

6. Ralph Gomory and William Baumol, *Global Trade and Conflicting National Interests* (Cambridge, Mass.: MIT Press, 2000).

7. Matthew Bidwell, "What Do Firm Boundaries Do? Understanding the Role of Governance and Employment Relationships in Shaping Internal and Outsourced IT Projects," PhD dissertation, MIT Sloan School of Management, 2004.

8. Isabel Ferandez-Mateo, "How Free Are Free Agents? The Relational Structure of High-end Contract Work," PhD dissertation, MIT Sloan School of Management, 2004.

9. John Schmitt, "The Rise in Job Displacement, 1991–2004," *Challenge* 47, no. 6 (November/December 2004): 46–68.

10. Paul Krugman, "Is Free Trade *Passé?*" *Journal of Economic Perspectives* 1 (1987): 131–144; Ralph E. Gomory and William J. Baumol, *Global Trade and Conflicting Interests* (Cambridge, Mass.: MIT Press, 2000); Paul Samuelson "Where Ricardo and Mill Rebut and Confirm Arguments of Mainstream Economists Supporting Globalization," *Journal of Economic Perspectives* 13 (Summer 2004): 135–146; Lester Thurow, "Do Only Economic Illiterates Argue That Trade Can Destroy Jobs and Lower America's National Income?" *Social Research* 71 (Summer 2004): 265–278.

11. "Hitting the Wall: Nike and International Labor Practices," Harvard Business School Case 9-394-189, 1999.

12. The Nike case is described in Richard Locke, "The Promise and Perils of Globalization: The Case of Nike," in Kochan and Schmalensee, *Management: Inventing and Delivering the Future*, pp. 37–70.

13. Barbara Hilkert Andolsen, *The New Job Contract* (Cleveland: Pilgrim Press, 1998), p. 142.

14. Nelson Litchenstein, *The Most Dangerous Man in Detroit* (New York: Basic Books, 1995).

15. For data on family income trends see Lawrence Mishel et al., *The State of Working America, 2001–2002*, pp. 43–56.

16. Barbara Ehrenreich, *Nickeled and Dimed* (New York: Holt, 2001), p. 218.

17. Beth Shulman, *The Betrayal of Work* (New York: The New Press, 2003), p. 149.

18. David K. Shipler, *The Working Poor* (New York: Knopf, 2004), p. ix.

19. Katherine S. Newman, *No Shame in My Game* (New York: Knopf, 1999).

20. Eileen Appelbaum, Annette Bernhardt, and Richard J. Murnane, eds., *Low Wage America* (New York: Russell Sage Foundation, 2003).

Chapter 5

1. Douglas McGregor, *The Human Side of the Enterprise* (New York: McGraw-Hill, 1960).

2. Arlie Hochschild, *When Work Becomes Home and Home Becomes Work* (New York: Metropolitan Books, 1997).

3. See for example, Amy Tsao, "The Two Faces of Wal-Mart," *Business Week Online*, January 28, 2004.

4. For examples of the key features of knowledge-based work systems and the evidence of their effects on performance, see Joel Cutcher Gershenfeld et al., *Knowledge Driven Work* (New York: Oxford University Press, 1998); or Jeffrey Pfeffer, *The Human Equation* (Boston: Harvard Business School Press, 1998); or Eileen Appelbaum and Rosemary Batt, *The New American Workplace* (Ithaca, N.Y.: Cornell ILR Press, 1994), or Casey Ichniowski et al., "What Works at Work," *Industrial Relations* 35, no. 3 (1996).

5. John Krafcik, "World Class Manufacturing: An International Comparison of Automobile Assembly Plant Performance," *Sloan Management Review* 30 (1988): 41–52.

6. Jody Hoffer Gittell, *The Southwest Airlines Way* (New York: McGraw-Hill, 2003).

7. Jody Hoffer Gittell and Charles O'Reilly, "JetBlue Airways: Starting from Scratch," Harvard Business School Case N1-801-354, August 2001.

8. This work is reported in Jody Hoffer Gittell, Andrew von Nordenflytch, and Thomas Kochan, "Mutual Gains or Zero Sum: The Effects of Airline Labor Relations on Firm Performance," *Industrial and Labor Relations Review* 57, no. 2 (January 2004): 163–180; "Options for Rebuilding Airline Labor Relations," *Perspectives on Work* 7, no. 2 (Winter 2004): 4–6; and *Options for Improving Negotiations and Dispute Resolution in the Airline Industry: A Report of the Airline Industry Working Group*, March 2004. http://web.mit.edu/iwer.

9. The studies cited in note 4 above summarize the evidence from studies carried out in these different industries.

10. Paul Osterman, "Work Reorganization in an Era of Restructuring: Trends in Diffusion and Effects on Employee Welfare," *Industrial and Labor Relations Review* 53, no. 2 (2001): 179–196.

11. Hirsh Cohen, "Studies of Industries and their People," *Perspectives on Work* 2, no. 1 (1998): 13–17.

12. John Kenneth Galbraith, *American Capitalism: The Concept of Countervailing Power* (Boston: Houghton Mifflin, 1956).

13. Henry S. Farber and Kevin F. Hallock, "Changing Stock Market Response to Announcements of Job Loss: Evidence from 1970–97," *Proceedings of the 51st Annual Meetings of the Industrial Relations Research Association*, 1999.

14. For a critique of this view of the CEO, see Rakesh Khurana, *The Search for a Corporate Savior: The Irrational Quest for Charismatic CEOs* (Princeton, N.J.: Princeton University Press, 2002).

15. Margaret Blair and Lynn Stout, "A Team Production Theory of Corporations," *Virginia Law Review* 85, no. 2 (March 1999): 248–328.

Chapter 6

1. "How Many People Lack Health Insurance and for How Long?" Congressional Budget Office Report, May 2003.

2. See Alice H. Munnell and Annika Sunden, "Private Pensions: Coverage and Benefit Trends," paper prepared for a Conversation on Coverage, Washington, D.C. Paper is available from the authors at Boston College.

3. Susan S. Bies, "Retirement Savings: Equity Ownership and Challenges to Investors," Speech to the National Economics Club, Washington, D.C., February 27, 2003.

Chapter 7

1. Daniel B. Cornfield, "Shifts in Public Approval of Labor Unions in the United States: 1936–99," *The Gallup News Service*, September 2, 1999.

2. See Thomas A. Kochan, "How American Workers View Unions," *Monthly Labor Review* 102 (April 1979): 15–22; Richard B. Freeman and Joel Rogers, *What Do Workers Want?* (Ithaca, N.Y.: Cornell University ILR Press, 1999); Seymour Martin Lipset and Noah Meltz, *The Paradox of American Unions* (Ithaca, N.Y.: Cornell University ILR Press, 2004).

3. *Fact Finding Report of the Commission on the Future of Worker Management Relations.* U.S. Departments of Commerce and Labor, Government Printing Office, Washington, D.C., 1994.

4. John Hoerr, *We Can't Eat Prestige: The Women Who Organized Harvard* (Philadelphia: Temple University Press, 1997).

5. Charles J. Morris, *The Blue Eagle at Work: Restoring the Right of Association to the American Workplace* (Ithaca, N.Y.: Cornell University ILR Press, 2004).

6. See Freeman and Rogers, *What Do Workers Want?*

7. For analysis of the changes in union management relations during the 1980s, see Thomas A. Kochan, Harry C. Katz, and Robert B. McKersie, *The Transformation of American Industrial Relations* (New York: Basic Books, 1986).

8. Charlie LeDuff and Steven Greenhouse, "Grocery Workers Relieved, If Not Happy at Strike's End," *New York Times*, February 28, 2004.

9. Joel Cutcher Gershenfeld, Thomas A. Kochan, and John Calhoun Wells "How Do Labor and Management View the Collective Bargaining Process?," *Monthly Labor Review* 121 (October 1998): 23–31.

10. Susan C. Eaton, Thomas A. Kochan, and Robert B. McKersie, "The Kaiser Permanente Labor Management Partnership: The First Five Years," MIT Institute for Work and Employment Research, 2003.

11. Saul Rubinstein and Thomas A. Kochan, *Learning from Saturn* (Ithaca, N.Y.: Cornell ILR Press, 2002).

12. Monami Chakrabati, "Labor and Corporate Governance: Testing a Theory of Social Embeddedness, *Working USA*, 2004.

13. Maureen Scully and Amy Segal, "Passion with an Umbrella," *Research in the Sociology of Organizations* 19 (2003): 125–168.

14. Lotte Bailyn, "Academic Careers and Gender Equity: Lessons from MIT," *Gender, Work, and Organization* 10, no. 2 (March 2003): 137–153.

Chapter 8

1. *Fact Finding Report and Final Report and Recommendations*, Commission on the Future of Worker Management Relations, U.S. Departments of Commerce and Labor, Government Printing Office, Washington, D.C., 1994, 1995.

2. Robert B. Reich, *Locked in the Cabinet* (New York: Knopf, 1997).

3. Letter from Admiral J. M. Loy, under secretary of transportation, to TSA security screeners, January 9, 2003.

4. David E. Card and Alan B. Krueger, *Myth and Measurement: The New Economics of the Minimum Wage* (Princeton: Princeton University Press, 1993).

5. Ross Eisenbrey and Jared Bernstein, "Eliminating the Right to Overtime Pay," Economic Policy Institute, Washington, D.C., 2003.

6. For a description of standards of due process see John T. Dunlop and Arnold M. Zack, *Mediation and Arbitration of Employment Disputes* (San Francisco: Jossey Bass, 1997), pp. 171–178.

Chapter 9

1. Annalee Saxenian, *Local and Global Networks of Immigrant Professionals in Silicon Valley* (Berkeley: Public Policy Institute of California, 2002).

2. Fei Qin, "Social Networks in the Case of Non-Network-Based Migration: A Study of Chinese Highly Skilled Immigrants in Boston," Working Paper, MIT Institute for Work and Employment Research, 2004.

3. Michael Harrington, *The Other America: Poverty in the United* States (Baltimore: Penguin, 1962); Daniel Patrick Moynihan, *The Negro Family: The Case for National Action* (Washington, D.C.: U.S. Department of Labor, 1965).

Index

401(k) pension plans, 4, 134, 138–139

Absenteeism, 123
Academic freedom, 12
Accountability, 119–120
ACORN, 168
AFL-CIO, 39, 43, 46, 141, 159, 178
  Americans Coming Together and, 144
  communication and, 161
  Department of Corporate Affairs, 167
  National Labor Relations Act and, 146
  New Deal and, 144
  Owens and, 214–215
  public debate and, 142–143
  Public Policy Department, 214
  recruitment and, 153
  SEIU and, 142–143
  Sweeney and, 146, 167
  Trumka and, 147–148
  U.S. Department of Labor and, 199
Agricultural Extension Services, 114
Agriculture
  Chavez and, 162, 164, 206
  child labor and, 19
  education and, 84, 86 (see also
    Education)
  farm life and, ix, 9, 50, 85
  unions and, 162, 164
Airline industry, 118, 161
  Transportation Security
    Administration and, 176
  worker's voice and, 108–113

Alcatel, 131
Alcoa, 161
Alfred P. Sloan Foundation, 17, 114,
  186, 220
Alliance, the (IBM group), 151
Alliance for Employee Growth and
  Development, The, 178
Amalgamated Clothing and Textile
  Workers Union, 161
Amati, Mike, 7, 207, 218
American Airlines, 161
American Federation of Labor. See
  AFL-CIO
American Federation of Teachers, 151
American Physical Therapists
  Association (APTA), 63–64
Americans Coming Together (ACT), 144
American Society for Training and
  Development (ASTD), 61
American values
  divisions over, 1
  erosion of, x
  fair wages and, 93–94
  innovative character of, 218–221
  morals and, x–xi, 1
  pragmatism and, x–xi
  trust and, xi–xii, 8 (see also Trust)
  working poor and, 94–99
Anagram Corporation, 81–82
"Analysis: Anxiety Still a Big Issue
  in 2004" (National Public Radio),
  86–87

Annan, Kofi, 8, 194
Ansolabehere, Paul, 82
Appelbaum, Eileen, 96
Arbitration, 183
AT&T, 178

Bailyn, Lotte, 28–30
Barnes, Jerry, 178
Baumol, William, 91
Bell South, 178
Beltram, Edward, 131
Benefits, 140, 204
  back-loaded, 129
  collective bargaining and, 132
  health-care issues and, 130–135
  layoffs and, 130
  paid family leave and, 26–28, 38–46,
    129, 187–189
  pensions and, 4, 129–130, 134–139,
    159, 167, 197
  Polaroid and, 127–128
  Portable Benefits Network and, 152
Berger, Suzanne, 82
Bernhardt, Annette, 96
Betrayal of Work, The (Shulman), 95
*Beyond the Part Time Partner: A Part
  Time Law Firm?* (Miller, Kochan, and
  Harrington), 31
Bidwell, Matthew, 77
Big Labor image, 145
Biotechnology, 49, 74
Black Caucus, 169
Blair, Margaret, 120–121, 219
Blue Eagle at Work, The (Morris), 150
Boeing Corporation, 64–66, 80
Bookman, Ann, 17
Boston Bar Association, 30
Boston Globe, 21, 52, 133, 171
Boyer, Robert, 85
Boyle, Ed, 163
Briscoe, Forrest, 32–33
Bubbles, economic, 2–4, 119–120
Bush, George W., 113, 160
  education and, 58–59
  family and, 176–177

  job creation and, 69–70
  overtime and, 195
Business sector
  accountability and, 119–120
  benefits and, 127–140
  CEO fiefdoms and, 57
  charismatic CEO and, xiv–xv, 119
  collective action and, 22
  command and cost-control mentality
    and, 105–107
  cooperation and, 13–14
  corporate philanthropy and, 161–162
  deregulation and, 118
  division of labor and, 102–103
  downsizing and, 12
  dual agenda and, 28–30
  education and, xiv–xv, 57–59, 61,
    63–66, 74–75
  fairness and, 41
  flexibility and, 10, 25–46
  future manufacturing and, 83–88
  joint programs and, 64–66
  knowledge-based organizations and,
    101–126 (*see also* Knowledge
    economy)
  market failure and, 61–62
  networking and, 102–103
  offshoring and, 70, 75–92
  policy directions for, 213–216
  restructuring and, 118–119
  scandals and, 102, 116
  sharing information and, 114
  stock prices and, 118–119
  tax incentives and, 73
  Taylor management and, 102
  team production view and, 120–121
  technology and, 74
  trust and, xi–xii, 8 (*see also* Trust)
  twenty-first-century governance and,
    116–124
  voice and, 158–159 (*see also* Voice)
  War Labor Board and, 132, 160
  worker satisfaction and, 2–4
  working poor and, 94–99
Business Week, 2

California, 10, 15, 42–43, 217, 220
CALPERS, 167
Carpenters Union, 141
Carter, Jimmy, 198
Cass, Susan, 36
Certified Nursing Assistants (CNAs), 170
Chaker, Ann Marie, 35
Chao, Elaine, 160
Chavez, Cesar, 162, 164, 206
Childcare, 6, 10, 17–18, 36
  flexibility and, 25–26
  paid family leave and, 26–28, 38–46, 129, 187–189
  unions and, 37–38
Child labor, 15
China, 81–82
Christensen, Kathleen, 17
Civil rights, 41, 92
Clark, Kathy, 85
Clark, Scott, 85
Class warfare, xi
Clinton, Bill, 40, 42, 62, 113, 175
Coalitions, 167–169
  family and, 206–211
  New Deal and, 205
  policy directions for, 205–221
Collective bargaining, 22, 174
  historical lessons of, 155–158
  interest-based negotiation and, 156–157
  majority rule and, 146–147
  modernizing labor laws and, 182–187
  National Labor Relations Act and, 146
  pensions and, 135–136
  policy directions for, 212–213
  Saturn Corporation and, 158
  security workers and, 176
  strikes and, 155–157
  United Farm Workers and, 162, 164
  voice and, 117, 132, 141–142, 155–158, 174
Collective Bargaining Forum, 161

Commission on the Future of Worker Management Relations, 175, 177–181, 200
Commons, John R., 205
Communications Workers of America (CWA), 151, 178
Community groups, 39–40, 216–217
"Companies Limit Health Coverage of Many Retirees" (Freudenheim), 131
Conference Board, 4
Congress of Industrial Organizations (CIO). See AFL-CIO
Continental Airlines, 109–111, 157
Cooperation, 22
  education and, 59–60
  health-care issues and, 21
Corporate Voices for Working Families, 39–40, 214–215
Corporations. See Business sector
Council of Economic Advisors (CEA), 71–72
Crime, 6
Cushing-Gavin Award, 163

Daimler Chrysler, 38
d'Arbeloff, Alex, 8
Deadweight losses, 72–73
Dean, Amy, 142
Declaration of Fundamental Principles and Rights at Work, 92
DeLancy, Kathy, 178
Deloitte & Touche LLP, 35–36, 219
Delta Airlines, 110, 179
Deregulation, 118
Dot-com bubble, 2–4
Drago, Robert, 29
Dual agenda, 28–30
Dunlop, John, 198, 200

Earned Income Tax Credit (EITC), 98, 189–190
Eastern Airlines, 109
Eaton, Susan C., xx, 24

Economic issues, ix, 173
  bubbles and, 2–4, 19–20
  deadweight losses and, 72–73
  dot-com era and, 2–4
  education and, 51–59, 62
  family toolkit for, 203–204
  free trade and, 91–92
  Great Depression and, 5, 12, 117, 205
  income inequality and, 1–2
  job creation and, 69–75
  jobless recovery and, 70
  knowledge economy and, xi–xii, 6,
    10–11, 49–67 (see also Knowledge
    economy)
  moral effects of, 1
  New Deal and, 19, 144, 146, 175, 197,
    201, 205–206
  offshoring and, 70, 75–92
  recession of 1990 and, 70
  standard of living, 1
  trust and, xi–xii, 8 (see also Trust)
  uneven wealth distribution and, 1–2
  U.S. Department of Labor and, 195,
    197–200
  U.S. manufacturing and, 83–90
  World War II era and, 117
Economic Justice for All (U.S. Catholic
  Bishop's Pastoral Letter), 1
Education, ix–x, 190, 198
  academic freedom and, 12
  American Federation of Teachers and,
    151
  bargaining power of, 207–208
  budget cuts and, 51–53
  business sector and, 61–66, 74–75
  career development and, 206–207
  challenges of, 53, 55–57
  early childhood, 58
  ECCLI and, 24
  economic issues and, 51–59, 62
  farm life and, 19
  flexibility and, 34
  globalization and, 107
  guarantees of, 75–76
  health-care issues and, 54–55

  importance of, 49, 51–59
  income and, 49–50
  jobs scare and, 12–13
  joint programs and, 64–66
  knowledge as power and, 164–165
    (see also Knowledge economy)
  life-long learning and, 12, 49, 60–67,
    164–165, 209
  market failure and, 61–62
  MBA flaws and, 115
  National Science Foundation and, 55
  "No Child Left Behind" and, 11, 58
  offshoring and, 70, 75–92
  parenting and, 11
  people skills and, 59–60
  politics and, 58–59, 62
  property taxes and, 52
  racial issues and, 55–56
  reforms and, 12
  school cutbacks and, 6
  sharing information and, 114
  technology and, 55–56, 60–61, 74
  top-down approach to, xiv, 57
  unions and, 64–65
  working poor and, 94–99
  young people and, 12–13
Ehrenreich, Barbara, 95, 166
Employee Freedom of Choice Bill, 183
Employee Stock Ownership (ESOP),
  121
Employment and Training
  Administration, 62
Enron, 116
Entrepreneurs, 75
Exit, 165–166, 173
Extended Care Career Ladder Initiative
  (ECCLI), 24

Fair wages, 93, 105
  Bush and, 176–177
  working poor and, 94–99
Family, xiv, 11, 172–173
  activism by, 205–221
  Bush and, 176–177
  business sector and, xii

childcare and, 6, 10, 17–18, 25–26, 36–38
coalitions and, 167–168, 206–211
collective bargaining and, 141–142
dual agenda and, 28–30
Earned Income Tax Credit (EITC) and, 98, 189–190
enabling of, 203–211
erosion of, x
farm life and, ix
flexibility and, 25–46
homemakers and, 9
interviews of, 206–207
job creation and, 190–193
market power and, 207–209
modernizing law for, 182–187
mothers/wives and, 17–18 (*see also* Gender issues)
national agenda for, 40–41, 182–202
paid family leave and, 26–28, 38–46, 129, 187–189, 220
Polaroid and, 127–128
single parents, 18
"special interests" label and, 45, 47
standard of living and, 6
state-level initiatives and, 200–201
stresses on, 7, 9–10, 17–18
toolkit for, 203–204
unions and, 150–154, 157
voice for, xv (*see also* Voice)
worker testimonials and, 177–182
Family and Medical Leave Act (FMLA), 40–41
Family and Work Institute, 25
Family/work integration, 47–48
community groups and, 39–40
demographics for, 17–18
flexibility and, 25–46
ideal worker and, 19–21
national policy for, 40–41
professional organization and, 38–39
single parents and, 18
state-level initiatives and, 42–46
unions and, 37–39

welfare reform and, 18
Farm life, ix, 9, 50, 85. *See also* Agriculture
Federal Mediation and Conciliation Service, 121, 186–187
Fernandez-Mateo, Isabel, 81
First contract negotiations, 183
Five Smooth Stones: Strategic Capacity in the Unionization of California Agriculture (Ganz), 162, 164
Flexibility, 10, 179, 204, 215
business case for, 34–37
community groups and, 39–40
dual agenda of, 28–30
education and, 34
family friendly programs and, 25–26
gender issues and, 25–46
health-care issues and, 32–34
ideal worker and, 26
industry and, 32–33, 35
law firms and, 26–32
management issues and, 36–37
Massachusetts and, 46
MIT and, 36–37
national policy and, 40–46
NUMMI and, 108–109, 111
paid family leave and, 26–28, 38–46, 129, 187–189, 220
professional associations and, 38–39
sabbaticals and, 34–36
Southwest Airlines and, 108–113
"special interests" label and, 45, 47
stigma and, 26–28
Sullivan, Weinstein & McQuay and, 30–32
sustainability and, 37
unions and, 37–39
universities and, 34–37
workplace regulations and, 195–196
Ford, Gerald, 113, 198
Ford Foundation, 152
Ford Motor Co., 38
Forrester Research, 76
Fortune Magazine, 93, 110
Frank, Barbara, 24

Freelancers Union, 152
Freeman, Richard, 165
Free trade, 91–92
Freudenheim, Milt, 131
Frontier Airlines, 109
Full Employment Act of 1946, 69
Full Employment and Balanced
  Growth Act of 1978, 69–70

Galbraith, John Kenneth, 117
Ganz, Marshall, 162, 164
Gender issues, x–xi, 11, 15, 218
  agriculture and, 19
  education and, 55
  flexibility and, 25–46
  ideal worker and, 19–21
  income and, 20
  Iron Man image and, 33
  MIT and, 171
  paid family leave and, 26–28, 38–46,
    129, 187–189, 220
  unions and, 149–150
  working wives/mothers and, 17–18
General Electric, 151
General Motors, 38, 93, 107, 161
Global Compact, 8
Global Compact (Annan), 194
Globalization, 6–7
  education and, 107
  free trade and, 91–92
  international standards and, 193–194
  Nike and, 92
  pros/cons of, 90–92
  UN International Labor Organization
    and, 91–92
Godlberg, Arthur, 198
Gomory, Ralph, 17, 91
Government, x
  Commission on the Future of Worker
    Management Relations and, 175,
    177–181
  communication and, 177, 179
  Council of Economic Advisors and,
    71–72
  deregulation and, 118

federal policy makers and, 217–218
health-care issues and, 23
job creation and, 69–75
knowledge-based work systems and,
  113
Manufacturing Extension Centers
  and, 75
Medicare Reform Bill and, 134
modernizing labor laws and, 182–187
National Labor Relations Act and,
  146, 150, 158–159
New Deal and, 19, 144, 146, 175, 197,
  201, 205–206
paid family leave and, 187–189
policy directions for, 217–218
Sarbanes Oxley bill and, 120
state-level initiatives and, 42–46,
  200–201, 217
tax incentives and, 73
U.S. Department of Labor and, 62,
  176–177, 195, 197–200, 202
War Labor Board and, 132, 160
Great Depression, 5, 12, 117, 205
Greater Boston Interfaith Organization
  (GBIO), 169–170, 216
Greenberger, Scott S., 134
Greenspan, Alan, 119

Haitian community, 169–170, 216
Hammer, Michael, 115
Harrington, Michael, 210
Harrington, Mona, 31
Harvard Union of Clerical and
  Technical Workers (HUCTW), 38–39,
  149–150, 219
Harvard University, 165
Health-care issues, 5, 128–129, 197, 220
  cooperation and, 21
  cost and, 130–131
  ECCLI and, 24
  education and, 54–55, 63
  flexibility and, 32–34
  government and, 23
  immigrants and, 170
  Iron Man image and, 33

mandatory overtime and, 21, 23
Medicaid and, 18, 41
Medicare and, 41, 134
nursing shortage and, 21, 23
reduced benefits and, 130–135
strikes and, 156
travel nurses and, 21, 23
universal coverage and, 135
voice and, 170
Healy, Kerry, 53
Highland Yarn Mills, 180
Hill, Jimmy & Florence, 179–181
Hochschild, Arlie, 103
Homemakers, 9
Horizontal Organization, The (Ostroff),
   104
Horvitz, Wayne, 121–122
Hospital and Health Care Workers, 157
Hotel, Entertainment and Restaurant
   Employees, 38
Hourly wages, 102–103
Human capital. *See also* Labor; Workers
   cooperation and, 13–14
   globalization and, 6–7
   investment in, 191–193
   knowledge economy and, 10–11
   technology integration and, 115–116
Human resources management, xiv
Human Side of the Enterprise, The
   (McGregor), 101–102
Humphrey-Hawkins Bill, 69–70
Hutchinson, Bill, 141
Hyatt, Amanda, 178
"Hybrid Institutions in the Labor
   Market: New Immigrants and Forms
   of Representation" (Yu), 170

Ideal worker, 9, 19–21, 26–28
Illinois, 18
Immigrants, 169–170, 209–211, 216–217
Income
   Bush and, 176–177
   CEOs and, 119, 124
   declining benefits and, 2–6
   decreasing of, 93–94

Earned Income Tax Credit (EITC)
   and, 189–190
education and, 49–50
fair wages and, 93–99, 105,
   176–177
flexibility and, 30–31
gender issues and, 20
hourly, 102–103
low wages and, 94–99
minimum wage and, 189–190
Nike and, 92
pensions and, 4, 129–130, 134–139,
   159, 167, 197
salaried, 102–103
skills and, 59–60
temporary agencies and, 81
two-income families and, 17–20
unequal distribution of, 1–2
working poor and, 94–99
"Income Gap Widens, Uncertainty
   Spreads, As" (Witte), 85
Industrial Areas Foundation, 168
Industrial era, 9
Industrial relations, xiv
Information technology (IT), 77
Innovation
   collective action and, 22
   knowledge-based work systems and,
      108–116
   McGregor and, 101–102
   networking and, 102–103
   offshoring and, 81
   technology and, 74–75 (*see also*
      Technology)
Institutional Shareholders Services
   (ISS), 167
Insurance, 5, 15
   health, 129–135 (*see also* Health-care
      issues)
   Temporary Disability Insurance and,
      42
   unions and, 129
*Integrating Work and Family Life: A
   Holistic Approach* (Bailyn, Drago &
   Kochan), 29

Interest-based negotiation, 156–157
Interfaith Alliance, 168
International Association of Machinists
    and Aerospace Workers (IAM),
    64–65
International Business Machines (IBM),
    35, 76, 151
International standards, 193–194
Invention, 6
Investment, 13–14, 201
  developing countries and, 193–194
  human capital and, 191–193
  pensions and, 135–139
  retirement savings and, 138
Iron Man image, 33

JetBlue Airways, 110–111
Jobs, 100. *See also* Labor
  availability and, 69–71
  benefits and, 127–140
  Council of Economic Advisors and,
    71–72
  creation of, 12–13, 69–75, 190–193, 201
  deadweight losses and, 72–73
  Declaration of Fundamental
    Principles and Rights at Work and,
    92
  education and, 84, 86 (*see also*
    Education)
  exiting and, 166, 173
  fair wages and, 93–99, 105, 176–177
  family adjustment policy for, 88–90
  free trade and, 91–92
  future knowledge economy and,
    73–75
  globalization and, 90–92
  human capital investment and,
    191–193
  international standards and, 193–194
  jobless recovery and, 70
  low wages and, 94–99
  macroeconomic policies and, 71–73,
    190–191
  manufacturing, 83–88
  networks and, 210

  offshoring and, 70, 75–92
  security for, 127–128
  sustainability and, 101
  trade and, 193–194
  voice and, 166 (*see also* Voice)
  working poor and, 94–99
John D. and Catherine T. MacArthur
    Foundation, 152
Johnson, Lyndon B., 198
Joint programs, 64–66
J. P. Morgan Chase, 152
Jungle, The (Sinclair), 94–95
Junk bonds, 118
Justice for Janitors, 156, 165

Kaiser Permanente, 123–124, 157, 161,
    212, 219
Kellog, Kate, 33
Kennedy, Edward, 183
Kennedy, John, 198
Khurana, Rakesh, xiv
Kim Dae Jung, 107
Klein, Donna, 39–40, 214–215
Knight, Phil, 92
Knocke, Ann, 64
Knowledge-based work systems
  diffusing of, 113–115, 185–186
  government and, 113
  NUMMI and, 108–109, 111
  Southwest Airlines and, 108–113
  technology and, 115–116
  trust and, 107–113
  twenty-first-century governance and,
    116–124
Knowledge economy, xi–xii, 6, 10, 204
  building organizations for, 101–126
  economic issues and, 51–59
  education and, 11–12, 49–67
  future jobs and, 73–75, 83–88
  income and, 49–50
  job creation and, 190–193
  job sustainability and, 101
  joint programs and, 64–66
  Manufacturing Extension Centers
    and, 75

Massachusetts and, 49–50
NUMMI and, 108–109, 111
offshoring and, 70, 75–92
sensible macroeconomic policies and,
  190–191
sharing information and, 114
skill mix and, 59–60
social abilities and, 59
social role of, 74–75
Southwest Airlines and, 108–113
technology and, 74
trust and, 102–107
twenty-first-century governance and,
  116–124
work systems and, 107–114
Kochan, Kathy, 54
Kochan, Loretta, xviii–xix
Krazinski, Lori, 86–87
Krugman, Paul, 91

Labor, x
  agriculture and, ix, 9, 19, 50, 84–86,
    162, 164, 206
  benefits and, 2–6, 127–140
  child, 15
  collective bargaining and, 22 (see also
    Collective bargaining)
  college degrees and, 49–50
  Commission on the Future of Worker
    Management Relations and, 175,
    177–181
  cooperation and, 13–14
  corporate governance and, 116–124
  creativity and, 6–7
  Declaration of Fundamental
    Principles and Rights at Work and,
    92
  demographics of, 4–6
  division of, 9, 102–103
  downsizing and, 12
  dual agenda of, 28–30
  ECCLI and, 24
  fair wages and, 93–99, 105, 176–177
  flexibility and, 25–46
  full employment and, 69–70

future solutions for, 211–213
health-care issues and, 18 (see also
  Health-care issues)
hour limits and, 10
ideal worker and, 9, 19–21, 26–28
inhumane treatment and, 94–95
innovation for, 13–16
insurance and, 5, 15
Iron Man image and, 33
joint programs and, 64–66
layoffs and, 117–118, 130
management partnerships and,
  186–187
manufacturing and, 83–90
media and, 165–166
modernizing law for, 182–187
National Labor Relations Act and,
  146, 158–159
New Deal and, 19
NUMMI and, 108–109, 111
offshoring and, 70, 75–92
overtime and, 195
paid family leave and, 26–28, 38–46,
  129, 187–189, 220
pensions and, 4, 129–130, 134–139,
  159, 167, 197
people skills and, 59–60
policy directions for, 211–213
Progressive Movement and, 95
safety and, 15
Saturn Corporation and, 158
security and, xi
single parents and, 18
skilled, 11–12, 59–61 (see also
  Education)
Southwest Airlines and, 108–113
"special interests" label and, 45, 47
stresses on, 7, 9–10
strong movement for, 14–15
team production view and, 120–121
temporary agencies and, 81
trust and, 102–107 (see also Trust)
twenty-first-century governance and,
  116–124
two-parent families and, 18

Labor (cont.)
  unions and, xii–xiii, 5–6, 37–38 (see
    also Unions)
  U.S. Department of Labor and, 62,
    176–177, 195, 197–200, 202
  voice for, 13–15 (see also Voice)
  War for Talent and, 69
  War Labor Board and, 132, 160
  worker satisfaction and, 2–4
  work hours and, 195
  working poor and, 94–99
  workplace regulations and, 195–196
Labor Guild of the Archdiocese of
  Boston, 162–163, 216
Land, Edwin, 127
Land of Plenty, The: Diversity as
  America's Competitive Edge in Science,
  Engineering, and Technology, 56
Lawyers, 26–32
Layoffs, 117–118, 130
Lewis, John L., 141
Lieberman, Joseph, 42, 188
Locked in the Cabinet (Reich), 62, 175
Lorenzo, Frank, 109
Lovell, Malcolm, 161
Low Wage America (Appelbaum,
  Bernhardt, Murnane, et al.), 96
Loy, J. M., 176
Lucent Technologies, 131
"Luring Moms Back to Work"
  (Chaker), 35

McCarthy, Billy, 145
McGregor, Douglas, 101–102, 105
McKersie, Bob, 161
Management, 125–126, 204
  accountability and, 119–120
  charismatic CEO and, xiv–xv, 119
  Commission on the Future of Worker
    Management Relations and, 175
  corruption by, 178–182
  Galbraith and, 117
  knowledge-based work systems and,
    108–124
  labor partnerships and, 186–187

  layoffs and, 117–118
  pensions and, 135–139
  Polaroid and, 127–128
  policy directions for, 213–216
  retention bonuses and, 128
  Sarbanes Oxley bill and, 120
  Taylor and, 102
  team production view and, 120–121
  technology and, 115–116
  Theory X and, 101–102, 125, 181
  trust and, 102–107
  twenty-first-century governance and,
    116–124
  unions and, 147 (see also Unions)
  voice and, 158–159
  workplace regulations and, 195–196
Manufacturing
  offshoring and, 70, 75–92
  working poor and, 96
Manufacturing Extension Centers, 75
Markets, xi
  bubbles and, 2–4, 119–120
  free trade and, 91–92
  globalization and, 6–7, 90–92
  international standards and, 193–194
  paid family leave and, 187–189
  trust and, 8
Marriott Corporation, 39
Marshall, Ray, 198
Massachusetts, 15, 21, 42, 217
  Attelboro, 51–53
  health-care issues and, 133–134
  knowledge economy and, 49–50
  unions and, 149
  Work-Family Council and, 46, 217
"Massachusetts Fiscal Crises Hit
  Education Hard" (Reschovsky), 52
Massachusetts Institute of Technology
  (MIT)
  Department of Political Science and
    Industrial Performance Center, 82
  flexibility guidelines and, 36–37
  gender issues and, 171
  job creation and, 74
  School of Engineering, 60

Sloan School of Management, xiv, 8
Workplace Center, 28, 32, 45, 170
Mead, Dana, 59–60
Media, 165–166
Mediation, 183
Medicaid, 18, 41
Medicare, 41, 134
Medicare Reform Bill, 134
Meisinger, Sue, 214–215
Mergers, 121–122
Mexico, 81–82
Miller, Brendan, 31
Miller, Gary, 86
Mineworkers Union, 141
Minimum wage, 189–190
Minnesota, 18, 81–82, 149
Minnette Mills, 181
Mirro Aluminum, 85
Mishel, Lawrence, 133
Morals. *See* American values
Morgan Stanley, 167
Morris, Charles, 150
Murnane, Richard, 96
"My Plan for Massachusetts Health
    Insurance Reform" (Romney), 133

National Academy of Sciences, 176
National Commission on Productivity
    and the Quality of Work, 113
National Council of La Raza, 168,
    216–217
National Education Association, 151
National Labor Relations Act (NLRA),
    146, 150, 158–159
National Partnership for Women and
    Families, 40–41
National Planning Association, 161
National Policy Association, 161
National Public Radio, 84, 86–87
National Science Foundation, 55
Neeleman, David, 110–111
Networks, 167–169, 210
New America Foundation, 214–215
New Deal, 19, 144, 146, 175, 197, 201,
    205–206

New economy, 2
Newell Rubbermaid Corporation, 86
New Jersey, 167
Newman, Katherine, 96
New United Motors Manufacturing
    Inc. (NUMMI), 108–109, 111
New York, 15, 217
New York Community Trust, 152
New York Hospital Association, 220
New York Times, 33, 105–106, 171
Nickled and Dimed (Ehrenreich), 95,
    166
Nike, 92, 165, 217
Nixon, Richard M., 113, 198
"No Child Left Behind," 11, 58
Nongovernmental organizations
    (NGOs), 92
North Carolina, 74, 180–181
Northwest Airlines, 110
No Shame in My Game (Newman),
    96
Nussbaum, Karen, 153–154

O'Donnell, Joe, 163
Offshoring, 70
    Boeing and, 80
    community policies and, 88–89
    cross-disciplinary teams and, 77
    decision-making policies and, 79–80
    economic effects of, 76–83
    education and, 75–76
    globalization and, 90–92
    group projects and, 77–78
    IBM and, 76
    intellectual property and, 82
    labor costs and, 79
    legal issues and, 77–78
    politics and, 80
    U.S. manufacturing and, 83–90
Ohio, 58, 88–89, 220
O'Neill, Tip, 15
*Options for Improving Negotiations
    and Dispute Resolution* (Working
    Group on Airline labor Relations),
    112

Osterman, Paul, 30, 113
Ostroff, Frank, 104
Other America, The (Harrington), 210
Otis, John, xviii–xix
Outsourcing, 5
Owens, Chris, 39–40, 214–215
Owens Community College, 58

Paid family leave, 26–28. *See also*
  Flexibility
  California and, 43, 220
  case for, 187–189
  national policy and, 40–46
  state-level initiatives and, 42–46
  unions and, 38–39
Paid Family Leave Coalition, 43
"Passion with an Umbrella" (Scully &
  Segal), 169, 171
Pennsylvania, 88–89, 220
Pensions, 130, 159, 167, 197
  401(k), 4, 134, 138–139
  collective bargaining and, 136
  overfunded, 129, 137–138
  portability for, 139
  reduced benefits and, 135–139
  U.S. Supreme Court and, 135–136
People Express, 109
Performance reviews, 29
Perkins, Frances, 159–160, 197–199
Personal Pursuits program, 35
Polaroid, 127–128
Policy
  absenteeism, 123
  benefits and, 127–140
  collective action and, 22
  Commission on the Future of Worker
    Management Relations and, 175
  cooperation and, 21–22
  deadweight losses and, 72–73
  dual agenda and, 28–30
  family toolkit and, 204
  flexibility and, 25–46
  full employment and, 69–70
  future directions for, 205–221
  globalization and, 90–92

innovation for, 13–16
job creation and, 69–75
knowledge-based work systems and,
  108–116
modernizing labor laws and,
  182–187
National Labor Relations Act and,
  146, 150, 158–159
national work-family policy and,
  40–46
New Deal and, 19, 144, 146, 175, 197,
  201, 205–206
"No Child Left Behind" and, 11, 58
NUMMI and, 108–109, 111
offshoring and, 70, 75–92
paid family leave and, 26–28, 38–46,
  129, 187–189, 220
pensions and, 139
sensible macroeconomic, 190–191
sick leave and, 44, 123
Southwest Airlines and, 108–113
state-level initiatives and, 42–46,
  200–201
U.S. Department of Labor and, 62,
  176–177, 197–200
U.S. manufacturing and, 83–89
voice and, 167–169 (*see also* Voice)
WARN Act and, 65
working poor and, 97–98
Politics, x, 15, 47–48, 221
  Bush and, 176–177
  class warfare and, xi
  cooperation and, 13
  education and, 58–59, 62
  job creation and, 69–75
  national work-family policy and,
    40–46
  New Deal and, 19, 144, 146, 175, 197,
    201, 205–206
  offshoring and, 80
  polarization of, x
  Progressive Movement and, 95
  "special interests" label and, 45–46
  state-level initiatives and, 42–46,
    200–201

U.S. Department of Labor and, 62,
  176–177, 195, 197–200, 202
Pope Leo XIII, 93, 169
Portable Benefits Network (PBN), 152
Poverty, 5
  health-care issues and, 18
  low wages and, 94–99
  minimum wage and, 189–190
  Nike and, 92
  welfare reform and, 18
  working poor and, 94–99
Primack, Phil, 83
Productivity. *See* Labor
Professional associations, 46. *See also*
  Unions
  exit and, 166
  family and, 38–39
  policy directions for, 211–213
Progressive Movement, 95
Provo, Lawrence, 85
Publicity, 165–166
"Putting People First" slogan, 175

Qin, Fei, 210
Quality through Training Program
  (QTTP), 65

Racial issues, x–xi, 11
  education and, 55–56
  health-care issues and, 170
  immigrants and, 169–170, 209–211,
    216–217
Reagan, Ronald, 198
"Rebuilding Bay State's Education
  Workforce" (Healy), 53
Reich, Robert, 62, 175
Religion, x, 1, 93, 183, 209
  coalitions and, 162–163, 167–170
  farm life and, 19
  policy directions for, 211–217
Rerum Novarum (Pope Leo XIII), 169
Reschovsky, Andrew, 52
Retention bonuses, 128
Retirement savings, 138
Rockefeller Family Fund, 152

Rockefeller Foundation, 96
Rogers, Joel, 165
Romney, Mitt, 134
Rondeau, Kris, 38–39
Roosevelt, Franklin D., 129, 159–160,
  197–199, 205
Russell Sage Foundation, 96

Safety, 15
Safford, Sean, 88–89
Salaries, 102–103
Samuelson, Paul, 91
Sarbanes Oxley bill, 120
Saturn Corporation, 158
Saxenian, Anna Lee, 209–210
Schultz, George, 198
Science, 11–12
  future jobs and, 73–75
  Taylor management and, 102
Scully, Maureen, 169, 171
Security, 176
Security and Exchange Commission,
  185
Segal, Amy, 169, 171
Seniority, 129
Service Employees International Union
  (SEIU), 37–38, 142–143, 157, 169–170,
  216
Sheinkman, Jack, 161–162
Shipler, David, 96
Shulman, Beth, 214–215
Sick leave, 44, 123. *See also* Flexibility
Silicon Valley, 74–75
Sinclair, Upton, 94–96, 98
Single parents, 18
Social security, 129, 139, 197
Society for Human Resource
  Management, 214–215
Soucy, Paul, 83
South Bay Labor Council, 142
Southwest Airlines, 108–113, 157, 219
Special interests, 45, 47
Standard of living, 1–2, 6, 8. *See also*
  Income
Stanford University, 74

Starting in Our Own Backyards
(Bookman), 17
State Disability Insurance (SDI), 43
"State Leaders Aim at Healthcare Gap"
(Greenberger), 133
State of Working America 2000–2001, The
(Mishel), 136
Stern, Andrew, 142, 144
Stock prices, 118–119
Stout, Lynn, 120–121, 219
Strikes, 155–157, 165
Sullivan, Bob, 30–31
Sullivan, Weinstein & McQuay (SWM),
30–32, 219
*Supporting Car Givers: Policy and
Practice in Long Term Care* (Eaton &
Frank), 24
Sweeney, John, 146, 167

Takeovers, 118
Taxes, 6, 25, 73
Council of Economic Advisors and,
71–72
Earned Income Tax Credit (EITC)
and, 98, 189–190
education and, 52
havens for, 120
high-income bracket and, 71–72
Taylor, Frederick, 102
Teamster's Union, 121–122, 145, 156
Technology, 11–12, 208
biotechnology, 49, 74
business sector and, 74
education and, 55–56, 60–61
future jobs and, 73–75
human capital integration and,
115–116
innovation and, 74–75
management and, 115–116
offshoring and, 70, 75–92
universities and, 74
working poor and, 94–99
Temporary agencies, 81
Temporary Disability Insurance, 42
Tenure, 117, 129

Teradyne, 8
Theory X, 101–102, 125, 181
Theory Y, 101–102, 125
Thurow, Lester, 91
Tocqueville, Alexis de, x
Toskes, Raffael, Sr., 85
Towers Perrin, 148
Toyota, 107–108
Trade programs, 193–194
Transportation Security
Administration, 176
Traveglini, Robert E., 134
Travel nurses, 21, 23
Trumka, Richard, 147–148
Trust, xi–xii, 8, 128–129
command and cost-control mentality
and, 105–107
corporate scandals and, 102
division of labor and, 102–103
fair wages and, 93–99, 105, 176–177
knowledge-based work systems and,
102–116
rebuilding of, 102–107
unions and, 147
Wal-Mart and, 105–107
working poor and, 94–99
TXU, 131
Tyco, 116
Tyson Foods Inc., 168, 216, 217

Undergraduate Practice Opportunities
Program (UPOP), 60
Unemployment, 5
insurance and, 15
jobs scare and, 12–13
tenure and, 117
Unions, xii–xiii, 5–6, 102–103, 120, 122,
207. *See also* Specific union
agriculture and, 162, 164
airline industry and, 108–113
Americans Coming Together and, 144
best, 143, 145–146
Big Labor image and, 145
child care and, 37–38
coalitions and, 167–169

collective bargaining and, 22, 117, 132,
141–142 (*see also* Collective
bargaining)
communication and, 161–162, 165–166
corruption in, 145
decline of, 118, 171–172
democracy and, 145
economic issues and, 142
education and, 64–65
family and, 157
future of, 142–143
Galbraith and, 117
gender issues and, 149–150
growth of, 129
health-care and, 21
hour limits and, 10
insurance and, 129
interest-based negotiation and,
156–157
knowledge as power and, 164–165
lifetime membership and, 150–154
media and, 165–166
modernizing labor laws and, 182–187
national approval of, 145–146
National Labor Relations Act and,
146, 150, 158–159
networks and, 167–169
New Deal and, 146
next-generation, 142–143, 165–166, 187
NUMMI and, 108–109, 111
paid family leave and, 38–39, 43
pensions and, 135–136
policy directions for, 211–213
Portable Benefits Network and, 152
public debate and, 142–143
reinventing, 146–155
Roosevelt and, 159–160
Southwest Airlines and, 108–113
strikes and, 155–157, 165
traditional organizing approach of,
146–147
turning points in, 141–142
vision and, 142, 149–150
voice and, 144 (*see also* Voice)
worker testimonials and, 177–182

working poor and, 94–99
worst, 143, 145–146
United Airlines, 110
United Auto Workers, 107, 220
family services and, 38, 157
NUMMI and, 108–109, 111
United Farm Workers, 162, 164
United Hospital Fund, 152
United Nations, 8, 91–92
United Parcel Service (UPS), 156, 165
United Steelworkers Local 6499, 86
University of Texas, 74
University of Wisconsin, 74, 205
US Airways, 110
U.S. Census Bureau, 35
U.S. Department of Labor, 62, 176–177,
195, 197–200, 202
Usery, William, 198
U.S. Supreme Court, 135–136

Vacations, 44. *See also* Flexibility
Vision, 142, 149–150
Voice, 204, 208
Americans Coming Together and,
144
building power sources for, 162–169
coalitions and, 167–169
collective bargaining and, 117, 132,
141–142, 155–158, 174 (*see also*
Collective bargaining)
Commission on the Future of Worker
Management Relations and, 175,
177–181
communication and, 165–166, 173
corporate governance and, 121–124,
184–185
decision making and, 158–159
direct participation and, 154–155
exit and, 166, 173
health-care issues and, 170
historical lessons for, 141–143
importance of, 121–124
knowledge and, 164–166
labor investment and, 167
media and, 165–166

Voice (cont.)
  national security and, 176–177
  needed changes for, 147–155, 172–174
  networks and, 167–169
  NUMMI and, 108–109, 111
  positive vision and, 149–150
  reinventing, 146–147
  Scully/Segal paper and, 169, 171
  in society, 159–162
  Southwest Airlines and, 108–113
  strategy for, 149–150
  strikes and, 155–157, 165
  union analysis and, 117, 143–146
  United Farm Workers and, 162, 164
  vision and, 142, 149–150
  worker testimonials and, 177–182

WAGE, 151
Walesa, Lech, 143, 145
Wall Street, 118–119. See also Business
  sector
Wall Street Journal, 115
Wal-Mart, 85, 105–107, 156
War for Talent, 69
War Labor Board (WLB), 132, 160
Washington Post, 84, 208
Washtech, 151
Welch, Jack, 8, 125
Welfare reform, 15, 18
Why the Garden Club Couldn't Save
  Youngstown: Social Capital the
  Transformation of the Rust Belt
  (Safford), 89
Wirtz, W. Willard, 198
Wisconsin, ix, 15, 18, 74, 85–87, 165,
  167, 217
Witte, Griff, 85
Women's Bar Association, 32, 218
Worker Adjustment and Retraining
  Notification (WARN) Act, 65
Workers
  accomplishment and, ix
  as assets, 101
  benefits and, 127–140 (see also
  Benefits)

collective bargaining and, 135–136,
  141–142 (see also Collective
  bargaining; Labor)
cooperation and, 21
Declaration of Fundamental
  Principles and Rights at Work and,
  92
demographics of, 148
dual agenda and, 28–30
education and, 55, 164–165 (see also
  Education)
fair wages and, 93–99, 105, 176–177
farm life and, ix, 19
flexibility and, 25–46
immigrant, 169–170, 209–211, 216–217
income inequality and, 1–2
information and, 120–121, 124–125
jobs scare and, 12–13
knowledge-based organizations and,
  101–126
layoffs and, 117–118, 130
legal rights of, 102–103
modernizing labor laws and,
  182–187
National Labor Relations Act and,
  146, 150
overtime and, 195
paid family leave and, 26–28, 38–46,
  129, 187–189, 220
pensions and, 4, 129–130, 134–139,
  159, 167, 197
people skills and, 59–60
Portable Benefits Network and, 152
retirement savings and, 138
seniority and, 129
sick leave and, 44, 123
social contract and, x
standard of living and, 1–2, 6, 8 (see
  also Income)
Taylor management and, 102
tenure and, 117, 129
testimonials of, 177–182
trust and, 102–107
voice and, 154–155, 158–159 (see also
  Voice)

Wal-Mart and, 105–107
work hours and, 195
Work-Family Council, 46, 217
Work-Family Task Force, 30
Work in America Institute, 161
Working America, 153–154, 220
Working Group on Airline Labor
    Relations, 112
Working poor, 5
  Earned Income Tax Credit and, 98,
    189–190
  job upgrades and, 97–98
  low wages and, 94–99
  policy for, 97–98
Working Poor, The (Shipler), 96
Working Today, 152, 220
WorldCom, 116
World Trade Organization, 194
World War II era, 117, 132, 135
Worth, Maurice, 179
Wright, Deborah, 179, 181

Xerox, 161, 169

Yu, Kyoung-Hee, 170